When the
WHITE HOUSE
Comes to ZION

MIKE WINDER & RONALD L. FOX

with foreword by Michael O. Leavitt

Published by Covenant Communications, Inc.
American Fork, Utah

Printed in China
First Printing: October 2011

18 17 16 15 14 13 12 11   10 9 8 7 6 5 4 3 2 1

ISBN 978-1-60861-232-1

When the
WHITE HOUSE
Comes to ZION

MIKE WINDER & RONALD L. FOX

with foreword by Michael O. Leavitt

Special Thanks To

Utah State Historical Society, Michael Homer, Phil Notarianni, Wilson Martin, Doug Misner, Michelle Elnicky, Heidi Orchard, Kristen Rogers-Iversen, and Greg Walz

Utah State Archives, Patricia Smith-Mansfield, Alan Barnett, Ken Williams, Tony Castro, and Heidi Stringham

The Church of Jesus Christ of Latter-day Saints Church History Library, Marlin Jensen, Richard Turley, Jr., Glenn Rowe, Grant Anderson, William Slaughter, Brad Westwood, and Anya Bybee

Brigham Young University, Harold B. Lee Library, Tom Wells, photo curator

The University of Utah, Marriott Library, Special Collections, Roy Webb

Ogden State Railroad Museum & Archives, Lee Witten

The Deseret News, Joseph Cannon, Rick Hall, Tad Walch, Michael De Groote, and their photographers: Chuck Wing, Tom Smart, Ravell Call, August Miller, Jeffrey Allred, Kristen Murphy, Scott Winterton, Mike Terry, Lennie Mahler, and all past photographers

The Salt Lake Tribune - The Ogden Standard - Provo Herald

Rutherford B. Hayes Presidential Library, Curator Nan Card

Benjamin Harrison Presidential Center, Curator Jennifer E. Capps

Union Pacific Railroad, Curator John E. Bromley

Library of Congress

The National Archives & Records Administration

The National Portrait Gallery

Helpful contributors, Scott and Julie Fisher, Douglas C. Pizac, Brent Ashworth, Anthony Christensen, Michael Kearns, Dick Richards, Kirk Jowers, Mike Leavitt, Olene Walker, Ralph Becker, John and Marcia Price, Mac Christensen, F. Michael Watson, Allyson Bell, Amy Hansen, and Set and Joan Momjian

&

The phenomenal team at Covenant Communications, editors Samantha Van Walraven and Kathy Jenkins; designers Jessica Warner, Margaret Weber, Jennie Williams, and Mark Sorenson; and marketing support Ron Brough, Robby Nichols, Kelly Smurthwaite, and Barry Evans

TABLE OF CONTENTS

— ❧ —

FOREWORD

To the readers,

O ne of the great honors of being governor of Utah is welcoming the chief executive of our nation to our great state. As governor, I had the opportunity to welcome Presidents Bill Clinton and George W. Bush to Utah on several occasions. Most of President Clinton's visits to Utah were with his family as they sought privacy at a friend's home near Park City. It was clear he valued the serenity of the Utah mountains.

I developed an especially warm relationship with President Bush. He and I used to sit next to each other at National Governor Association meetings because they would seat us alphabetically, and Utah always came next to Texas. We grew closer on a trip to Israel together. Later, I was honored to serve in his Cabinet.

One of the highlights of presidential visits to Utah was when President Bush came to preside over the February 2002 opening ceremonies of the Olympic Winter Games. I remember the spectacular ceremony we had in the capitol rotunda preceding the opening ceremonies, where Bush became the first U.S. president to visit the inside of our capitol building (although President Woodrow Wilson did come as far as the exterior).

One of my most prominent memories of that visit was meeting the president at the Salt Lake International Airport. Air Force One has a breath-taking presence. Its shining blue and white majesty is a spectacular symbol of American greatness and goodness.

On that very special day in Utah history, the sky was clear and the mountains to the west of the airport were dusted with fresh snow, making a perfect match to the airplane's blue and white. That image symbolized for me that Utah's moment had arrived, and the leader of the free world was there to honor the significance for our state, country, and world.

An important role of the president of the United States is to get out among the people of this great nation—whether in campaign mode, helping friends at fundraisers, interacting at town hall meetings, or participating in historic events. It is the people of our republic that make it great, and there are no better people than the good citizens in Utah. This is why I am pleased that presidents have made a point of coming to Utah since the days of President Ulysses S. Grant.

Every presidential visit to Utah is memorable in its own way, and I applaud Mike Winder and Ron Fox for putting together this amazing collection of photographs and stories from over a century of presidential visits to the Beehive State. This book demonstrates the ever-progressing relationship between Utah and the White House and underscores the important role Utah has played in our nation's existence.

DESERET NEWS

I have had an even longer relationship with author Ron Fox. Ron and I met during my first campaign for governor in 1992, and he has been a good friend of mine and of the state ever since. He served as executive director for two of my inaugurals ceremonies and helped with several major events, including the solemn remembrance for the victims of September 11. Ron was also instrumental in organizing the 2002 Olympic Winter Games welcome ceremony at the capitol, the School Trust Lands transfer announcement, and the visits of the president and vice president to our state.

I have always joked with Ron that I know he always carries red, white, and blue bunting, a flag or two, bungee cords, and duck tape in the trunk of his car, so he can be ready to tackle any event. He also witnessed my last act as governor by being the legal witness to my letter of resignation as I embarked into federal service as EPA administrator and later as secretary of Health and Human services.

May Utah continue to play an important role in America's future, and may future presidents continue to enjoy the warmth and hospitality of the Beehive State.

Michael O. Leavitt

I first met author Mike Winder during my first campaign for governor in 1992, when, as a young leader of the Teenage Republicans, he helped hammer in yard signs for me throughout the Salt Lake Valley. He later spoke alongside me at Southern Utah University's commencement event for the Governor's Honors Academy in the summer of 1993. Mayor Winder is a prominent and rising leader in the Republican Party and has made an important historical contribution with this book.

Michael O. Leavitt served as Utah's fourteenth governor from 1993–2003. He later served in President George W. Bush's Cabinet as administrator of the Environmental Protection Agency and secretary of Health and Human Services.

Section I

VISITS TO THE UTAH TERRITORY

1872–1901

LEADING UP TO A PRESIDENTIAL VISIT

MANY OF OUR FOUNDING FATHER PRESIDENTS dreamed of traveling to the West. George Washington whetted his appetite for the West as a young man when Lord Fairfax sent him to survey his extensive land holdings. This project sent young Washington beyond the source of the Potomac River and into the Ohio Valley. For the rest of his life, Washington dreamed of ways to make the Potomac more navigable so they could open the vast American West for trade and commerce. He was even the founding president of the Patowmack Company, which set out to accomplish that very task. Yet Washington would never venture too far west and would never know of the Great Salt Lake or its unique environs.

Thomas Jefferson had a more active role in initiating the discovery of the West's potential when he executed the Louisiana Purchase in 1804, thrusting the young nation's future westward. His yearning to explore the West led him to dispatch the Corps of Discovery that Lewis and Clark headed. But Jefferson never let go of his desire to personally venture farther West. "I have never ceased to wish to descend the Ohio & Mississippi to New Orleans," he once mused to his younger sister while in the White House, "and when I shall have put my home in order,

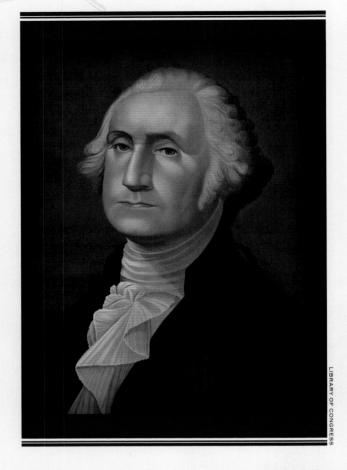

(Right) George Washington, lithograph.   *(Opposite) Lewis and Clark.*

Period Map of the United States and Mexico. 1849.

"I always had a liking for Abe Lincoln, and if he had come out here and known us, he would have understood us and liked us . . ."

I shall have the leisure and so far I have health also, to amuse myself in seeing what I have not yet seen."[1]

The eventual twelfth president of the United States, Zachary Taylor, ventured farther west than all of the previous presidents when he commanded troops throughout Texas in the Mexican-American War in 1846. The fourteenth president, Franklin Pierce, also led soldiers in the Mexican War, but neither of the men made it as far as Utah.

President Millard Fillmore was president when the Territory of Utah was created in 1850, and James Buchanan sent the U.S. Army to replace Brigham Young as governor with his appointee Alfred Cumming in 1857. Yet despite both presidents' interest in the area, they never expressed a desire to personally make the trek to Utah.

Abraham Lincoln, however, did think of the West, and desired at some point to visit. He was a driving force behind initiating the transcontinental railroad in 1863 but was too preoccupied with the demands of the Civil War to venture far from Washington. Had he managed the journey, he would have ranked among numerous other notable visitors Brigham Young entertained, such as author Mark Twain, explorer Richard Burton, and first Republican presidential candidate John C. Fremont.

"I always had a liking for Abe Lincoln," Brigham Young related a few years after Lincoln's assassination, "and if he had come out here and known us, he would have understood us and liked us, and I'd have told him 'another' [story] to match his every time, and then we wouldn't have heard so much rot about our ways."[2]

Lincoln's successor, Andrew Johnson, did venture westward but only made it as far as St. Louis on the rail journey.[3] With the 1869 completion of the transcontinental railroad culminating with a golden spike in Promontory, Utah, the possibilities of presidential visits to the West—and specifically to Utah—finally entered the realm of plausibility; however, the first presidential visit wouldn't take place until six years later in 1875.

UTAH STATE HISTORICAL SOCIETY

2007 UTAH COMMEMORATIVE QUARTER *(Inset) The Utah quarter was officially released in a ceremony hosted by the Governor of Utah, Jon Hunstman, Jr., Utah First Lady Mary Kaye Huntsman, and U.S. Mint senior level executive Gloria Eskridge on Nov. 9, 2007. Thousands of Utahns attended, including more than 2,500 schoolchildren (each received a free quarter to remember the day.) The date on the top of the coin, 1896, is the date of Utah's admission to the Union. More than 133,000 Utah residents voted on the quarter's design (one design featured a beehive, another a snowboarder) which celebrates this great event that linked the East to the West.*

TRANSCONTINENTAL RAILROAD *(Left) After a seven-year sprint and major—heroic—human effort, the first phase of construction of the transcontinental railroad had its watershed moment on May 10, 1869, when the Central Pacific and the Union Pacific railways joined at Promontory Point, Utah. Coast-to-coast travel time was reduced from four to six months to six days. Soon after, our nation underwent a phase change, thenceforth becoming a unified whole in its political, economic, and now even cultural affairs.*

LIBRARY OF CONGRESS

The first nationally elected official to visit Utah was not the president of the United States but rather the vice president. On October 3, 1869, fewer than five months after the railroad was completed at Promontory Point, Vice President Schuyler Colfax arrived for a brief visit to assess the situation in Salt Lake City and to warn the Mormons to obey the law. He had come to Utah in 1865 as Speaker of the House, but this was his first time as a nationally elected figure. Colfax reported back to President Ulysses S. Grant that "the golden moment has arrived" to appoint tough officials for the territory to subdue the Saints.[4] Brigham Young was clearly not impressed with the new administration and quipped, "Who goes to the White House these days? A gambler and a drunkard. And the Vice-President is the same."[5]

UTAH STATE HISTORICAL SOCIETY

Above — *Schuyler Colfax visits Utah Territory. October, 1869.*
Inset — *Vice President Schuyler Colfax*

JAMES A. GARFIELD

JAMES GARFIELD WAS PRESIDENT of the United States in 1881 and served at the same time Eli H. Murray was territorial governor of Utah and John Taylor was president of the Church. Garfield came to Utah twice in the 1870s as a congressman, making him the first future president to visit the Utah Territory.

LIBRARY OF CONGRESS

Aug 7 1872 James F. Bradley Chicago Ill.

C. M. Onmston S. Joseph Mich

K. Schussler San Francisco Cal

Geo. Harrod Cincinnati O

John Wilson San Francisco

Aar Harris Cincinnati O

Mary Harris

Edmund Wilkes Hutter Mining & Smelter

John S. Cowell " "

K. C. Barker Detroit

Mrs K. C. Barker

John Fremantle London England

E. L. Coleman M.D Salt Lake City

Mrs E. H. Swain Chicago Ill.

I. D. Armstrong & Wife Brooklyn N.Y.

Livingston Stone. Commissioner of Fisheries. Charlestown N.H

Elof... Benhouse Manchester

W Brown Nelis Michigan

Tho. B. Van Horne Fort Vancouver W.S.

O. P. Mason Nebraska City

E. Stebbings Leavenworth Kas

J. A. Garfield Hiram. Ohio

D. G. Swain U. S. Army

Geo. W. Smith Newark N.J.

Mrs Geo W Smith " "

UTAH TERRITORIAL SEAL (Above)

A PAGE FROM THE FIRST PRESIDENCY'S GUEST BOOK (Left) James A. Garfield, a former Civil War general, current congressman from Ohio, and future president, stopped in Salt Lake City with Major Swain of the U.S. Army while en route to Montana for a meeting with the Flathead Indians. They arrived by rail on Sunday, August 11, 1872, and Garfield wrote in his diary that they "immediately went out to one of the Ward meetings and heard [John] Taylor, one of the Apostles, preach." The following day he recorded, "After breakfast, G. Q. Cannon, one of the Twelve Apostles and the Delegate-elect to Congress, took us in a carriage to the various points of interest in the city. The Tabernacle, the Temple, Brigham [Young]'s house and Camp Douglas. After dinner he took us to the depot, where we met Brigham just coming in from Ogden. Mr. Young held our train 15 minutes for a chat."[6] While at "Brigham's house" on Monday the 12th, Congressman Garfield and Major Swain signed the First Presidency's guest book (shown here).

TRAIN UNLOADING AT THE RESORT AT BLACK ROCK ON THE GREAT SALT LAKE *Railway excursions to the beaches of the Great Salt Lake for relaxation in the sun and sand were common in the 1870s and made an obvious itinerary choice for the Utahns hosting future President Garfield in 1875.*

A SAIL ON THE GREAT SALT LAKE *Visitors to the Utah Territory were intrigued with the largest salt lake in the western hemisphere, and exploring it by boat was an attraction for many. Even Congressman Garfield and his party enjoyed a "sail on Salt Lake," according to the newspaper reports of his 1875 visit.*

SALT LAKE TRIBUNE

GARFIELD STANDING ON SECOND FLOOR BALCONY OF THE CARTER HOTEL IN LAKEPOINT *On June 4, 1875, Congressman James A. Garfield made a second visit to the Utah Territory. A VIP party, including Governor Samuel Axtell, Salt Lake City Mayor Daniel H. Wells, and Territorial Delegate and Apostle George Q. Cannon, greeted him at the depot in Ogden. They rode with the congressman to Salt Lake, arriving at 11:00 AM In the afternoon, about 200 of the Territory's prominent men and women joined Garfield for an excursion on the Utah Western Railroad out to the beaches of the Great Salt Lake. The group enjoyed the hospitality of the newly opened Carter Hotel on the beach, and Congressman Garfield had the pleasure of sailing on the Great Salt Lake. The following day, Garfield enjoyed a similar day trip to Provo and back.[7]*

J. A. Garfield
1881

RONALD FOX COLLECTION

IN MEMORY
OF OUR
LAMENTED
PRESIDENT
J. A. GARFIELD
Sept. 19th. 1881.

When President Garfield was assassinated mere months after taking the oath of office, many in the East thought the Mormons had killed him as retaliation for the anti-polygamy references he made in his inaugural address. To show that there was no ill will toward the slain president, Utah Governor Eli H. Murray suggested to the legislature that they change the name of a proposed new county from Snow County to Garfield County, which they did.[8] Garfield Beach, in the area of the Carter Hotel where he had visited on the Great Salt Lake, was also named for the twentieth president.

President Garfield Memorial Ribbons

INAUGURATION BALL

Programme.

MUSIC BY THE GERMANIA ORCHESTRA OF PHILADELPHIA.
WILLIAM STOLL, JR., CONDUCTOR.
HENRY FEHLING, ASSISTANT.
AND
U. S. MARINE BAND.
JOHN PHILIP SOUSA, CONDUCTOR.
CHAS. THIERBACH, LEADER.
Music under the Direction of . . . . . Mr. Sousa

PROMENADE CONCERT.
RECEPTION OF THE PRESIDENT.
9 to 11 o'clock.

1 INAUGURATION MARCH.
Respectfully dedicated to President Garfield by John Philip Sousa.
PERFORMED BY COMBINED BAND AND ORCHESTRA.

2 OVERTURE, "Fest," . . . . Leutner
ORCHESTRA.

3 GRAND SELECTION, "Mephistophele," . . Boito
BAND.

4 FANTASIA, "Boccaccio," . . . . . Suppé
ORCHESTRA.

5 NATIONAL AIRS OF ALL COUNTRIES, . . Anon
BAND.

6 BALLET MUSIC FROM FERAMOIS, . Rubinstein
ORCHESTRA. { a. Wedding March.
{ b. Dance of the Bayadiers.

7 MELANGE, "In Parlor and Street," . . Sousa
BAND.

8 MARCHE FLAMBEAU, ... Meyerbeer
ORCHESTRA.

Order of Dancing.

Dancing commences at 11 o'clock.

1 LANCIERS, "Pirates of Penzance," . . Sullivan

2 WALTZ, "Pleasure Trip," . . . . Strauss

3 PROMENADE, "Whirlwind Polka," . . Levy
CORNET DUET, JAEGER AND PETROLA.

4 QUADRILLE, "Militaire," . . . . . Strauss

5 POLKA, "My Lady," . . . . . . Faust

6 PROMENADE, Xviophone Solo, . . . Michaelis

INAUGURATION BALL PROGRAM   When James A. Garfield was elected president in 1880, many in Utah were hopeful that he would treat them well because of his visits to the territory and the personal relationships forged. "He has been one of my allies in Congress. I have appealed to him a number of times when I needed help,"George Q. Cannon wrote. [9] "He had visited this [Salt Lake] city twice; he had become acquainted with the people, seen them at their homes, and had frequently conversed upon our doctrines. I know therefore, he understood our question [of what it would take for us to be accepted by the Union] probably better than any man in public life."[10]

ULYSSES S. GRANT

U LYSSES S. GRANT WAS PRESIDENT of the United States from 1869–1877 and served at the same time Charles Durkee, John Shaffer, Vernon Vaughan, George Woods, and George Emery served as governors of the Utah Territory and Brigham Young as president of the Church. He came to Utah twice, including once as president.

On Sunday, October 3, 1875, Ulysses S. Grant became the first president of the United States to visit Utah. *The Salt Lake Herald* captured the significance of this visit: "Utah is highly honored by this presidential visit, the first one we believe ever made to the territory. It is at once an official recognition of the growing importance of this section, and the president's desire to become somewhat better acquainted with the people and affairs of Utah, than he possibly could be from individual reports received through interested, if not prejudiced, parties."[11]

GRANT PARTY IN FORT SANDERS, WYOMING *President Grant was en route to Denver and took a detour to Utah Territory to confer with his new appointee, Governor George W. Emery. This was the farthest west a United States president had ever been, and remarkably, no known photographs exist of his visit to Utah. The closest we have is this photo of the president and his entourage at Fort Sanders, Wyoming (near present-day Laramie), en route to Utah. Grant has a hat on and both hands on the fence. Remarkably, this is also the only know photograph of famed Civil War generals Grant, Philip Sheridan, and William Tecumseh Sherman together. (Sheridan is to the left of the woman in the white dress and has his hand in his pocket. Sherman is in the center, with his coat over his arm.)*

UTAH TERRITORIAL GOVER-NOR GEORGE EMERY *(opposite top)* **FIRST LADY JULIA GRANT** *(opposite bottom) At the mouth of Echo Canyon, Governor Emery and a few of the federal officials joined the presidential party, traveling together to Ogden. The Ogden depot was filled with an eager crowd, and they were thrilled when the special train carrying President Grant rolled in at 12:30 PM. Grant was standing on the rear platform of the Pullman car, where the large crowd instantly recognized him. They waved their hats in excitement, and the President responded by taking off his hat and bowing. The Ogden brass band struck up "Hail to the Chief" during the excitement as the patriotically decorated train slowed to a halt.*[12]

The presidential party then rode the forty miles from Ogden to Salt Lake City in a special train. President Grant, Governor George Emery, and George Q. Cannon stood on the platform to view the countryside, while Brigham Young remained inside conversing with the First Lady.[13] *En route, Julia Grant told Young that she admired the accomplishments of the Mormons, though she objected to the practice of polygamy. The U.S. president's son, Col. Fred Grant, also accompanied the group.*[14]

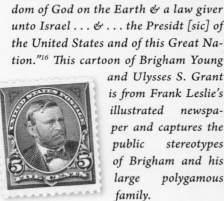

CARTOON OF YOUNG AND GRANT MEETING *Federal officials and Church leaders competed to host Grant, resulting in a rather clumsy meeting at the train station in Ogden. There, Brigham Young and a committee of prominent citizens and Church leaders from Salt Lake City met them. George Q. Cannon said to Grant, "Mr. President may I have the pleasure of introducing to you President Brigham Young." They then shook hands, but Young did not understand at first who it was, and Cannon had to quickly tell him that it was President Grant. Both presidents removed their top hats in respect, and Brigham Young then exclaimed, "President Grant, this is the first time I have ever seen a President of my country."*[15] *Wilford Woodruff penned in his diary that it was notable to witness the meeting of "the Presidet [sic] of the Kingdom of God on the Earth & a law giver unto Israel . . . & . . . the Presidt [sic] of the United States and of this Great Nation."*[16] *This cartoon of Brigham Young and Ulysses S. Grant is from Frank Leslie's illustrated newspaper and captures the public stereotypes of Brigham and his large polygamous family.*

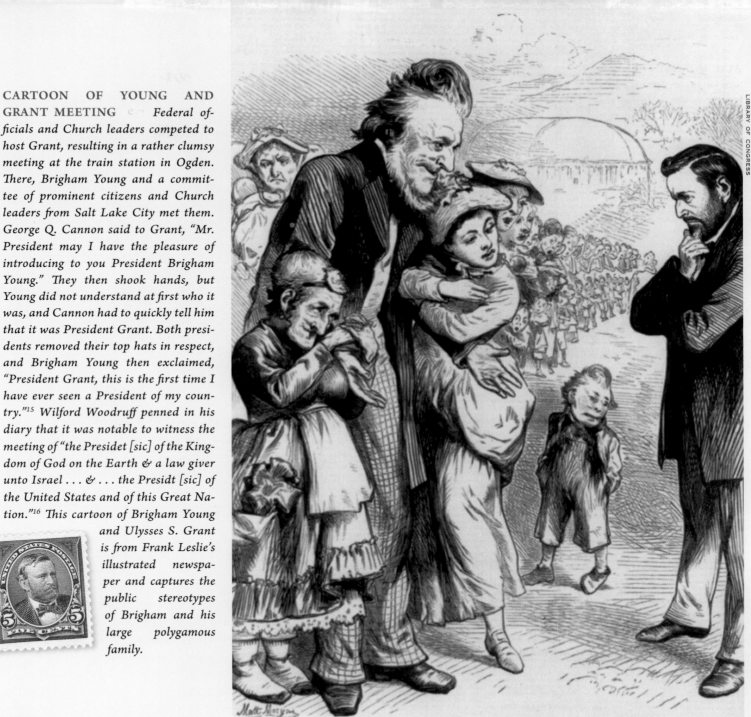

Ulysses S. Grant made a brief return trip to Utah on October 30, 1879. It had been four years since he'd become the first president to visit Utah and more than two years since he left office. Grant and his family left the U.S. on a two-year world tour in May 1877 and were working their way back home after a triumphant circumnavigation, where they were greeted by enormous crowds on three continents. They had dined with Queen Victoria in England and Otto von Bismarck in Germany. They had steamed up the Nile, called on Prince Chulalongkorn in Siam (Thailand), mediated a dispute between China and Japan, and enjoyed the hospitality of Emperor Meiji at the Imperial Palace in Tokyo. They arrived back in the States in San Francisco, and the train heading east made a brief stop in Ogden. Three carloads of dignitaries had come up from Salt Lake to greet

"General Grant," including Governor Emery and Church Apostles. At Ogden, Grant gave brief remarks to the cheering crowd at the train depot. Despite straining his back earlier in the morning on the train, General Grant made his way to a Pullman Palace Car, where he sat in the doorway and shook hands with well-wishers for an hour before steaming eastward to complete his round-the-world journey.

Above: Ogden Union Train Depot, East Front, 1879. Taken by C.R. Savage. Right: A Palace Car was a premium service offered by the Railroad. The cars featured plush carpeting, individual gas lamps for the passengers, and at night, individual fold-down berths.

WALKER HOUSE   *(Right) When a carriage took the presidential party from the Salt Lake railway station to Grant's hotel, the Walker House in Salt Lake City (shown opposite), the streets were lined with throngs of white-clad children singing and throwing flowers before the president's carriage. As the presidential entourage slowly made its way down South Temple Street to Main Street, Grant asked Governor Emery, "Whose children are these?" When he learned that they were Mormon children, "for several moments the president was silent, and then he murmured in a tone of self-reproach, 'I have been deceived!'"[17]*

A large crowd of curious onlookers patiently waited outside the Walker House for a glimpse of the chief executive. They were delighted when President Grant and Governor Emery went out on the balcony to greet them. The governor was pleased to introduce to the Salt Lake crowd "the first President of the United States that had ever visited Utah." He also bade him a hearty welcome to the Territory on behalf of all the people and explained that due to the fatigue of the journey, President Grant would not address the crowd at that time.[18]

PRESIDENT ULYSSES S. GRANT

While Governor Emery took President Grant to Camp Douglas, George Q. Cannon was left to entertain Julia Grant and her son at an organ recital at the Tabernacle. During the visit to the Tabernacle, Mrs. Grant offered a prayer for the Mormons. She was deeply moved by what she saw and heard and told ex-delegate William H. Hooper, "Oh, I wish I could do something for these good Mormon people." The group later reunited and left on the train for Ogden, escorted once more by Brigham Young and a delegation of Mormon leaders as well as Governor Emery and a delegation of non-Mormon officials. En route, Mrs. Grant enjoyed talking with the LDS women of the group, where she left an impression of being very friendly. As the group boarded the departing train in Ogden, Col. Fred Grant told

President Cannon, "If there is anything I can do for you let me know. I don't believe all that is said about the people of Utah."[22]

Ultimately, Ulysses S. Grant returned to the White House, but his visit had left an impact. After the presidential visit, Brigham Young wrote about it to his son Alfales, who was away at Ann Arbor, Michigan: "We have had a pleasant little excitement this week in the visit of Pres. Grant and party to our city and territory. The ring [of anti-Mormons] attempted to corral him but signally failed, and he very impartially bestowed his attentions on all persons and parties alike, at which they, fancying themselves his especial pets, feel very much chagrined. The party—the ladies especially—expressed themselves very much delighted with their visit to the home of the Latter-day Saints."[23]

GUEST REGISTER OF THE TABERNACLE   *(Opposite) The following day, October 4, the presidential party visited the Temple Block and the Tabernacle. Here they signed the guest register (shown opposite). From there, President Grant left in a buggy to visit one of the nearby hills, where he could take pleasure in a view of the city.[19] He called on the soldiers at Camp Douglas and enjoyed lunch at the home of Colonel O.A. Patton, where the president was especially delighted with the Pattons' four-day-old son, who seemed to like the president right away.[20] Grant gave some advice to Governor Emery, where he urged him to identify himself with Utah's non-Mormon community and not try to ally himself with the Mormons. Emery ended up being a moderate Grant appointee, neither antagonizing nor siding with the Mormons.[21] A public reception was held for the President in the early afternoon at the Walker House, with numerous ladies and gentlemen coming through to pay their respects.*

RUTHERFORD B. HAYES

RUTHERFORD B. HAYES WAS PRESIDENT of the United States from 1877–1881 and served at the same time George Emery and Eli Murray were governors of the Utah Territory and John Taylor was president of the Church. He came to Utah once while he was president.

President and Mrs. Hayes visited Utah September 5–6, 1880. It was a visit marked by the power struggle between the Mormon and non-Mormon parties of the state to host him. Hayes was on a train trip west to Seattle and became the first president to travel west beyond the Rocky Mountains to the Pacific Coast. His travel party included First Lady Lucy Hayes, two of their sons, Secretary of War Alexander Ramsey, and General William Sherman, who led the famous march on Atlanta, Georgia, during the Civil War.

OIL PAINTING OF RUTHERFORD B. HAYES *The presidential party was greeted at the train station in Ogden by the Ogden Brass Band, an enthusiastic crowd, and various Utah dignitaries. Governor Murray introduced the president to the crowd, but because it was the Sabbath, the dignitaries uttered only a few sentences of appreciation in response to the warm welcome and declined to give any speeches. Hayes recognized Territorial Delegate George Q. Cannon, who introduced him to Church President John Taylor and Apostle Daniel H. Wells. The VIPs then transferred to the two coaches of the special train and traveled south to the capital.*

UTAH TERRITORIAL GOVERNOR ELI MURRAY   *Upon hearing that President Hayes would be making a trip to the West, Governor Eli H. Murray (shown here) wrote him: "I am glad to know of your proposed [visit] to the west and write now in advance to express the hope that you will stop, take a look at this great Territory and dwell for awhile within the gates of the City of the Saints." The governor defended, "Salt Lake City is a good halfway place, a sojourn here would prove both refreshing and interesting." The President agreed and added the "City of the Saints" to his itinerary.[24]*

Mayor Feramorz Little and the Salt Lake City Council assembled a committee to welcome the president but were shut out by Governor Murray, who had assembled his own committee of non-Mormon dignitaries. President Hayes ignored Mayor Little's first invitation to host him, and when he received a second invitation, he simply replied: "By prior arrangement I am to be the guest of the Governor, and hope you are acting in concert."[25] Governor Murray made a great effort during the presidential visit to keep Hayes away from Church officials and to meet only with the anti-Mormons of the city. Historian B. H. Roberts believed that "this visit, under the conditions prevailing when it was made, and the president's association with the anti-'Mormon' party while in the city—deepened his prejudices."[26]

CITY *of* SAINTS

RUTHERFORD & LUCY HAYES   *(Right)* **ELIZA R. SNOW**
(Inset) On the train journey south, Mrs. Hayes invited the ladies of the welcoming party into the president's car, where they had an enjoyable visit. Some of the ladies from the Relief Society presented her with an elegant white silk collarette made from Utah-grown silk, and Eliza R. Snow presented her with a copy of her poems and the new Primary Hymn Book.[27]

When the train stopped at Farmington, a large number of children were there to cheer the presidential party, and President Hayes had Mrs. Hayes called for to come see the sight of the many children who were there to greet them. The Deseret News noted: "Mrs. Hayes as well as the President took great pains to reach down from the cars and shake hands with the little folks, not neglecting even the smallest of them. A similar scene took place at Wood's Cross, and the President and party were highly gratified at the marks of respect from the people of Utah."[28]

UTAH WELCOMES OUR CHIEF MAGISTRATE.

Long Life and a Pleasant Trip to our Distinguished Guests.

DINNER
In Honor of our Worthy President,
Rutherford B. Hayes.
WALKER HOUSE,
C. S. ERB, Prop'r.
Salt Lake City, Sept 5th, 1880.

SUNDAY, SEPT'R 5th, 1880.
Menu.

Soups
Fresh Oyster   Chicken

Fish
Baked Bear Lake Trout, Madeira Sauce
Brook Trout, Boiled, Norman Matalotte Sauce

Entrees
Lamb's Cutlets, Garnished with French Peas
Fricassee of Spring Chicken, Mushroom Sauce
Roast
Stuffed Turkey, with Currant Jelly
Surloin of Beef, Brown Sauce
Baked Apples, Wine Sauce

Game
Teal Duck, with Marangue Tarts
Canvass Back Duck, Apple Sauce

Salads
Shrimp   Chicken Mayoneise
VEGETABLES IN SEASON.

Pastry
New York Plum Pudding, Hard Sauce
Sliced Apple Pie   Lemon Custard Pie
Raspberry Jam Tarts
Neapolitan Cake   Ravoli Cake
Almond Fruit Cake   Petits Choux au Caramel
Assorted Fancy Biscuits

Dessert
Pyramids of Macaroons
Lemon Ice Cream   Vanilla Ice Cream
Damson Fruit Water Ice   Grape Fruit Water Ice
Peach Marangue   Pine Apple Marangue
Gateau de Anana a la Porcupine
Strawberry Jelly   Assorted Confectionery   Orange Jelly

FRUIT
CAFE

Star Job Print, Romney Block.

"One Country, One Constitution, O

20th July 1877

R B Hayes

WALKER HOUSE DINNER PROGRAM   When the president arrived in Salt Lake, thousands of Sunday School children lined the streets from the depot to the Walker House, where the presidential party stayed. From the portico of the hotel, Governor Murray introduced the guests to the crowd. Again, because of the Sabbath, the greetings were brief, and the dignitaries refrained from making any speeches. The president did say that he was astonished at what he had seen as he travelled through the Territory and that this civilization in the desert and the appearance of the people was beyond anything he had seen in the West. The party then enjoyed a fine dinner at the Walker House.

HAYES SIGNATURE FROM ELIZA R. SNOW'S AUTOGRAPH BOOK   (Top right) President Rutherford B. Hayes distributed preprinted cards with his signature beneath one of his hallmark phrases and the date that the last Reconstruction troops left the South. He likely gave this one to Eliza R. Snow, who was the president of the Relief Society, during his Utah visit. She placed it in her autograph book.

WALKER HOUSE   (Right) Main Street, Salt Lake City, looking north, 1889.

INTERIOR OF MORMON TABERNACLE   *(Below)* **TABERNACLE GUEST BOOK WITH HAYES'S SIGNATURE**   *(Right)*

Monday morning, Hayes and his party saw the various sites of the city and were greatly impressed with the Tabernacle on Temple Square. General Sherman stood on one end of the Tabernacle and President Hayes on the other, and they were amazed that they could carry on a conversation due to the remarkable acoustic properties of the building. Like modern tourists, they heard the pin-drop demonstration from the end of the building. To this, Hayes remarked, "extraordinary" and said he had never before seen anything like it. While there, they met the builder of the Tabernacle, Superintendent Henry Grow. Hayes said, "I am pleased to meet with the man who could erect such a building. Who was the architect?" "President Brigham Young was his own architect," was the reply. To which, Hayes was completely speechless.[29]

HAYES AND WHEELER.

HAYES AND WHEELER BANNER FROM 1876 PRESIDENTIAL CAMPAIGN

PRESIDENT HAYES IN DOORWAY OF HOME AT FT. DOUGLAS *(Left) After the military salute, the presidential party enjoyed lunch at Fort Douglas and posed for a photograph before they left. The President can be seen in the center of the doorway. By 1:30 PM, they were on the special train back to Ogden. Shortly after leaving Salt Lake, President Hayes entered the rear cars, shook hands with all present, and then took a seat near President John Taylor, where the two presidents conversed until they reached Ogden.*[30]

MILITARY SALUTE AT FT. DOUGLAS *A public reception for the guests was held at the Walker House from 10–11 AM, where Governor Murray introduced most callers. Hayes's party then loaded the carriages and went to Fort Douglas, where General John E. Smith welcomed them with a salute of artillery on the fields of Fort Douglas, which is shown in the accompanying photo.*

Rutherford B. Hayes was the last president to visit Utah for eleven years; the next visit would not take place until 1891. Because of the controversy over plural marriage, relationships between Utah

and the White House were especially hostile in the 1880s. James A. Garfield, who followed Hayes, did not have a chance to visit Utah as president before he was assassinated in his first year (although he came twice as a congressman). His successor, Chester A. Arthur, did not make it to Utah in the three and

a half years he served in office to finish out Garfield's term. The next president, Grover Cleveland (who was both the 22nd and 24th president) ironically never made it to Utah in either of his terms, despite signing the

enabling act that made Utah the 45th state in 1896.

BENJAMIN HARRISON

Benjamin Harrison was president of the United States from 1889–1893 and served at the same time Arthur Thomas was governor of the Utah Territory and Wilford Woodruff was president of the Church. He came to Utah twice, including once as president.

As a result of the 1890 Manifesto by President Wilford Woodruff renouncing polygamy, President Harrison assumed a more moderate attitude toward the Saints and announced in 1891 that he would visit the Utah Territory.[31] Included in the presidential party were First Lady Caroline Harrison, her secretary and niece Mrs. Dimmick, Russell B. Harrison and his wife, Mary McKee (the Harrison's daughter), Carter B. Harrison and his wife, Postmaster General John Wanamaker, Secretary of Agriculture Jeremiah McClain Rusk, and Marshall Dan Ransdell. It was Harrison's only visit to Utah as president, but he had been through once before, in 1881, as a new senator from Indiana and as a member of the Senate Committee on Territories.

IS ENDORSED.

The People Accept the Manifesto!

THE VOTE UNANIMOUS

President Cannon Gives the Reasons For Its Issuance.

PRESIDENT WOODRUFF SPEAKS.

He Is Thankful the Saints Have Sustained Him in His Action in Issuing It.

THE SALT LAKE HERALD: TUESDAY, OCTOBER 7, 1890   (Opposite) President Harrison assumed a more moderate attitude toward the Saints due to the 1890 Manifesto renouncing polygamy.

HARRISON IN CARRIAGE TRAVELING DOWN MAIN STREET, SALT LAKE CITY   (Right) In the early morning hours of May 9, 1891, President Benjamin Harrison arrived in Salt Lake City, where he met with civic leaders and President Wilford Woodruff, George Q. Cannon, and others.[35] They went directly to the Walker House for a breakfast but enjoyed a route lined with immense crowds of people. Gentlemen waved their hats, ladies waved their handkerchiefs, and the crowd cheered as they glimpsed the president, who cordially responded by removing his hat and tipping his head. This is the only known photograph of Harrison while he was in Utah.

TOUR OF
THE PRESIDENT,
TO THE PACIFIC COAST.
April 14th to May 16th
1891

ITINERARY

ITINERARY PROGRAM COVER   (Left) Utah leaders wanted to make a good impression, but the Church leaders were especially anxious to help create goodwill in post-Manifesto Utah to help advance the cause of statehood. With the presidential visit to Utah within days, First Presidency member George Q. Cannon sent Elder John Henry Smith of the Twelve south to Utah County to "ask the people to make a showing as the President passed through."[32] In Salt Lake City, the Gardo House, Beehive House, and other Church-owned buildings were "profusely decorated" with flags and patriotic bunting. Signs covered the Juvenile Instructor building declaring, "Welcome to the Grandson of Tippecanoe" and "Under Harrison freedom dawned on Utah." Even the temple had a huge banner covering an entire side of the building that said, "Fear God, Honor the President."[33]

In advance of the presidential visit, Governor Arthur Thomas, Territorial Delegate John T. Caine, Provo Mayor John E. Booth, and some of the federal appointees in Utah traveled north into Idaho. They were introduced to President Harrison and then joined the overnight train south.[34]

"IN HONOR OF HARRISON," *SALT LAKE HERALD*, **MAY 10, 1891.** *A parade formed behind the presidential procession, and along South Temple Street, the VIPs passed a large group of children, who were cheering and were each waving a flag. The group of about 7,000 children sang "My Country 'Tis of Thee" and "The Star Spangled Banner." President Harrison was touched and stopped to talk with them.*[36] *"I have not seen in all this long journey," the president later said, "anything that touched my heart more than . . . when the children from the free public schools of Salt Lake City, waving the one banner that we all love and singing an anthem of praise to that beneficent Providence . . ., gave us their glad welcome."*[37] *He later added, "I have seen nothing more beautiful and inspiring than this scene which burst upon us unexpectedly. The multitude of children bearing waving banners makes a scene which can never fade from our memories."*[38]

At Liberty Park, state and Church leaders sat on the stand with the president while he spoke to a large crowd.[39] *"We are a people organized upon principles of liberty," Harrison told the cheering crowd. "But, my fellow countrymen, it is distinguished from license; its liberty within and under the law. I have no discord as a public officer with men of any creed, religious or political, if they will obey the law." He then went to participate in the opening of the new Chamber of Commerce building.*

> *"I have not seen in all this long journey anything that touched my heart more than . . . when the children from . . . Salt Lake City . . . gave us their glad welcome."*

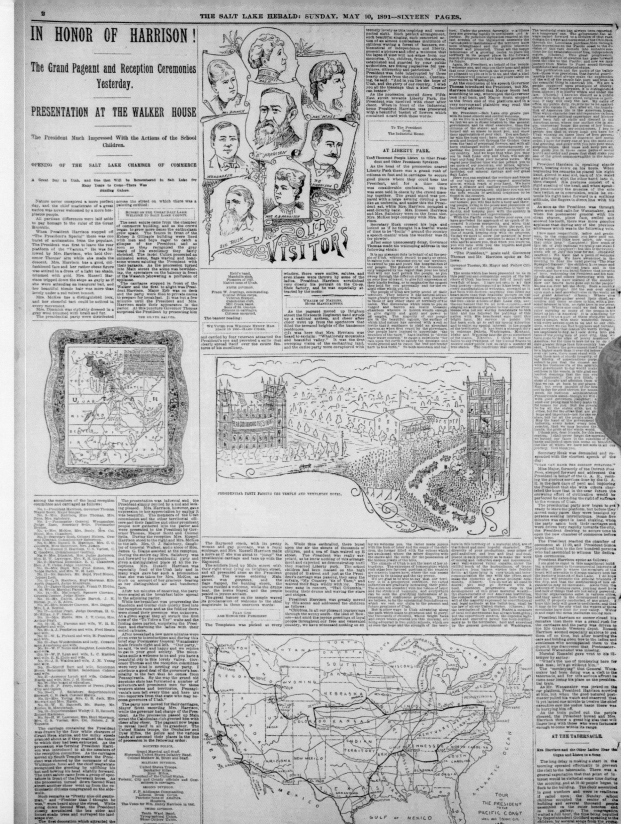

Welcome to the

President

Walker House

Salt Lake City,   Saturday, May 9, 1891.

To the President

By Salt Lake City Corporation.

Mayor Scott,   Mrs. Harrison,
President Harrison,   Mrs. Salisbury,
Governor Thomas,   Mrs. McKee,
Gen. Wanamaker,   Mrs. R. Harrison,
Gen. Rusk,   Mrs. Zane,
R. Harrison,   Miss Thomas,
Judge Zane,   Mrs. Dimmick,
Major Sanger,   Miss Robertson,
Col. Sells,   Mrs. Boyd,
Col. Godfrey,   Mrs. Blunt,
Governor Robertson,   Mrs. Sells,
Col. Blunt,   Marshal Ramsdel,
M. Boyd,   Chas. Saunders.
C. D. Harrison,   Ladies.

BREAKFAST.

COFFEE,
VIENNA
ROLLS.

FRENCH
TOAST.

CUCUMBERS,
RADISHES,
SLICED
TOMATOES.

CORN BREAD.

GRAHAM
BREAD.

STRAWBERRIES AND CREAM.

—

OAT MEAL MUSH.

—

BROILED BROOK TROUT.

SARATOGA CHIPS.

LAMB CHOPS,

WITH FRESH MUSHROOMS.

SPRING CHICKEN ON TOAST,

WITH BREAKFAST BACON.

TENDERLOIN STEAK,

BAKED POTATOES.

EGG OMELETTES, WITH PARSLEY,

GERMAN WAFFLES.

WALKER HOUSE COVER AND INSIDE OF BREAKFAST PROGRAM   *The breakfast at the Walker House began promptly at 8:00 AM, and the party enjoyed a variety of local delicacies.*

TOP HAT BELONGING TO BENJAMIN HARRISON   *A host of Sunday School children and the Mormon Tabernacle Choir waited patiently for hours in the Tabernacle to perform patriotic music for the president; however, the anti-Mormons of the city, including Governor Arthur Thomas, worked hard to "keep the virtues and progress of the 'Mormon' people as far as practicable in the shade." Harrison was therefore kept far away from Temple Square, to the disappointment of many Saints.[40] Nonetheless, from the view of Church leaders, "it could have been worse," considering the nation's chief was hosted by "the Tribune ring."[41] The presidential train continued south, making stops and brief speeches in Lehi, American Fork, Provo, and Springville. "It has been very pleasant to-day to ride through this most extraordinary valley," Harrison said in Springville after a day traveling through the Mormon settlements of Utah County, "and to notice how productive your fields are and how genial and kindly your people are."[42]*

Harrison's visit to Utah was part of the longest journey ever undertaken up to that time by any president while in office. The 9,232-mile rail trip lasted one month and three days. The trip was partly planned and largely financed by the former Governor of California, Leland Stanford. The pioneer railroad builder had invited the president to his ranch in Palo Alto to discuss a professorship at the newly built Stanford University and to participate in the dedication of that institution.

Above ❧ *Harrison family aboard the* Presidential Special *at Royal Gorge.* *Below* ❧ *Booklet detailing President Harrison's Tour to the Pacific Coast, showing him in Utah on Saturday, May 9th, 1891.*

TOUR OF THE PRESIDENT TO THE PACIFIC COAST, APRIL 14th to MAY 15th, 1891

PRESIDENT VISITS OGDEN

Crowds Throng the Vicinity of the Union Depot—The President is Greeted by Governor Wells, Senator Kearns and Many Prominent Citizens of Utah.

The citizens of Ogden had been kept in touch with the movements of the presidential special by Standard bulletins yesterday and as a result the crowds did not begin to assemble at the Union depot until about twenty minutes before the time for the arrival of the train.

The special had been delayed one hour and twenty minutes on the Sacramento division caused by the fact that the train made the circuit by the way of Stockton instead of crossing the bay at Port Costa. The special entered the Salt Lake division at Wadsworth exactly that one hour and twenty minutes late and failed to make up any of the time, but all along the division the stations were made on the schedule time and not a moment was lost. As stated before in the Standard the most disagreeable portion of the journey across Nevada was made in the night time. In the early hours yesterday morning a heavy rain storm came up which beat down the dust, a usual feature of this journey, and cooled the atmosphere. As a consequence the otherwise disagreeable trip was rendered pleasant.

From Carlin into Ogden engine 1100 pulled the train with Engineer Thomas Lindsay at the throttle. In charge of the train were Conductor Coates and Brakemen Hancock and Cross.

The train pulled into Ogden at exactly 7:23. There were seven coaches, including in the train, the private car of General Manager Kruttschnitt being included in the presidential special, next to the baggage car. The fourth car was the private car of the President and Mrs. McKinley and as it passed the multitude assembled caught a glimpse of the pale face of Mrs. McKinley at the window.

The President occupied the rear car, the "Olympia," with Secretaries Long, Hitchcock, Postmaster General Smith and Private Secretary Cortelyou.

The train moved in slowly to avoid accidents as the dense crowds assembled continually pushed across the track, ebbing and flowing like a mighty sea. All the neighboring buildings were covered with crowds who wished to catch a glimpse of the President. In the crush several men, women and children were crowded to the ground and fainting women were conveyed clear of the mass of struggling humanity at several points.

The special had barely come to a stop when the well-known features of Gov. Wells was seen to appear above the closed gate at the west side of the car platform. He was stopped for a moment by the detective at the rear of the train but upon disclosing his identity he was allowed to pass into the car, closely followed by Senator Kearns, both of whom clambered over the gate to the platform. The gate was then opened and Judges Miner and Bartch, Adjutant General Burton, W. C. Weaver and Angus Wright were allowed to enter the car.

At the other end of the car Secretary Hitchcock had appeared and after some conversation invited C. O. Whittemore, R. B. Whittemore, Parley P. Christensen and Mayor Browning to enter and meet the President. After the party had been presented to the President in the interior of the car, Gov. Wells stepped to the rear platform and spoke as follows, as soon as the applause which greeted his appearance had subsided:

"Fellow citizens: Owing to the fact that today is the Sabbath and to the further fact of the illness of Mrs. McKinley, the President especially requests that no applause or noise be rendered when he appears. Owing to these facts also he does not desire to address you, but will step to the platform and acknowledge your greeting."

Governor Wells retreated to the car and Senator Kearns appeared and said:

"My Fellow Citizens: I have the honor to introduce to you the greatest statesman of the modern age, our beloved chief executive,—William McKinley."

The President appeared immediately, and with bared head bowed his acknowledgment to the tumultuous applause received. He then stepped to the lower steps of the car platform in order to shake hands with the school children and others gathered on the west side. After about seven minutes of hand-shaking here the President returned to the platform. Just at the rear of the car the Logan-Dix G. A. R. post was assembled and from among the number a veteran climbed upon the platform and insisted upon shaking hands with the President despite the fact that the detective on guard tried to prevent him.

During all this time W. C. Weaver was in evidence on the platform, much to the dismay of the kodak fiends, who in endeavoring to catch a picture of the President, only succeeded in obtaining an active likeness of Mr. Weaver.

About five minutes before the train left for the east the President again entered his car and was there presented by Governor Wells with a flag as a souvenir of the esteem in which the chief executive is held by the people of Utah. The President assured Governor Wells and Senator Kearns that he would again visit Utah before the end of his presidential term if circumstances would so permit.

Before the train moved out Governor Wells was made the object of piteous appeals by the politicians from Salt Lake, who had accompanied the party to Ogden in order to meet the President, but who had been refused admission to the car. The governor made his escape from the car as soon as possible and with the members of his party boarded a waiting Short train for return to Salt Lake.

The presidential train was made ready for the continuation of the journey and started eastward at 7:55, the President, Secretary Cortelyou and other members of the party bowing farewell to the people from the rear platform.

WILLIAM McKINLEY

WILLIAM McKINLEY WAS PRESIDENT of the United States from 1897–1901 and served at the same time Heber M. Wells was governor of Utah and Wilford Woodruff and Lorenzo Snow were presidents of the Church. He came to Utah once as president for a brief stop.

President William McKinley and his wife, Ida, visited the West in May 1901; however, because of the first lady's ill health, they cancelled the segment to the Pacific Northwest and remained in San Francisco for two weeks until her doctors felt she was stable enough to travel. This delay bumped plans for a longer visit to Utah, where Senator Thomas Kearns was preparing to host the First Family in his Kearns Mansion (future Utah Governor's Mansion). Instead, a very brief stop at the depot in Ogden on Sunday evening, May 26, 1901, became the first presidential visit to Utah after the territory achieved statehood in 1896.

"PRESIDENT VISITS OGDEN," *THE STANDARD*, MAY 27, 1901   (Opposite) Governor Wells emerged from the president's rail car and instructed the crowd: "Fellow Citizens: Owing to the fact that today is the Sabbath and to the further fact of the illness of Mrs. McKinley, the President especially requests that no applause or noise be rendered when he appears. Owing to these facts also he does not desire to address you, but will step to the platform to acknowledge your greeting." The excited masses promptly ignored these instructions after Senator Kearns addressed them by saying, "My Fellow Citizens: I have the honor to introduce to you the greatest statesman of the modern age, our beloved chief executive,— William McKinley."[43]

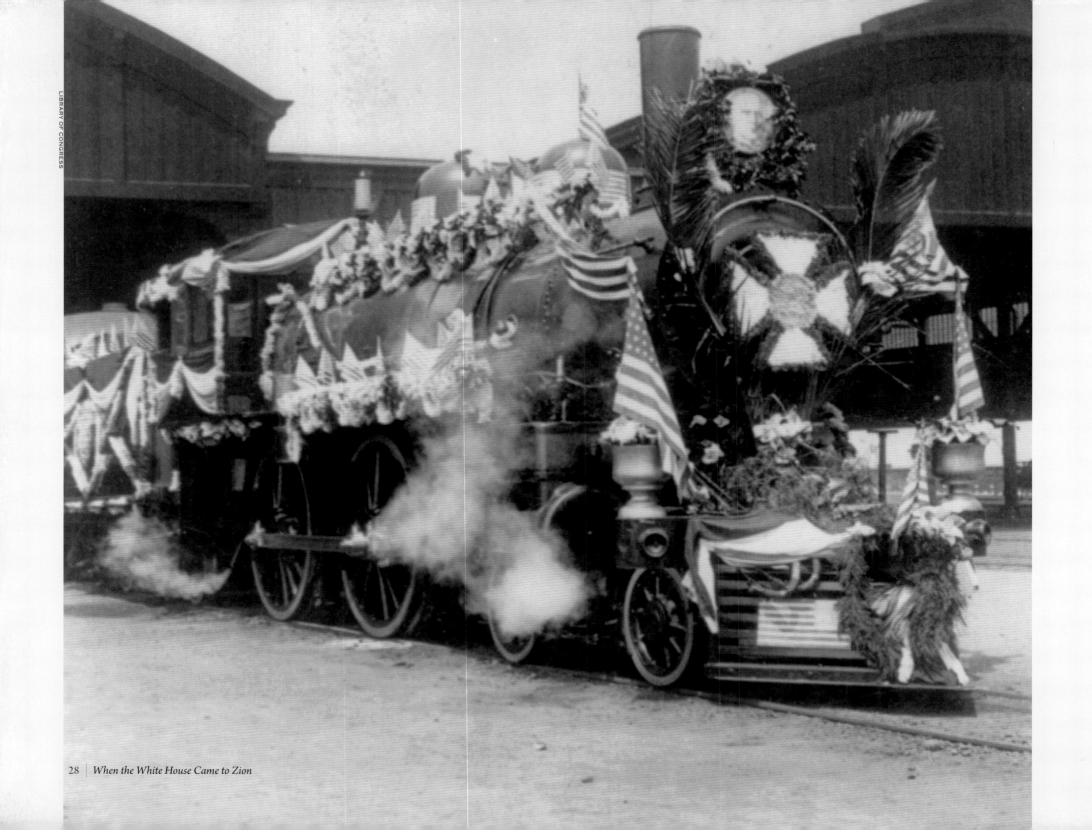

ILLUSTRATION OF THE *PRESIDENTIAL SPECIAL* ON ITS WAY TO OGDEN *President McKinley appeared and bowed his head in acknowledgment of the applause. He then stepped down to the lower steps of the platform and spent seven minutes shaking hands with the school children who had come before returning to his rail car. Once inside, Governor Wells presented him with an American flag with forty-five stars that was made from Utah-grown silk. The president promised Governor Wells and Senator Kearns that he would return to Utah for a proper visit before the end of his term "if circumstances would so permit."*[44] *The train departed eastward once more at 7:55 PM after a thirty-two–minute stop.*

MCKINLEY TRAIN LEAVING OAKLAND FOR OGDEN *(Opposite) A large crowd assembled in the Ogden depot as the seven-car Presidential Special arrived at 7:23 Sunday evening. As it slowed, some caught sight of Mrs. McKinley's pale face as she looked out the window of the fourth car. As soon as the train stopped, the crowd rushed forward, the Utahns hoping for a glimpse of the president. The newspapers reported, "In the crush several men, women, and children were crowded to the ground and fainting women were conveyed clear of the mass of struggling humanity at several points."*[45] *Both Governor Heber Wells and Senator Thomas Kearns jumped the railing and were allowed by the detective present to enter the presidential car.*[46] *This photograph is the actual train of McKinley's trip as they were departing east from Oakland, California.*

ASSASSINATION OF PRESIDENT McKINLEY

WM McKINLEY

McKinley would never make good on his promise to return to Utah because of his assassination. Just twelve weeks after returning from the West, on Sept. 6, 1901, President McKinley was shot twice by anarchist Leon Czolgosz while visiting the Pan-American Exposition in Buffalo, New York. Apostle and future President George Albert Smith happened to be in the Music Hall and "heard the shot that killed McKinley."[47]

McKinley's vice president, Theodore Roosevelt, would become the new president.

Above   Wash drawing by T. Dart Walker of the assassination of President McKinley. At a reception the day after the President had delivered an important speech modifying his high-tariff policy, Czolgosz pretended to extend his hand in congratulations but instead pulled out a concealed revolver and shot the president twice.

A NEW STATE IN A NEW CENTURY

1902–1945

THEODORE ROOSEVELT

T HEODORE ROOSEVELT WAS PRESIDENT of the United States from 1901–1909 and served at the same time Heber M. Wells and John C. Cutler were governors of Utah and Joseph F. Smith was president of the Church. He came to Utah three times, including once as president.

"ROOSEVELT SPENDS A DAY IN SALT LAKE"   *Theodore Roosevelt first visited Utah while campaigning as President McKinley's running mate, on September 20–21, 1900. At that time he was the governor of New York. Roosevelt toured the Agriculture College in Logan (now Utah State University) and spoke at the Logan Tabernacle, Brigham City, and Saltair on the shores of the Great Salt Lake.*

GOVERNOR ROOSEVELT AT SALTAIR   *(Opposite) Theodore Roosevelt (far left) visited the Saltair with Utah's first governor, Heber M. Wells (center). They both took a swim in the lake while there, and it happened to be the last day of the season and one of the coldest days of the year to date. "I admire the way you have come into the wilderness and made it blossom like the rose," he said in Brigham City. "I admire what you have done here in building up the country—the farms, ranches, the cities you have built."[48] He called on the First Presidency of Lorenzo Snow, Joseph F. Smith, and George Q. Cannon, enjoyed a performance at the Tabernacle, lunched at the Alta Club, and led a parade of 300 horsemen. However, the reception was lukewarm; Roosevelt's voice was tired and strained on the trip, and the people of Utah—who had overwhelmingly backed William Jennings Bryan over McKinley in 1896—were skeptical about the McKinley-Roosevelt support for the gold standard versus silver.[49]*

ROOSEVELT SPENDS A DAY IN SALT LAKE

Takes Part in a Parade, Makes Two Speeches and Has Swim in the Lake.

Entire Affair Was a Frosty One—Cowboy Feature Developed Into Turnout of Sheepmen.

RECITAL AT TABERNACLE.

Candidate and Party Hear Some Good Music.

ARRIVAL OF ROOSEVELT.

Parade Was Received With Considerable Coolness.

SALT LAKE HERALD.

Weather Today.
Forecast for Salt Lake Today is Fair and Warmer.

SALT LAKE CITY, UTAH: SATURDAY, SEPTEMBER 2 , 1900   NUMBER 109

ELT'S DAY OF STRENUOUS ENDEAVOR IN SALT LAKE

AN EXHIBITION RIDE   CALL ON PREST SNOW   AT THE BEACH   THE EVENING SMILE

"I admire the way you have come into the wilderness and made it blossom like the rose."

PRESIDENT ROOSEVELT ARRIVING IN SALT LAKE CITY

The president's visit to Salt Lake City on Friday, May 29, 1903, was a whirlwind of activity, and the people received him extraordinarily well. He arrived at the depot in Salt Lake on a special train at 8:30; rode through the solidly lined streets to the City and County Building; addressed the school children gathered there at 9:00; reviewed a big parade there from 9:15–9:45; drove to the Tabernacle on Temple Square, where he attended a great meeting from 10–11 (speaking for 30 minutes of it); traveled to the home of Senator Thomas Kearns for a reception and breakfast from 11:15–1:15; and then made it back to the train depot for the 1:25 departure to Ogden.

MAYOR THOMPSON, PRESIDENT ROOS-EVELT, AND GOVERNOR WELLS *(Left to Right): Salt Lake City Mayor Ezra Thompson, President Roosevelt, and Utah Governor Heber M. Wells. Wells was so excited to host the president that he refrained from naming his newborn baby boy, hoping to bestow the honor of naming the child on the president. Wells arranged for the babe's nurse to take him to the City and County Building and remain in waiting until the perfect opportunity arrived. As the president left the reviewing stand to return to his carriage, Governor Wells presented the infant in his arms to the president. Roosevelt held the boy a moment, tickling him under the chin and delighting him. However, no name came to mind in the brief moment, and the president handed the little one back to the nurse and sped on to his speech at the Tabernacle.[50]* **ROOSEVELT'S TOP HAT** *(Opposite)*

ROOSEVELT'S SPURS *(Above) Roosevelt had been second-in-command of the 1st United States Volunteer Cavalry in the Spanish-American War, 1898. When his commanding officer was given command of another unit, this one became known as "Roosevelt's Rough Riders."*

PRESIDENT REINS IN THE ROUGH RIDERS *On the west yard of the City and County Building (see below right), hundreds of school children lined up in rows to greet the president, with the smallest children against the rope line and the larger children in back. Only twelve feet separated the rope line where the smallest children were watching the parade from the presidential reviewing stand, and it was in this narrow chute that the procession came through. When a division of Rough Riders came through, they were bucking and maneuvering their horses to show off for the President, but it was creating quite a threat for the young children watching. Seeing the terrorized faces of the little children hanging over the rope in front, the President raised his right hand and cried, "Boys, don't gallop your horses; the little folks might get hurt!" The men on horseback obeyed, but a number of children had already fainted from terror and exhaustion.[51]*

SAN JUAN HILL

NEWSPAPER COVER, *SALT LAKE TELEGRAM,* **MAY 29, 1903.**

The president's second visit to Salt Lake City was a whirlwind of activity, and the people received him extraordinarily well. When he arrived at the Tabernacle, President Roosevelt was introduced to President Joseph F. Smith and his counselors, John R. Winder and Anthon H. Lund (see far right), who all sat with him on the stand during the meeting. The Tabernacle was filled to capacity. In his remarks, Roosevelt said of the state:

The fundamental element in building up Utah has been the work of the citizens of Utah. And you did it because your people entered in to possess the land, and to leave it after them to their children and to their children's children. You here, whom I am addressing, and your predecessors, did not come here to exploit the land and then go somewhere else. You came in, as the governor of the state has said, as home makers, to make homes for yourselves and for those who should come after you. And this is the only way in which a state can be built up. And I say to all of you, and all of your people, from one ocean to another, especially the people of the arid and semi-arid regions, the people of the great plains, the people of the mountains, approach the problem of taking care of the physical resources of the country in the spirit that has made Utah what it is.[52]

J. F. Smith family

Prest. Roosevelt
RECEPTION
Tabernacle, Friday, May 29, 1903

RESERVED SEAT   ADMIT ONE

ROOSEVELT PROCESSION DOWN MAIN STREET   (Below) *After Roosevelt traveled down Main Street (shown here in front of the Oregon Front Line Railroad Building), he said, "I believe the crowds were larger than in any other city of similar size. But nowhere on the trip have I seen the crowds handled by the police better than they were in Salt Lake. The demonstration in the tabernacle was also unique, taking place as it did, in a house of worship. I wish we were going to stay longer in Salt Lake."*[53]

To meet
The President of the United States.
Mr. and Mrs. Thomas Kearns
request the pleasure of the company
of
Pres. and Mrs. Joseph F. Smith.
on Friday morning, May the twenty-ninth.
at half after eleven o'clock.

Breakfast.

ROOSEVELT AND LOCAL DIG-
NITARIES OUTSIDE THE KEARNS
MANSION (Opposite) President Roosevelt
enjoyed a late-morning breakfast at the one-year-
old home of Senator Thomas Kearns, which
would become Utah's Governor's Mansion in
1937. As a thank you gift for his hospitality,
Roosevelt gave Senator Kearns this horned
hat rack (Left), which remains today in the
Governor's Library at the mansion. As his own
souvenir from the breakfast, President Joseph F.
Smith picked up one of the little decorative American
flags from the table décor as the event ended and saved
it with his own invitation from the historic meal.

MIKE WINDER COLLECTION

You see JOHNSON all over the world.

113 THE CROWD AT SENATOR KEARNS
ROOSEVELT DAY IN SALT LAKE, MAY 29 1903.

The Johnson Co's Stereoscopic Views.

THOMAS F. KEARNS FAMILY COLLECTION

A New State in a New Century 1902–1945 | 37

SAGAMORE HILL NATIONAL HISTORIC SITE

THE OGDEN STANDARD, **MAY 29, 1903** ∘ *(Left)* **ROOSEVELT ADDRESSED A HUGE CROWD IN OGDEN** ∘ *(Above) The people of Ogden held a parade for the president and dignitaries from the train depot to the City Hall square at Twenty-fourth Street and Grant Avenue, where Roosevelt spoke to an enormous crowd. After the rally, the president's party departed by rail to Evanston, Wyoming.*

SECRETARY OF NAVY MOODY ANNOUNCES *USS UTAH* TO BE NEW BATTLESHIP FOR THE NATION'S FLEET ∘ *(Opposite) Sitting on the dais at the rally in Ogden are Secretary of the Navy William H. Moody, President Roosevelt, and Utah Senator and Apostle Reed Smoot. While accompanying the President in Utah, Secretary Moody announced that* USS Utah *would be the name of one of the new battleships being added to the nation's fleet. (Opposite top) The* USS Utah, *a Florida-class battleship, was launched on 23 December 1909 under the sponsorship of Miss Mary Alice Spry, daughter of Utah Governor William Spry; it was sunk when hit by a torpedo during the attack on Pearl Harbor on December 7, 1941.*

THE NEWS FIFTEEN HOURS AHEAD OF THE MORNING PAPERS

The Ogden Standard.

THE STANDARD FIFTEEN HOURS AHEAD WITH THE WORLD'S NEWS

Thirty-third Year—No. 128 OGDEN CITY, UTAH, FRIDAY EVENING, MAY 29, 1903. Price Five Cents.

OGDEN, A RADIANT CITY, GREETS THE NATION'S CHIEF

A Demonstration That Far Exceeds Anything Before Witnessed in This City Welcomes President Roosevelt to Ogden--Glad Tribute From the People--Beneath an Azure Sky He Speaks to a Multitude of Loyal Citizens of Utah.

ROOSEVELT IS WILDLY CHEERED IN SALT LAKE

Chief Magistrate Praises the Sturdy Pioneers of Utah--80,000 People Greet Him as He Drives Along Streets of the City --Secretary Moody Promises to Name a Battleship "Utah."

AMBASSADOR MYER HURT IN AUTOMOBILE ACCIDENT

OUR WELCOMED GUEST.

FLOODS INUNDATE THE UNION PACIFIC

UNDERWOOD & UNDERWOOD, LIBRARY OF CONGRESS

ROOSEVELT IN SOUTHERN UTAH *(Above) Theodore Roosevelt, the person farthest out on the ledge, was a naturalist and conservationist. While here in 1913, he enjoyed the splendor of southern Utah.*

OGDEN RAILROAD MUSEUM

MIKE WINDER COLLECTION

WOMEN OF THE MOOSE

Roosevelt made a brief stop in northern Utah three and a half years after leaving the White House. Desiring to return to the White House, he challenged President William Howard Taft for the Republican nomination, and when he came up unsuccessful, he founded the Progressive Party, known popularly as the "Bull Moose Party." On September 13, 1912, he stopped briefly in Ogden to speak at the Progressive State Convention as part of his campaign for a return to the presidency. There, he spoke for thirty minutes while gripping his soft black hat and "smilingly acknowledging the applause with his famous double row of molars gleaming beneath his moustache."[54] En route to Ogden, Roosevelt made a quick stop in Brigham City, where the newspapers recorded, "He came, shook hands with a great many, made a short address, waved his hat, beamed to the people with that famous smile, and was gone."[55]

(Above) Teddy Roosevelt, a big gun collector, (shown in last car by himself) enjoyed a tour up the canyon near Ogden with the John M. Browning family—arms inventors.

WHITE HOUSE COLLECTION

WILLIAM HOWARD TAFT

WILLIAM HOWARD TAFT WAS PRESIDENT of the United States from 1909–1913 and served at the same time William Spry was governor of Utah and Joseph F. Smith was president of the Church. He came to Utah seven times, including three times as president.

WILLIAM HOWARD TAFT IN THE BLUE ROOM, 1911   *Official White House portrait, oil on canvas by Anders Leonard Zorn (1860–1920).*

TAFT AND SMOOT RIDE TOGETHER DURING THE PRESIDENT'S VISIT *William Howard Taft first visited Utah when he passed through Salt Lake City in 1900 en route to the Philippines. President McKinley had appointed Taft to be the first governor-general of the Philippines, following the acquisition of the islands during the Spanish-American War.*[56]

On June 22, 1909, Apostle-Senator Reed Smoot requested that the president make a stop in Utah as part of his autumn western trip, and Taft agreed to come.[57] *The Apostle later worked with the president to schedule the details of his first visit to Utah as president.*[58] *Taft rode with Smoot on his visit.*

ENJOYING THE VIEW FROM TEMPLE HILL IN PROVO *After a brief stop in Helper, President Taft's train wound its way north to Provo, arriving at 12:45PM on September 24, 1909. The streets were filled with cheering crowds, and school children lined Academy Avenue, shouting for the president. They enjoyed the view from Temple Hill, where Taft stood in his vehicle (far left), along with Senator Smoot (third from left) and Major Archibald Butt (second from left with his back to photographer). Major Butt was Taft's closest military aide and was his constant associate. When he drowned aboard the sinking RMS Titanic in 1912, it sent a mourning Taft into a deep depression.*

TAFT IN PROVO TABERNACLE *(Below Left) Taft stopped at the Provo Tabernacle, where the people greeted him with cheers and waving handkerchiefs. After two choir numbers and a warm introduction by Reed Smoot, the president spoke for about thirty minutes and then joined the choir and congregation in singing "The Star-Spangled Banner." He took time to shake hands with many in the Provo Tabernacle and on the surrounding grounds before boarding the train for Salt Lake at 3:00. "The President and party were delighted with reception and President said it was the best he had received since leaving Beverly, [Ohio]," wrote Smoot.[59] Apostle George Albert Smith (then thirty-nine years old) was the chairman of the entertainment committee for Taft's presidential visit. Elder Smith recalled the events held in the president's honor, shaking hands with him, and his "goodly girth and walrus mustache."[60]*

LDS CHURCH HISTORY LIBRARY

RONALD FOX COLLECTION

"TAFT IN MIDVALE" BY KEN BAXTER *(Above) Taft's train stopped in American Fork, Lehi, and Midvale so he could make brief remarks from the back of the train to the assembled crowds.*

TAFT REVIEWING TROOPS AT FORT DOUGLAS *(Opposite) They arrived in Salt Lake at 4:30PM and proceeded to Fort Douglas, where Taft reviewed the troops and spoke at a reception. The following morning, Taft was introduced to the First Presidency—Joseph F. Smith, John R. Winder, and Anthon H. Lund—at a breakfast at the Commercial Club. The presidential party proceeded to admire the Great Salt Lake at Saltair, attend an organ recital in the Tabernacle, and have lunch at the Salt Lake Country Club.*

BLACK ROCK
Great Salt Lake

Saltair

FROM "ZION: HER GATES AND TEMPLES," 1890

UTAH STATE HISTORICAL SOCIETY

LUNCH AND GOLF AT THE SALT LAKE COUNTRY CLUB *At the Club, the president did not play a round of golf, but he did joke around with the caddies, and the VIPs hit one ball each. Governor Spry hit a drive to the eighty-yard line; Senator Smoot hit to the 100-yard mark; Senator George Sutherland's left-handed drive went 125 yards; and Taft "had not exerted himself in making the drive, yet the ball reached the 210-yard mark."[61] Here, Taft is shown in his car leaving the Country Club with Governor Spry and Major Butt. In the afternoon, he spoke to a large crowd at Liberty Park, and he spent the evening with prominent Church and civic leaders at the Alta Club, where Taft spoke.[62]*

TAFT'S WHIRLWIND VISIT ❦ *The Sunday morning of September 26, President Taft arrived to a Temple Square packed with people. Once inside the Tabernacle, Apostle-Senator Smoot introduced the president, who gave a forty-minute sermon to the congregation on the proverb "A soft answer turneth away wrath, but grievous words stir up anger." During the address, the president pled for cooperation between Mormons and non-Mormons. Smoot wrote, "I never heard a better sermon . . . The President was delighted with the meeting and so were the people."[63] The President then departed Temple Square, heading east on South Temple. It was a whirlwind visit, as shown in this cartoon from the Salt Lake Tribune. Taft made a brief visit to the YMCA that Sunday morning, attended the 11:00 service at the Unitarian church, and then boarded the train for Ogden. There he spoke in the City Park (see below), and traveled on to make brief stops in Brigham City and Cache Valley, where thousands came out in the rain to hear from the Republican president. As he was leaving Utah, Taft told his entourage that his visit there "was one continual round of pleasure and a continual revelation . . . the people so healthy and prosperity was evident on all sides."[64]*

"SEEING SALT LAKE"

GATES AND TEMPLES," 1890

"LIVING FLAG" IN SALT LAKE CITY

(Also Opposite) As the entourage traveled from the Tabernacle, they observed some 20,000 children lining the street, waving flags and cheering for the president. A host of young people had formed a "living flag" with their colored outfits to greet the president. The president paused to stand and pay respect to the flag.

RONALD FOX COLLECTION

HOTEL UTAH

The very best of everything at sensible prices

THE HOTEL UTAH IS ONE OF THE TRULY GREAT HOTEL BUILDINGS OF THE UNITED STATES AND THE FURNISHINGS AND EQUIPMENT THOROUGHLY IN KEEPING WITH THE BUILDING ITSELF.

Under the Management of
GEO. O. RELF

TAFT STAYS AT THE NEWLY OPENED HOTEL UTAH *Smoot asked President Taft to visit Salt Lake City again, a visit which took place October 5, 1911.* [65] *He was greeted in the morning in Ogden by Governor William Spry, Senator Reed Smoot, Congressman Joseph Howell, Salt Lake City Mayor John S. Bransford, and Ogden Mayor William Glasmann. Taft arrived in Salt Lake City an hour later and was impressed with Hotel Utah, which had been completed since his last visit. Taft was the first real VIP guest for the new hotel. Records show that his suite cost $6 a night and that his breakfast included cantaloupe, sliced peaches, broiled sirloin steak, bacon, eggs, potatoes mashed in cream, crescents, toast, and rolls—all for $2.15. The press picked up Taft's compliments about the extraordinary hospitality of the new hotel, which helped build its reputation.* [66]

TAFT SPEAKS IN TABERNACLE *(Right and opposite bottom) Taft then spoke to an assembly of senior citizens in the Tabernacle.*

UTAH STATE HISTORICAL SOCIETY

TAFT SPEAKING AT FAIRPARK

After the his visit to the Tabernacle, Taft lunched at the Alta Club, visited Fort Douglas, spoke to 40,000 people at the state fairgrounds and reviewed a prize livestock parade there, and took dinner at the Commercial Club. Smoot's summary of the hectic day was that "the President has made many friends . . . and was pleased with his visit. . . . A great day for Utah."[67]

Taft made a fourth visit to Utah two weeks later on October 18, 1911, while returning from California. He stopped again in Salt Lake and spoke to great crowds in Ogden, Brigham City, and Logan.[68]

Presidential Reception
tendered to the
Old Folks of Utah
irrespective of Creed, Race or Color,
on the occasion of
President William Howard Taft's
Visit

Salt Lake Tabernacle
October 5th, 1911

Programme—Continued

5. Greetings to the Old Folks and Introduction of the Chief Executive of the Nation
   Bishop C. W. Nibley

6. Address to the Old Folks
   President William H. Taft

7. Song, "Dear Heart, We Are Growing Old"
   Horace S. Ensign and Tabernacle Choir

8. Selection
   Old Folks' Choir
   Thos. Butler, Conductor

9. Organ Solo, "The Old Folks at Home"
   J. J. McClellan, Tabernacle Organist

10. Chorus, "Glory and Love to the Men of Old"
    Tabernacle Choir and Organ

11. National Anthem, "Star Spangled Banner"
    Tabernacle Choir and Organ

12. Selections by
    Fort Douglas Military Band

An incident occurred at the Tabernacle in 1911 when President Taft's hat disappeared during his remarks. Major Butt, Secretary Hilles, and Chief of Staff Jimmy Sloan were perturbed and frantically looking for it while Senator Smoot and Governor Spry were busy introducing Taft to the First Presidency of the Church. *The Salt Lake Herald-Republican* reported that "President Taft's head is of a size to conform with the rest of his body, which means that his hat must be some hat. Unlike a needle, it would be prominent in a haystack. Yet, it couldn't be found." The rest of the day, Taft wore a golf cap. It turned out that during the president's address, the hat had rolled off the peg on which it hung, and a member of the Choir put it in a safer place and then left the Tabernacle before remembering the safely hidden presidential top hat.

President Taft leaving the Commercial Club before his top hat was lost at the Tabernacle.

TAFT CONTINUES TO VISIT UTAH FOR MANY YEARS

In August 1915, Taft arrived in Salt Lake City for a fifth visit to the state, his first as a former president. The Church put him up in Hotel Utah's presidential suite and held a reception for him at the hotel upon his arrival on the eighteenth. On the nineteenth, Taft spoke at a banquet for the American Bar Association at Hotel Utah. On the twentieth, Taft asked Elder Smoot to take him to see President Smith. There, the former U.S. president met with Joseph F. Smith and his counselors, along with Presiding Bishop Charles W. Nibley. Taft had lunch at the Newhouse Hotel and gave a speech to the Bonneville Club there on America's unpreparedness in case of war.[69]

A Mountain Congress to promote the League of Nations was held in Salt Lake City, Feb. 21–22, 1919. During this conference former President Taft attended and spoke at the Tabernacle.[70] This image of Taft in Utah from a previous visit shows the goodly girth of America's heaviest president. The chef at the Hotel Utah commented in 1919 that former President Taft was the largest eater he had ever seen and ate more in one meal than four other VIPs combined—a foot-long sirloin steak, ham, eggs, potatoes, three or four sets of rolls and cakes, and four cups of coffee.[71]

Former President Taft traveled to Utah for a seventh visit in 1920 to encourage voters to return Reed Smoot to the Senate and to campaign for Warren G. Harding.[72] President Heber J. Grant reflected on the visit: "I remember when ex-President Taft was here he said, with that little chuckle of his that made us all laugh, 'And to think that when he [Reed Smoot] first came down to Washington nearly everybody tried to keep him out of the senate. Now I have come all the way to Utah to plead with the people to be sure and send him back again.'"[73] In 1921, Taft was appointed chief justice of the United States Supreme Court, the only man to head both the executive and judicial branches of the government.

UTAH STATE HISTORICAL SOCIETY

LDS CHURCH HISTORY LIBRARY

"When [Reed Smoot] first came down to Washington nearly everybody tried to keep him out of the Senate. Now I have come all the way to Utah to plead with the people to send him back again."

WOODROW WILSON

Woodrow Wilson was president of the United States from 1913–1921 and served at the same time William Spry and Simon Bamberger were governors of Utah and Joseph F. Smith and Heber J. Grant were presidents of the Church. Wilson came to Utah once, and it was while he was president.

On September 23, 1919, President and Mrs. Wilson visited Utah as part of the president's national tour to drum up support for the League of Nations. They came by train from the west over the Nevada desert and arrived first at Ogden at 2:30 PM. Mayor and Mrs. T. S. Browning greeted them and took them on an hour-long automobile tour of some of the highlights of the Junction City. At 3:30, the Wilsons were headed south by rail to Salt Lake.

WILSON PARADE THROUGH SALT LAKE CITY (Above) *President and Mrs. Wilson arrived at Union Station in Salt Lake City at 4:30 and were greeted in their private car by Governor Simon Bamberger, Salt Lake City Mayor W. Mont Ferry, and President Heber J. Grant, and their wives. The presidential party then climbed into various vehicles for a parade through the city—east on South Temple to Main Street, south to Fourth South, up to Camp Williams, and over to the state capitol. The largest crowds ever assembled in Utah history up to that time were there that day to steal a glimpse of the man who had led America through the Great War.*

The Salt Lake Telegram noted: "The roads leading into the city from all directions were marked during the day by long caravans of autos. Garfield, Bingham, Park City, Murray, Midvale, Sandy and other small communities in close proximity to Salt Lake were almost deserted of citizens. Many stores and business houses in these places declared a holiday in order that employees might visit the city and get a glimpse of the president."[76]

GOVERNOR **WILSON** SUITS ME

THE MAN OF THE HOUR

WOODROW WILSON

WILSON GREETING OGDEN RESIDENTS (Above) *Fully 50,000 persons from every section of the northern half of the state gathered to greet the presidential party in the Junction City.*[74] *The tightly wedged crowd that lined the streets of Ogden acknowledged every movement and smile of the "man of the hour" with deafening cheers. Mr. R. B. Porter represented the Federated Clubs of Ogden, and Mrs. J.G. Falck represented the Women of American Patriots, with a basket of flowers and a basket of fruit which she presented to President and Mrs. Wilson.*[75]

WILSON PRESENTS BOY SCOUTS CERTIFICATES OF RECOGNITION AT CAPITOL BUILDING *(Above)* **CARS GATHERING AT CAPITOL** *(Left) At the state capitol, 300 Boy Scouts warmly greeted President Wilson. He had a certificate for each boy in recognition of their work during the Liberty loan drives to help raise money for the war effort. Time did not allow for a personal presentation to each boy, but he gave the certificates to General Richard W. Young, who was charged with making sure each boy received his.[77] (Left inset) This 1915 poster promoted the Third Liberty Loan Campaign run by the Boy Scouts of America. J. C. Leyendecker did the artwork for the poster.*

AMERICAN LITHOGRAPHIC CO., NEW YORK CITY, 1915

RECEIVED
MAR 17 '13
PRESIDENT'S OFFICE

THE WHITE HOUSE
WASHINGTON
March 11, 1913

My dear Mr. Smith:

The President directs me to acknowledge
the receipt of your letter of March 4th and
to assure you of his deep appreciation of your
kind words of congratulation and good wishes.

Thanking you warmly in the President's
behalf for your courtesy in writing him, I am

Sincerely yours,

J. P. Tumulty

Secretary to the President

Mr. Joseph F. Smith,
Salt Lake City, Utah.

WILSON VISITS EMMELINE B. WELLS

At 6:00PM, President and Mrs. Wilson arrived at the Hotel Utah for a rest and a private dinner; however, they first called on the Hotel Utah apartment of the general Relief Society president, 91-year-old bed-ridden Emmeline B. Wells. Woodrow Wilson wanted to congratulate Sister Wells and the Relief Society for the sale of more than 205,000 bushels of Relief Society wheat to the U.S. government during World War I.[78] "Aunt Em," as she was affectionately known, noted that he was the twelfth president of the United States of whom she had the pleasure to meet, but that he was the first one who had called on her.[79]

WILSON'S FIRST INTERACTION WITH THE CHURCH

(Above) Though this was Wilson's first and only visit to Utah, it wasn't his first interaction with the Church. Six years earlier, President Joseph F. Smith sent a letter to Wilson, congratulating him on winning the presidential election. President Smith received the above acknowledgment and thanks for his letter from President Wilson's secretary, Joseph P. Tumulty.

SPEECH AT TABERNACLE

At 8:10PM, the president and Mrs. Wilson left Hotel Utah for the Tabernacle, where the president gave a stirring speech, advocating for the League of Nations, to more than 15,000 people who had packed in for the occasion. He emphasized that the whole world was waiting to see if the American government would accept the peace treaty or not.

WILSON TOURS CHURCH ADMINISTRATION BUILDING WITH PRESIDENT HEBER J. GRANT

After the rousing speech at the Tabernacle, President Heber J. Grant took President Wilson on a tour through the new Church Administration Building (left), which had just been completed two years prior. "This is a room where a man can think," Wilson said of Grant's private office.[80] He referred to the building's reception area, with its weighty marble columns, as "the most beautiful room in the United States."[81] The Wilsons left Salt Lake City at 10:30PM on their special train headed east.

GOVERNOR SIMON BAMBERGER AND WIFE, IDA, TAKE EDITH AND WOODROW WILSON SIGHTSEEING   *When asked "What does President Wilson think of Salt Lake?" Governor Bamberger smiled broadly and replied, "Why, I showed him so many things of interest and told him so much about this wonderful city that he's decided to come back here and live." After a laugh, the governor went on to explain that Wilson asked many questions and said he had read and been told much about the state and the Mormon people but had never set foot here to see for himself. Mrs. Wilson was impressed with the wide streets and the proximity of the mountains.[82] In this photo they are near the University of Utah.*

Woodrow Wilson's day in Utah was one of the last days in his presidency spent at full physical and mental capacity. Just two days later, September 25, the president collapsed in Pueblo, Colorado. A massive stroke just a few days later left him almost completely incapacitated, paralyzed on his left side and blind in his right eye. For the remainder of his presidency, his wife, Edith, served as his steward and screened business coming and going in the White House. She worked with friendly reporters to help shield the public from the full extent of Wilson's disability until his death in 1924.

Above   President Wilson was sightseeing with his wife and the Bambergers at Ft. Douglas just days before he suffered a massive stroke.

WARREN G. HARDING

W ARREN G. HARDING WAS PRESIDENT of the United States from 1921–1923 and served at the same time Charles R. Mabey was governor of Utah and Heber J. Grant was president of the Church. He came to Utah once, and it was while he was president.

President and Mrs. Harding visited Utah on June 26, 1923, where they made a few stops in northern Utah, spent some time in Salt Lake, and then headed to southern Utah for a visit to Zions National Park the next day. The morning of the twenty-eighth, the president greeted crowds at Brigham City and Logan.[83]

HARDING ON STEPS OF BOUNTIFUL TABERNACLE *(Right) As the president, governor, and first ladies drove south, they made a brief stop in Layton. There, Elizabeth Ellison (the future Mrs. Roy Simmons), the six-year-old daughter of the mayor, presented a bouquet of roses to Florence Harding. The party also made a brief stop at the Bountiful Tabernacle for a short speech on the steps. Governor Mabey is seen waving to the crowd as he introduces Warren G. Harding.*

HARDING GIVING A BRIEF SPEECH FROM GOVERNOR MABEY'S CAR *(Above) The presidential party arrived in Ogden's Union Station at about 8:00 AM, where a large cheering crowd and Ogden Mayor Frank Francis greeted him. He was driven to Lester Park for a short speech, and while there, he met three-year-old triplets. "I've never had the privilege of shaking hands with triplets," Mrs. Harding said of young Willard, William, and Willis Jensen. The presidential party then drove ninety minutes south to Salt Lake in Governor Charles Mabey's new Lincoln touring car with the governor and his wife. Governor Mabey can be seen standing next to the car, holding his hat, while President Harding makes a short speech at one of the stops en route.*

FOR PRESIDENT WARREN G. HARDING

HARDING AND COOLIDGE

"I love, above all else, the boyhood and girlhood of marvelous Utah."

HARDING REMOVES HAT TO THE CROWD IN FRONT OF HOTEL UTAH *(Right) After the rally at Liberty Park, the president went to Hotel Utah for a luncheon and reception. He enjoyed the young people's cheering the most in Salt Lake: "I have found a new slogan in your wonderful country, which I am delighted to adopt, namely, the one which refers to 'Utah's best crop.' I do not know when I have seen so many happy, smiling, sturdy children in so short a period of travel. A thousand delights have come to us in getting more intimately acquainted with your wonderful country . . . but I love, above all else, the boyhood and girlhood of marvelous Utah."[84]*

SALT LAKE CITY CROWDS GREET HARDING *(Above) A crowd of 100,000 people cheered as the presidential entourage entered Salt Lake City and paraded down Main Street. When the entourage stopped at Liberty Park for a speech, President Harding was visibly moved: "Words are unable to express my appreciation of the warm friendly spirit of this reception."[85] Among the thousands of children who lined the streets and cheered was thirteen-year-old Gordon B. Hinckley, who always remembered standing with his siblings and waving flags as the president's motorcade drove by. This was the first, but by no means the last, presidential encounter for the future Church president.[86]*

A HISTORIC ROUND OF GOLF *After lunch, President Harding played eleven holes at the Salt Lake Country Club. His partner was President Heber J. Grant, and the two presidents were triumphant over their opponents, Lee Charles Miller (president of the Country Club) and Joy Johnson (president of the Bonneville Club). There had been some rumors that Harding was not very good, but he played a terrific game, out-driving the rest most of the time; although, President Grant's drive to the green on the second hole saved the pair when President Harding drove into the rough. The victorious president of the United States and president of the Church collected a dollar from Miller and Johnson at the end, a small wager of the historic round.[87]*

PRESIDENT COMING TO IRON COUNTY.

According to an announcement made by Senator Reed Smoot after his arrival in Salt Lake City from Washington, D. C., President Harding will deliver a public address at the Salt Lake tabernacle on the evening of his visit to Utah's capital, which probably will be Monday, June 2?

The president will reach Salt Lake in the morning. The day's program has not yet been determined, but definite arrangements have been made for the address at the tabernacle according to the senior senator. If tentative plans are followed, the president and his party will leave for Cedar City after the meeting. The next day will be spent at Cedar Breaks and Zion National park.

Plans provide for a short reception [...] night at Cedar [...]

PRESIDENTIAL TRAIN FIRST TO USE NEW LUND TO CEDAR CITY RAILROAD SPUR *(Right) That evening, President Harding spoke in the Tabernacle and enjoyed music from the organ before boarding a train for an overnight journey south to Cedar City. The presidential train was the first to use the new spur on the main line that had just been finished between Lund and Cedar City thirty-five miles to the southeast. It was hoped that the new rail spur and the publicity surrounding the president's maiden trip on it would bring more tourists to southern Utah's parks. Eager local residents waited with flags in hand for the train to pull into Cedar City.*

PRESIDENT AND MRS. HARDING GREET PAIUTE INDIANS *(Below) Among the crowd greeting President and Mrs. Harding in Cedar City was a band of seventy-five Paiute Indians. The president insisted on shaking hands with everyone there before the traveling party piled into thirty cars that were waiting to take them on the sixty-five-mile trip to Zions National Park. It would take four hours over dusty dirt roads to get there.*

UNION PACIFIC COLLECTION

UNION PACIFIC COLLECTION

HARDING WITH ELIZABETH STAPLEY, FIRST PIONEER CHILD BORN IN UTAH *(Below) Between Cedar City and Zions National Park, they made a stop in Toquerville, where they were given a basket of locally grown "Dixie fruit." The president made a brief speech, and he and Mrs. Harding were photographed with seventy-five-year-old Toquerville resident Elizabeth Stapley (shown left of Pres. & Mrs. Harding), who was the first white woman born in Utah on August 9, 1847. The presidential entourage also stopped briefly in Rockville and Springdale, where a pipe and drum corps performed. The residents of these small towns along the way had spent much of the previous night carrying buckets of water to sprinkle the roads through their towns to help keep the dust down for their distinguished visitors.*

DAUGHTERS OF THE UTAH PIONEERS

LUND TO CEDAR ROAD OPENED

Town Jubilant as Locomotive Steams In

CEDAR CITY, June 12.—The residents of Cedar City and the surrounding country were jubilant Monday when they saw a big locomotive of the Salt Lake, Los Angeles railroad driven by N. A. Williams, general superintendent of the line, steaming into town. The day marked the completion of the road from Lund to Cedar City.

Nearly every person in the whole section was present at opening of the road. The mayor and a committee of townspeople welcomed the [...] greeting was held [...] the luncheon [...] made by the mayor [...] rail officials [...] party with [...] rius de Braba [...] manager of [...] em; T. C. Pe [...] agent at Los A [...] Jones, assist [...] the system.

A New State in a New Century 1902–1945 | 57

Harding died on his western trip mere weeks after his visit to Utah. After leaving Utah, the president and first lady made stops in Yellowstone National Park, Montana, and Washington State, and President Harding became the first president to visit Alaska. Harding died suddenly on August 2 in San Francisco. His bronze casket stopped in Ogden the following day as it carried the president eastward. Governor Mabey went aboard the train to lay a wreath and share the state's condolences with the widow. A memorial service to President Harding was held August 12 in the Tabernacle.

Calvin Coolidge, Harding's successor, was the only twentieth-century president to not visit Utah while in office, despite serving from 1923–1929. Coolidge did, however, almost build his "western White House" in Pinecrest in Emigration Canyon because of Reed Smoot's solid salesmanship, but in the end, he built his summer home in the Black Hills of South Dakota.

"I wouldn't have missed it for anything."

HARDING ENJOYS ZIONS NATIONAL PARK ON HORSEBACK

At Zions Park, in a place called Wylie's Camp (where the Zion Lodge now stands), President Harding put on cowboy chaps, mounted a saddle horse, and took a two-hour ride up the narrows of the canyon. The large traveling party followed suit and had lifelong bragging rights of going horseback riding through Zions National Park with a president of the United States. (Inset) Several VIPs rode with the president. Pictured here are: Utah Governor Charles R. Mabey, President Warren G. Harding, Salt Lake City Mayor Charles C. Nelsen, Senator Reed Smoot, and President Heber J. Grant. As he left Cedar City that evening, President Harding told the gathered crowd, "We have had a wonderful day today—wonderful in many ways. We have come to have, perhaps, even a greater reverence for the Creator, a new wonderment at His purposes, and a new curiosity to know when we ourselves are going to fully understand God's purpose." Mrs. Harding made her first speech of the trip and added, "It was the greatest experience of my life. I wouldn't have missed it for anything."

HERBERT HOOVER

HERBERT HOOVER WAS PRESIDENT of the United States from 1929–1933 and served at the same time George Dern was governor of Utah and Heber J. Grant was president of the Church. He came to Utah at least twenty-three times, including once as president.

LIBRARY OF CONGRESS

Herbert Hoover visited Utah more than any other president—twenty-three times in his public life and countless other times as a young man. "This is by no means my first visit to Salt Lake City," Hoover said in his 1932 visit (his only visit while serving as president). "I came from the West and one of my first professional engagements was the responsibility of carrying a chain and driving stakes on a ditch line in this State," he said of his time as a surveyor. "So I come to your State as no stranger."

STANFORD UNIVERSITY

Hoover (seated left) attended the newly established Stanford University in Palo Alto, California. He majored in geology and participated in the Surveying Squad (shown here in 1893).

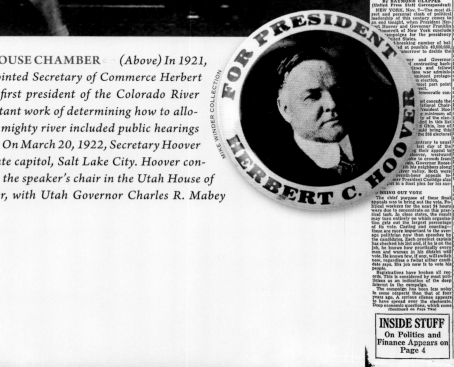

CORBIS

HOOVER IN UTAH HOUSE CHAMBER *(Above) In 1921, President Harding appointed Secretary of Commerce Herbert Hoover to serve as the first president of the Colorado River Commission. The important work of determining how to allocate the resources of the mighty river included public hearings in several western states. On March 20, 1922, Secretary Hoover held a hearing in the state capitol, Salt Lake City. Hoover conducted the meeting from the speaker's chair in the Utah House of Representatives chamber, with Utah Governor Charles R. Mabey to his left.*

FOR PRESIDENT HERBERT C. HOOVER

MIKE WINDER COLLECTION

Weather Forecast
FAIR
UNSETTLED
WARMER
COOLER
RAIN

UTAH'S INDEPENDENT NEWSPAPER — FIRST IN EVERYTH

Salt Lake Teleg.

VOL. XXXI, NO. 242.

SALT LAKE CITY, MONDAY EVENING, NOVEMBER 7, 1932.

HOOVER PLEDGES SILVER,
S. L. Throngs Gree

Chief Executive Receives Hearty Welcome in City

Citizens Turn Out En Masse, Line Route Through State to Catch Glimpse of of Mr. and Mrs. Hoover

Salt Lake and Utah threw care to the winds Monday to turn out almost en masse to welcome President Hoover on his first visit here since he has been the nation's chief executive.

Hoover was the name on everyone's tongue. He was the hero of the day from the time his official train pulled into Echo, Utah, shortly before 10 a. m. until he departed for the west coast from Ogden at 2:30 p. m.

The president came here to make a final bid for votes in the Republican cause, but partisanship was discarded by Utah's citizens—everyone, Republicans and Democrats alike, sang Hoover's praises to the skies.

The chief executive welcomed his first Utah crowd at Echo, where more than 1000 school children from the North Summit district turned out to catch a brief glimpse of the president as the special train made a short stop for the official Utah delegation to board.

SCHOOL BAND PLAYS

A band from the North Summit high school, led by Appollo Hansen, sent the strains of "America" and "The Star Spangled Banner" echoing through the rock walls of the canyon as the train pulled out of the station. And as the train slowly continued on its way to Salt Lake rousing cheers for Hoover echoed after it.

Schools were dismissed in the district and enthusiastic children and newspeople from Wanship, Rockport, Hoytsville, Coalville, Upton, Grass Creek, Echo and Henefer lined the tracks on either side of the special.

The president stood on the rear platform and smiled as the throng but made no speech. Before the train arrived Senator Reed Smoot mounted the baggage wagon and addressed the throng and characterized President Hoover as "a remarkable man—the only president of the United States who has been faced with such conditions."

Included in the party which boarded the train at Echo were Senator and Mrs. Smoot, Ernest Bamberger, national committeeman; Byron D. Anderson, state chairman; John E. Booth, chairman of the state speakers bureau; E. R. Callister, Salt Lake county chairman; A. L. Glassman, copublisher of the Ogden Standard Examiner; John Hart of Rigby, Idaho, former national committeeman of that state; R. P. Lafayette, passenger traffic manager of the Southern Pacific railroad; Mrs. Jeanette M. Morrell of Ogden, national committeewoman; Mrs. M. A. Dunyon and Mrs. Jesse F. Cannon, associate vice chairwomen; Mrs. John B. Stewart, Salt Lake county chairwoman; Henry C. Taggart and Miss Hunting-ton Lindbourow.

President Hoover remained in his private compartment during the trip to Salt Lake and was engaged most of the time in revamping his speech delivered in the tabernacle.

Mrs. Hoover granted the women of the official party an audience and shortly before arriving at Ogden, President Hoover conferred with the Utah party leaders.

PRESENTS FLOWERS

Mrs. Smoot presented Mrs. Hoover with a basket of chrysanthemums and with a basket of roses on behalf of the Girl Scouts of Utah. Miss Loofbourow also presented the first lady with a bouquet of roses.

Mrs. Hoover told the group of the work she had done in founding a school near the president's Rapidan camp in Virginia and discussed the organization of Republican women's clubs through the country.

She also related how she had risen at 5 a. m. Monday and had alighted in Green River, Wyo., to greet a small party of ranchers and children who had driven for miles to watch the official train pass through.

"It was a touching sight, indeed," she said.

STOPS IN EVANSTON

Before arrival in Echo, the train also stopped at Evanston, Wyo., where a large crowd gathered at the station. The president greeted the group from the rear platform, but delivered no speech.

The president talked informally during his brief conference with Utah party leaders and expressed his appreciation of the gala welcome accorded him. Those who attended the
(Continued on Page Two)

PARTY CHIEFS NEAR END OF FIERY BATTLE

Record-Breaking Ballot Is Expected to Decide Result

By RAYMOND CLAPPER
(United Press Staff Correspondent)
NEW YORK, Nov. 7.—The most direct and personal clash of political leadership of this century comes to an end tonight, when President Herbert Hoover and Governor Franklin D. Roosevelt of New York conclude campaigns for the presidency of the United States.

A record-breaking number of ballots cast—estimated at possibly 40,000,000—tomorrow to decide the

Neither Hoover and Governor Roosevelt of contrasting backgrounds, views and fellow men admonition on election.

The most part point velt, Democratic nom

Neither would concede the national Chairman President Hoover a minimum of the election led in this fight Ohio, loss of the 266 electoral votes

Contrary to usual last day of their appeal to Hoover, westward making to crowds from train, Governor Roosevelt with his neighbors along river valley. Both were seventh-hour appeals to President Coolidge also put in a final plea for his successor.

BRING OUT VOTE

The chief purpose of these final appeals was to bring out the vote. Political workers for the next 24 hours were due to concentrate on this practical task. In close states, the result may turn entirely on which organization gets out the largest percentage of its vote. Casting and counting—these are more important to the average politician now than speeches by the candidates. Each precinct captain has checked his list and, if he is on the job, he knows how practically every man and woman in his district will vote. He knows few, if any, will switch now, regardless of what either candidate says. His job now is to vote his people.

Registrations have broken all records. This is considered by most politicians as an indication of the deep interest in the campaign.

The compaign has been less noisy in some respects than that of four years ago. A serious silence appears to have spread over the electorate. Deep economic questions, which come
(Continued on Page Two)

INSIDE STUFF
On Politics and Finance Appears on Page 4

AS SALT LAKE GAVE CHIEF EXECUTIVE TUMULTUOUS WELC

OGDEN CITIZENS HEAR PRESIDENT

By Staff Correspondent
OGDEN, Nov. 7.—Reviewing the economic strife with which the country has been faced during his administration, President Hoover told 5000 Ogden citizens who gathered at the station that he "always has the interest of the working people at heart" and appealed to them to vote for the Republican party.

The presidential special train arrived at Ogden at 2:10 p. m. from Salt Lake and the president delivered his address from the rear platform.

President and Mrs. Hoover were on the platform with Senator and Mrs. Reed Smoot and George W. Lowe, Weber county Republican chairman.

Mrs. Hoover was presented with a bouquet of roses by Mrs. Milton H. White, first commissioner of Girl Scouts of Ogden, and Mrs. J. G. Falk, organization secretary of Girl Scouts in Utah.

In his speech President Hoover said:

"We are, I am confident, on the way out of the depression."

EMPHASIZES TARIFF

"Every Utah industry is dependent upon proper tariff protection. My opponents, if placed in power, may change these things. They say different things concerning the tariff in the west than they do in the east.

"One of the great aims of this administration has been to provide work for the people. Ogden, being an industrial center, should realize that this is the first of 15 depressions which have swept the country in which wages were not reduced.

"The depression continued for two years and my agreement between employes and industrial leaders still holds."

His continued policy of protecting the workers by putting more teeth in the immigration laws had also helped
(Continued on Page Two)

It was a day of prolonged shouting, flag waving, military and civic display Monday as the city turned out to pay tribute to President Herbert Hoover, who, in the closing hours of the campaign, brought his message to Salt Lake and Utah. Views during the president's hour and a half visit here are shown above.

Top, a view of the parade from the Union Pacific station on West Temple street.

The arrow shows the president's automobile just before he left it to enter the tabernacle grounds through the west gate.

Lower left, President Hoover and Mrs. Reed Smoot snapped as the presidential party was escorted from the depot. Thousands lined West Temple street for a glimpse of the chief executive as he rode in an open automobile.

Lower right, Mrs. Louis Marcus, wife of Salt Lake's mayor, as she presented a huge basket of flowers to Mrs. Hoover at the station.

Suspicious Looking Sack Holds Lunch
Utah Celery Given to President
Mrs. Smoot Almost Gets Left at Echo

Visions of an attack on the president or one of his party marred the peace of mind of city detectives at the depot shortly before the president's train arrived.

Luscious, crisp Utah celery will grace the dinner table of President Hoover and his party Monday night. The celery was given to the president by representatives of the chamber of commerce on his arrival here Monday noon.

A flowering individual, dressed in a dark suit and carrying a suspicious looking paper sack began making his quirks as to just which officials were to be in each of the cars.

Suspicions were put to rest, however, when his most good-naturedly explained to the detectives that he was merely carrying his lunch.

When President Hoover's special train pulled out of Echo, Utah, the first stop on his invasion of the state Monday morning, one important member of the official welcoming party almost was left behind.

Because of the frigid early morning temperature, Mrs. Reed Smoot had remained in the automobile which had carried her from Salt Lake. She was not on the platform when the train was ready to leave.

It was only because of the expert
(Continued on Page Two)

COURT R
LIND

FLEMINGTON
John Hughes Cu
Lindbergh kidna
today, Judge Ada
was imposed on
against him lifted
walked from cou
on bail pending an
against sentence.

Curtis was con
justice by giving
to Colonel Charle
the police concern
tiations with t
Lindbergh baby,
found dead.

Today's hearing
utes, Defense Cou
asked the judge t
consider the judg
ests of justice."

The state conc
motion and cons
The judge then
pension of the p
was immedi

Rehearing
In Oil

WASHINGTON
supreme court tod
American Petrole
hearing in its app
held valid three
the Elk Hill oil
which were obtai
Secretary Fall.

Today's action
refuse the appea
order a rehearing
from a ruling ha
tained with w

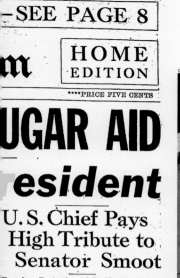

HOME EDITION

****PRICE FIVE CENTS**

UGAR AID
esident

U. S. Chief Pays High Tribute to Senator Smoot

Promises Protection of State's Key Industries in Speech Before 10,000 Utahns in Tabernacle

Protection of Utah's key industries—silver and sugar—was promised by President Herbert Hoover Monday in one of the most forceful speeches of the current campaign.

Addressing 10,000 cheering Utahns in the L. D. S. tabernacle, the nation's chief executive received ovation after ovation as he outlined the Republican platform, attacked the campaign policies of the Democratic party and paid tribute to Utah's senior senator, Reed Smoot.

His speech, the next to the last major address of his campaign, was brief, but it left no doubt in the minds of his enthusiastic audience just how the speaker stood on the major issues confronting the people and particularly those issues affecting Utah.

The tariff, world peace and other issues were brittly presented, but when the speaker swept into a discussion of the question in which his listeners were vitally interested, his remarks were hailed with shouts, cheers, whistles and other enthusiastic response that shook the ceiling of the historic tabernacle.

That part of the speech touching on silver was preceded by the explanation that the Democrats were waging a campaign of "misrepresentation" as to his stand on the question. His eyes flashed and his jaw squared as he pounded the rostrum and in ringing tones said:

"While it has been long since determined that there can be but one standard of monetary value — gold — we should restore silver to greater use for subsidiary coinage."

Here the audience arose with a mighty yell and it was minutes before the president could continue. Outside the

(Continued on Page Three)

Highlights of Hoover Speech

"Two senators in your neighboring states have told me they would be glad to have Senator Smoot on the ticket in their states.

"In his term of service, longer than any other member of the senate, he has acquired a great knowledge of the workings of the United States government, unparalleled by any other man in the United States.

"I regret that agriculture has been lagging behind industry in this march to recovery.

"Our first duty now is to repair this breach in order that agriculture may march forward with industry.

"That we shall do, either through the flexible tariff provision or, if necessary, through legislation.

"We propose to preserve the American market for the American farmer.

"The Republican tariff proposal gives immediate relief to the beet sugar grower and brings about a safe basis for Philippine independence.

"Increase in the value of silver would relieve us from strain of cheap production of goods which flow over our borders; it would rehabilitate the buying power of many foreign nations for our goods.

"We have long since determined that there can be put one standard on monetary value, but yet we should restore silver to greater use for subsidiary coinage and purposes in those countries which have traditionally used it and to do it without undermining the gold standard.

"It thus becomes a problem that cannot be solved without international action.

"I have given assurances to the people of the intermountain region that I shall appoint a representative on the American silver delegation who will carry their point of view to that conference.

"I will join no movement that proposes to use military or economic force in its attempt to prevent war. For that is a contradiction of method.

CORBIS

OGDEN RAILROAD MUSEUM AND ARCHIVES

RONALD FOX COLLECTION

Senator Smoot and His Bride On Honeymoon at White House

SALT LAKE TELEGRAM, JULY 1930

Senator Reed Smoot and his bride, the former Mrs. Alice Taylor Sheets of Salt Lake City, Utah, are pictured here on the White House grounds, where they are enjoying their honeymoon until the White House on the London naval treaty. They planned to go to Honolulu, but President Hoover asked them to stay as his guests until the treaty question is settled.

HOOVER'S VISIT AS PRESIDENT, NOVEMBER 5, 1932 *(Left) Hoover's only visit to Utah as president was a brief stop on the day before he was voted out of office as the nation embraced Franklin D. Roosevelt and his plans for a New Deal. He arrived at noon on November 7, 1932, and went to the Tabernacle on Temple Square for a thirty-minute speech in which Hoover not only campaigned for himself but also for the entire Republican ticket, especially his friend Apostle-Senator Reed Smoot (left of Hoover, clapping). Following his address, Hoover then boarded the train for Ogden (Left Below), where he made a fifteen-minute platform address before heading west toward California.*

It was Smoot who persuaded President Harding to appoint Herbert Hoover as Secretary of Commerce back in 1921, and it was Hoover who insisted that Smoot and his bride spend a two-week honeymoon in the White House when the newlyweds had to cancel their plans for Hawaii after Smoot was called back to the Senate for a key vote. Both Hoover and Smoot were swept out of office the following day in the Roosevelt landslide.

HOOVER VISITS UTAH EIGHT TIMES THROUGHOUT THE 1930s *After leaving the White House, Hoover came to Utah seventeen times. He had a brief train stop in Ogden on March 20, 1933, came to visit Reed Smoot on September 29, 1933, spoke at an event in Ogden on the Townsend Plan (a forerunner idea to Social Security) on December 19, 1935, made remarks in Ogden on April 7, 1936, participated in a campaign rally in Ogden on September 5–6, 1936, and stopped by Salt Lake City on June 14, 1937, and again on April 8, 1939.[88] Hoover and his wife, Lou Hoover (right), stayed in the Hotel Utah while on a vacation on August 12, 1940.*

DESERET NEWS

A New State in a New Century 1902–1945 | 61

HERBERT HOOVER AND SON ALLAN MEET UP IN UTAH *Hoover's many visits to Utah continued into the 1940s, with stops in Salt Lake City on June 12, 1943, August 7, 1944, July 1, 1945, and August 5–8, 1949. The former president met up with his second son, Allan Hoover, in Salt Lake in the 1940s. Allan was a Harvard MBA and banker who helped run the Hoover Institute at Stanford University for a number of years.*

HOOVER VISITS THE TOOELE ARMY DEPOT IN 1950 (Left) President Herbert Hoover (center) stands with Col. James D. Barnett and Lt. Col. F.E. Rogan during his visit to the Tooele Army Depot seventeen years after leaving office. His swing through the state took place August 1–4, 1950, and included stops in Ogden, Salt Lake, and Tooele County. George Diehl, who served as mayor of Tooele from 1983 to 1994, after working for thirty-three years as the executive assistant at the Tooele Army Depot, recalled Hoover's visit: "Hoover referred to us at the depot as 'his neighbors,'" Diehl said. "He was no longer the president of the United States, and he appeared to be just a regular Joe."

Hoover, who was a mining engineer, was in Tooele County to inspect the Bauer Mine that the Combined Metals Company owned, which was a firm Hoover had a major interest in. In his younger years in the mining industry, Hoover once served as the managing director of Consolidated Zinc Corporation, an Australian company that eventually merged with other mining interests to create the Rio Tinto Group in 1997—the current owner of Utah's Kennecott Copper Mine.[89]

Hike Youth Fun Facilities, Hoover Tells S. L. Chiefs

SALT LAKE CITY, Aug. 3 (AP)—Former President Herbert Hoover had a suggestion yesterday for the people of Salt Lake City.

They "should take it upon themselves to provide more adequate recreational and training facilities for the city's youth," he said.

The former president, chairman of the board of directors of National Boy's Clubs of America, briefly inspected the city's Jaycee Boys and Girls club.

"The youth leaders here are doing a fine job with the facilities they have," he observed, "but their job is handicapped by lack of proper equipment and recreational meeting places."

As an example of progress in youth development, Hoover cited Bridgeport, Conn.

"The city," he pointed out, "with only a population of 90,000, subscribed one million dollars for boy's club work. It seems to me Salt Lake City, with a population well over twice that of Bridgeport

could afford to take more interest in its young people."

He observed that the majority of the people do not recognize importance of proper training youth.

DESERET NEWS

HOOVER AND GOVERNOR J. BRACKEN LEE AT LAGOON RALLY On July 31, 1951, Hoover addressed a Republican rally at Lagoon and spent the night at Salt Lake. The former president spent some time with Utah Governor J. Bracken Lee at the Lagoon rally. Hoover stopped by Utah twice more, on July 13, 1952, for a press conference in Salt Lake and on August 23, 1956, to meet with a group of Republican women.

DESERET NEWS

FRANKLIN D. ROOSEVELT

Franklin Delano Roosevelt was president of the United States from 1933–1945 and served at the same time Henry H. Blood and Herbert B. Maw were governors of Utah and Heber J. Grant was president of the Church. Roosevelt came to Utah five times, including twice as president.

BINGHAM GIRL ONCE AGAIN WINS ROOSEVELT SIGNATURE, *SALT LAKE TRIBUNE,* SEPTEMBER 18, 1932 *Franklin D. Roosevelt first visited Utah on August 26, 1920, when he was campaigning unsuccessfully for the vice presidency as the running mate of James Cox. He spoke to rail workers, as well as to a group gathered in the Tabernacle, promising to return in October.[90] Later, as governor of New York, Roosevelt came to Salt Lake for the annual meeting of the National Governor's Association that ran from June 30–July 2, 1930. While here in 1930, an eight-year-old girl from Bingham, Utah, named Athens Jimas, rushed up to him and said, "I wish you were our president!" A tickled Governor Roosevelt autographed a card for her and told that if he ever was, she could come see him in the White House. Two years later, in 1932, ten-year-old Athens again demonstrated her loyalty to Gov. Roosevelt, getting another card signed and saying, "I know you are going to be our president!"*

Bingham Girl Once Again Wins Roosevelt Signature

Governor Roosevelt, for the second time in two years, autographs a card for Athens Jimas, 10-year-old Bingham girl, and again invites her to the White House, should he be elected president.

Child Proudly Shows Card Given Her Two Years Ago; Gets White House Bid

Two years ago, when Governor Franklin D. Roosevelt was in Salt Lake attending the governors' conference, 8-year-old Athens Jimas of Bingham rushed up to him and said—"I wish you were our president."

Farley Makes Things Hum in Visit to S. L.

Loses No Time in Calling Friends; Youth Interviews Roosevelt

Who is Jim Farley?

James A. Farley, popular Democratic national chairman, will make friends in Salt Lake as he has all over the country and friends for Farley means votes for Roosevelt, political observers say.

Governor Roosevelt, who presumably had the same wish in his mind, took a card out of his pocket, signed his name and told Athens that if he ever did become president and she would present the card at the White House he would see that she received a real reception.

Athens, now 10, presented the card Friday to Governor Roosevelt again, but this time she said: "I know you are going to be our president."

Governor Roosevelt, his face beaming with the famed family smile, signed the card again, affectionately patted Athens on the shoulder and renewed the promise that she would be fittingly received at the White House if he is elected president.

While party leaders from several states patiently waited, Governor Roosevelt chatted a few minutes with Athens and had her pose with him for pictures.

Mr. and Mrs. James Jimas, parents of the girl, pridefully looked on from the anteroom.

ROOS

The famou... velt for h...

The famo...

ROOSEVELT MAKES A CAMPAIGN VISIT *Governor Roosevelt made a campaign stop in Utah September 17–18, 1932, en route to his election as president that November. On Saturday, he lunched at the Newhouse Hotel, took dinner at Hotel Utah, and made a major campaign address in the Tabernacle about the current railroad problem. On Sunday, he attended services at St. Paul's Episcopal Church, had lunch at the home of Governor George Dern, and attended a public reception at the state capitol. While in Salt Lake City, the Democratic nominee met with Dr. Elbert D. Thomas, Democratic candidate for U.S. Senate from Utah (standing), and Henry H. Blood, Democratic nominee for Utah's governor (right). All three were successful that fall.*

TALKS IN UTAH

The Weather

UTAH—Fair Saturday and Sunday; cooler Sunday.
NEVADA, IDAHO—Fair, cooler Sunday.
WYOMING—Fair, cooler Sunday.
(Detailed Report on Page Twenty-five)

The Salt Lake Tribune

Local Metal Prices

Silver ...... 27¾c   Zinc 3.50c
Copper ...... 5.37c   Lead 2.60c

VOL. 125, NO. 156. Entered at the postoffice at Salt Lake City as Second-Class Matter SALT LAKE CITY, SATURDAY MORNING, SEPTEMBER 17, 1932. 26 PAGES—FIVE CENTS

ROOSEVELT ARRIVES IN SALT LAKE

ROOSEVELT TALKS IN UTAH, *SALT LAKE TRIBUNE*

"My visit here in Salt Lake City is, I assure you, one of the brightest spots of a happy trip," he said at the beginning of his remarks. "As I have viewed the scene in this valley, it is easy to see how a distinguished citizen of your State, arriving in this place eighty-five years ago, exclaimed: 'This is the place.'" The president's remarks in the Tabernacle about the railroads were later packaged into a campaign brochure by the Democratic National Committee.

The RAILROADS

★

Republican Mistakes
and
Democratic Remedies

★

Governor
Franklin D. Roosevelt's Speech
Delivered at
Salt Lake City, Utah
Sept. 17, 1932

★

Issued by
THE DEMOCRATIC NATIONAL COMMITTEE
Hotel Biltmore, New York City

ECONOMIC SECURITY
ROOSEVELT   BLOOD

Money Pours In for G.O.P., Aide Reports

Treasurer Says Democratic Victory in Maine Brings Heavy Receipts

(By Associated Press)
WASHINGTON, Sept. 16.—President Hoover was informed today by Joseph R. Nutt, treasurer of the Republican committee, that the Democratic victories in Maine had increased campaign contributions and brought in sight the Republican goal of a $1,500,000 fund.

The party treasurer said he reported to Mr. Hoover that attainment of a hoped for total of between $1,000,000 and $1,500,000 previously had seemed doubtful, but that in the last week money had "poured in from every section" of the country.

Conserve Funds

Due to the necessity for money saving by the national committee, however, he added, no funds are to be advanced to Republican state organizations nor any money given to the senatorial campaign committee, which received about $150,000 in 1928.

He said the Republican congressional campaign committee, which was given $250,000 in the last campaign, would receive a percentage of all contributions.

Nutt's visit climaxed a day in which the chief executive conferred with a number of political callers, but in which the White House announced declined to comment upon reports that Mr. Hoover would go beyond the previously agreed total of three campaign speeches.

Letters Received

Among the president's visitors today was Senator Hastings of Delaware, assistant manager of the eastern campaign, who said he had discussed the entire political situation, particularly the Democratic gains in Maine.

Hastings said he had received a number of letters concerning the Maine vote, some of which he asserted indicated to him "that the Democrats are depending upon a campaign of prejudice and their ability to capitalize the depression."

Among the other callers were Joseph Scott of Los Angeles, who placed Mr. Hoover's name in nomination, and Representative Moore, Republican, New York. Both said they told Mr. Hoover their position would be in the Republican column in November.

Nutt said he attributed the sudden shifting of campaign contributions almost entirely to the Democratic success in Maine.

"I told the president," he said, "that I felt pretty good over the Maine elections, anyhow. As I interpret it, people want to maintain the present administration and are coming forward with money to help. Many of our contributors now decided they didn't give us a cent in 1928.

Although Nutt said the Republican party would be able to spend more if it had it, he added he believed it the campaign could be conducted satisfactorily on $1,500,000.

He estimated this figure with the fund of about $3,500,000 in 1928, of which, he said, about $300,000 was left after the campaign. During the present drive, he added, many requests have been made of Republican state organizations, but all of them have been turned down.

They have their own organizations," he said, "and I believe they should be able to support themselves.

Brings Democracy's Message

FRANKLIN DELANO ROOSEVELT

Nominee Speaks Here Saturday On Rail Problem

Democratic Standard-Bearer Will Deliver Second Major Address of Trip at L. D. S. Tabernacle

Conferences With Party Leaders Arranged

New York Governor Receives Rousing Welcome From Crowds at Station and Hotel on Arriving at Midnight

ROOSEVELT'S PROGRAM IN SALT LAKE

Here is the program for Governor Roosevelt's visit in Salt Lake Saturday and Sunday:

SATURDAY
11 a. m. to 12 o'clock noon—Conferences with various groups, Newhouse hotel.
12:30 to 1:30 p. m.—Luncheon at Newhouse hotel, as guest of the chamber of commerce board of governors and past presidents.
3 to 5 p. m.—Conferences with various groups, Newhouse hotel.
6:45 p. m.—Program at L. D. S. tabernacle, where he will speak at 7:15 o'clock.
8:30 to 10 p. m.—Dinner at Hotel Utah, as guest of Utah Democrats.

SUNDAY
11 a. m. to 12:15 p. m.—Attend services at St. Paul's Episcopal church.
12:30 p. m.—Guest at luncheon at residence of Governor George H. Dern.
2:15 to 4:30 p. m.—Public reception at state capitol.
5 p. m.—Train leaves for Butte, Mont.

Governor Franklin D. Roosevelt, Democratic nominee for president, was given a rousing welcome when he arrived here Friday midnight to deliver the second major address of his western tour.

In spite of the late hour of his arrival, the Union Pacific station was packed with spectators, who gave the presidential nominee one of the most enthusiastic receptions of his trip thus far. Governor Roosevelt, displaying the famous family smile and leaning on the shoulder of his handsome son, James Roosevelt, waved his hat at the crowd, posed for pictures with Governor George H. Dern for a few moments and was then rushed away to his headquarters in the Newhouse hotel.

The hotel lobby, like the station, was packed with cheering people, who stood on chairs and davenports to get a glimpse of the Democratic standard-bearer.

Governor Roosevelt gave no talk at the station because of the fact that he will deliver one and probably two important speeches during his two-day visit here.

SIGNIFICANT SPEECH EXPECTED

His address at the tabernacle Saturday night will deal with the railroad problem and many members of his party expect that it will be the most significant and important of his western tour.

The New York governor said that he would likewise have something to say about the silver question before departing from Salt Lake. He did not announce when he would speak on this in at the chamber of commerce luncheon Saturday noon rather than at the mass meeting in the tabernacle.

The throng that greeted him upon his arrival here included enlisted men of the national guard, under the leadership of Adjutant General W. G. Williams; J. Bruce Kremer, national committeeman from Montana; Orman W. Ewing, national committeeman from Utah; Delbert M. Draper, Democratic state chairman; candidates on the Democratic state ticket and party leaders from every section of the state.

The Democratic nominee for president, while declining to elaborate his views on the silver question, evinced a lively interest in the subject. He pointed out that prosperity in the west is dependent upon the mining industry and that prosperity in the national sense is dependent upon prosperity in every section. His attitude is that rehabilitation of mining is therefore one of the essential steps toward economic recovery, just as is restoration of the purchasing power of agriculture.

Governor Roosevelt's address is scheduled to start at 7:15 p. m., elaborate his views on the silver question, evinced a lively interest in the talk being broadcast by two national radio systems.

Other features of the New York governor's visit in Salt Lake

R. F. C. APPROVES DOTSERO FUNDS

$3,850,000 Loan Authorized to Build Cutoff; Quick Start Promised

WASHINGTON, D. C., Sept. 16.—The Reconstruction Finance corporation today authorized a loan of $3,850,000 to the Denver & Rio Grande railroad to be used in building the Dotsero cutoff. The corporation acted wholly in accord with the recommendation of the interstate commerce commission, last Monday, the commission, at the same time, extending until November 15 the date on which construction shall begin, but

Hoover Takes Lead in Poll Of Ten Cities

NEW YORK, Sept. 16 (UP)—Returns from the cities in the Literary Digest's presidential poll, announced today, showed President Hoover leading Governor Franklin D. Roosevelt by 283 votes. The figures:

	H.	R.
Palo Alto, Cal.	118	77
Sacramento, Cal.	94	325
Hartford, Conn.	698	379
Fitchburg, Mass.	65	48
Springfield, Mass.	446	238
Newark, N. J.	878	641
Reading, Pa.	234	355
Charleston, W. Va.	111	219
Wheeling, W. Va.	33	91
Salt Lake City	186	380
Totals		

DERN LAUDED BY ROOSEVELT

Governor and Wyoming Man Credited With Aiding in Nomination

By STAFF CORRESPONDENT
WITH GOVERNOR ROOSEVELT'S SPECIAL IN SALT LAKE—Governor George H. Dern of Utah and Fred Johnson of Wyoming were introduced by Governor Franklin D. Roosevelt at stops between Cheyenne and Salt Lake Friday as two of the men largely responsible for his being a candidate for president.

Tabernacle was used by Gov. Franklin D. Roosevelt. Photo shows part of crowd and the speech. Inset, a closeup of Roosevelt.

> "No sight in the United States gives me so much of a thrill as when I ... find myself coming down into the Salt Lake Valley."

The Inaugural Committee
requests the honor of the presence of
Miss Muriel Thompson
to attend and participate in the Inauguration of

Franklin Delano Roosevelt
as President of the United States of America
and
John Nance Garner
as Vice President of the United States of America
on Saturday the fourth of March
one thousand nine hundred and thirty-three
in the City of Washington

Please reply to Ray Baker
Chairman Committee on Reception of Governors of States
and
Special Distinguished Guests
Washington Building, Washington, D.C.

Cary T. Grayson
Chairman, Inaugural Committee

THOUSANDS WELCOME THE PRESIDENT   On September 29, 1935, President Roosevelt made his first visit to Utah as president on a twenty-five-minute rail stop in Salt Lake City. He and First Lady Eleanor Roosevelt were en route to southern Nevada for the dedication of Boulder Dam (now Hoover Dam). They stood on the rear platform of the train to greet the people. A crowd of 20,000 at the Union Pacific Depot heartily welcomed him. "My friends, it is good to be in Salt Lake City again on this beautiful day," Roosevelt said. "I am happy to be greeted by my friends, the governor of Utah and the mayor of Salt Lake City." "No sight in the United States gives me so much of a thrill as when I wake up on the train and find myself coming down into the Salt Lake valley," he said to the crowd. "I had that same thrill this morning. I am happy to see from your faces that things are a lot better with you than when I was here three years ago."[91]

(Right) Paul Hard, Secret Service; Pres. Franklin D. Roosevelt; Gus Gennerich, Secret Service; First Lady Eleanor Roosevelt; Utah Governor Henry H. Blood.

Salt Lake Girl Presents Bouquet to First Lady

Eleven-year-old Dixie Rose Giles, daughter of Mr. and Mrs. G. R. Giles of 1469 Stratford avenue, can thank a representative of The Telegram for the distinction of presenting a bouquet of flowers to Mrs. Roosevelt, as she stood with the president on the rear platform of the presidential car.

Dixie Rose, a sixth grade pupil of Highland Park school, wearing a blue checked gingham dress, was whisked through police lines with the aid of a Telegram reporter, and handed the first lady a large bunch of home-grown black-eyed Susans. Dixie Rose received a gracious "thank you, my dear" from the first lady for her trouble.

A beautiful basket of pink gladioli and yellow chrysanthemums, the gift of Governor and Mrs. Henry H. Blood, was handed to Mrs. Roosevelt at the same time.

SALT LAKE UTAH CITY

KEY TO THE CITY *(Above)*

Salt Lake City Mayor Louis Marcus presented Roosevelt with a large, five-pound "key to the city" made of Utah copper.[92]

NO THIRD TERM

Policemen Wrestle Ribbon Tying First Lady's Bouquet

Two policemen wrestled with ribbon and string in the crowded Union Pacific depot Sunday so that President and Mrs. Franklin D. Roosevelt might be presented a huge bouquet of flowers and a box of candy.

The flowers were from Governor and Mrs. Henry H. Blood. It was the job of Brigadier General W. G. Williams, adjutant general of Utah and chief of the governor's staff, to see that the gifts were delivered.

But the flowers wouldn't stay together. The general called on Patrolmen H. K. Record and A. C. Reese to see what they could do. Using a baggage truck for a work bench, the officers wrestled with ribbon and string.

President and Mrs. Roosevelt got the gifts.

THE SALT LAKE TELEGRAM, SEPT. 30, 1935

ROOSEVELT RETURNS TO UTAH TO MOURN *President Roosevelt made his final visit to Utah on September 1, 1936, to pay his last respects to George Henry Dern (Above left)—Utah's sixth governor—who had served as Roosevelt's Secretary of War from 1933–1936. Roosevelt had strict instructions that he make no public speeches, media interviews, or anything to be construed as political during the visit. He was there to mourn his friend and advisor. His party whisked him directly to the Tabernacle for the afternoon funeral; took him, with the family and friends, to the graveside service at the cemetery; and had him back aboard his special train all within just a little more than three hours. (Above right) President Roosevelt rode in the same car as two of George Dern's children—Mary Dern and John Dern—as they made their way to the Tabernacle for the funeral service.*

After President Roosevelt's death in 1945, Eleanor Roosevelt continued to make visits to Utah. The former first lady served as the first United States delegate to the United Nations, as chair of the UN Commission on Human Rights, and as the first chair of President Kennedy's Presidential Commission on the Status of Women. On one of her visits to Utah, Salt Lake City Mayor Earl J. Glade accompanied her around town.

(Above) Program from the memorial service held in Utah for FDR. (Right) Mayor Glade and Eleanor Roosevelt, getting a bite to eat at a lunch counter.

Section III

POSTWAR UTAH COMES OF AGE

1946–1969

HARRY S TRUMAN

NATIONAL PORTRAIT GALLERY

Harry S Truman was president of the United States from 1945–1953 and served at the same time Herbert B. Maw and J. Bracken Lee were governors of Utah and George Albert Smith and David O. McKay were presidents of the Church. He came to Utah at least eight times, including three times as president.

UTAH STATE HISTORICAL SOCIETY

THE OGDEN
Standard-Examiner

OGDEN CITY UTAH, TUESDAY EVENING, JUNE 26, 1945 — 12 PAGES — FINAL EDITION

Delegates Sign Peace Charter; Truman to Close Conference

Ratification Next Job; President To Visit Missouri

SAN FRANCISCO, June 2 (AP)—Delegates of 50 unite nations began signing at o— p. m., Mountain war time, t— day a world charter designe— to maintain peace and secu— ity.

Dr. V. K. Wellington Koo, c— nese ambassador to London, c— the first delegate to affix a s— nature to the historic docum— hammered out here in nine wee— of deliberations.

The ceremony—expected to l— several hours with 153 delega— signing—was held in the audi— ium of San Francisco's veter— memorial building. Delegates ga— ered around a blue, oval tab— surrounded by the flags of all t— united nations.

Delegates Witnesses

The only witnesses were t— delegates, themselves and phot— graphers and newspapermen.

Dr. Wellington Koo of Chi— brushed his name down the pa— of history—and the first of t— united nations to be invaded b— the axis became the first to aff— a signature.

Thus began an hour's long cer— mony in which 153 delegates move— in alphabetical order—after Chin— Russia, Britain and France ha— signed—to the great blue tab— surrounded by the flags of all t— united nations, centering the kie— lighted auditorium of San Fra— cisco's veterans' building.

U. S. Waits Until Las—

The United States preferred t— wait until last—partly because i— is host country, but largely b— cause it wanted to sign in the la— ernoon, so that President Trum— might witness the ceremony mo— conveniently.

The delegates, as they gathere— in the auditorium, found a co— mon appreciation in the words — an old Negro spiritual which p— claims: "I ain't gwine study wa— no more, no more."—

One by one, the delegates we— called to the table upon whi— lay the blue leather-bound cha— ter that their top spokesman s— represents the hopes of the livi— and a promise of "never again."— the fallen dead.

Truman Speaks Tonight

After the formal signing, Pre— dent Truman will close the co— ference with an address at abo— six p. m. mountain war time.

A triumphant meeting of t— united nations conference—its la— working session—last night a— proved the final version of t— charter. The signatures went — today; next come the slower pro— ess of ratification.

Rapping last night's session — its close, Britain's tall delegate— chief, the Earl of Halifax, w— presided, solemnly told the co— ference: "I think we all agr— we have taken part in a histor— moment in world history."

Controversy had been cleared aw— days before this final action. a— the vote of approval was unan— mous.

Officials estimated that the sig— ing would require about ei— hours. A last minute change — plans pushed Argentina out of i— phabetical first place and put t— conference sponsoring powers a— France at the head of the ord— of signers.

These ceremonies complete — months and a day of intense, — bate-studded conference wo— They make this symbolically — of the great days for which t— allied world has fought a— planned since the second Wor— war started—the day on whi— the victorious governments s— scribe to a plan for preventing — third World war.

Truman Lauds Nimitz

President Truman today cal— Fleet Admiral Chester W. N— itz and congratulated him on — long string of victories in the — cific war against Japan.

The man who commands t— greatest fleet in world histo— talked with the president in h— suite in the Fairmont hotel. N— itz is scheduled to return t— headquarters at Guam when — has completed his official busine— here. The reason for his trip t— San Francisco was not disclos—

President Truman also confer— briefly with Field Marshal J— Christian Smuts, prime minister — the Union of South Africa, w— is to be a guest at the Wh— House next Monday.

The president plans to leave S— Francisco immediately after h— speech closing the united natio— security conference. En ro— east, President Truman will — overnight at a city which can— be revealed in advance beca— of security reasons, then proce— tomorrow to Independence, Mo— his home town, for a celebrat—

San Francisco Welcome . . Ticker tape showers down on President Harry S. Truman as he moves along Montgomery street in San Francisco's financial district on his arrival from Portland June 25 to attend the closing session of the united nations conference. At side President Truman is greeted by Secretary of State Edward R. Stettinius, Jr., at nearby Hamilton field.

Here's Outline of Peace Program

SAN FRANCISCO, June 26 (UP). Here is an outline of the new world organization adopted by the united nations:

General assembly: the "town meeting of the world." To be composed of representatives from all nations; each member to have not more than five representatives but only one vote. Site of headquarters for annual meetings to be selected later.

Security council: The "policeman" of the world. To be composed of 11 nations. The United States, Britain, Russia, China and France to have permanent seats; six other nations to be elected for two-year terms with special attention to their ability to help keep the peace and to geographical location. To meet continuously at a site to be selected.

Economic and social council: The "eradicator" of causes of war. To be composed of 18 nations elected for three-year terms. No special privileges for big powers but recognition to be given by the general assembly in electing council members to their economic, cultural and social importance.

Trusteeship council: The "guardian" of dependent peoples. To be composed of members administering trust territories, members of the Big Five not holding trusteeships, and enough other nonadministering members to make the council equally divided between those who hold trusteeships and those who don't. The elected members to serve for three-year terms.

International court: The world court for legal disputes. To be composed of 15 judges, each from a different nation, for nine-year terms. Judges to be nominated by the national groups in the existing permanent court of arbitration and elected by the general assembly and the security council. The seat of the court will be The Hague in The Netherlands—the seat of the old permanent court of international justice.

Military staff committee: The
(Continued on Page Two) (Column Seven)

How New Peace Pact Will Work

(Editor's Note: Here is one of six stories explaining how the united nations—just fashioned at San Francisco to keep world peace—will work.)

WASHINGTON, June 26 (AP)— The bonecrusher of the united nations is the security council. It's a pistol, fully loaded.

To keep peace that pistol can be used against the head of any member of the united nations except the Big Five: United States, Britain, Russia, France, China.

If some smaller nation starts to shove a neighbor around, the council can throw an economic headlock on it by isolating it from the rest of the world.

This can be done by shutting off commerce, telephone, telegraphic, cable, air and rail communication with it.

If this isn't enough, if that same aggressor nation ignores the economic blockade and moves in on a neighbor, then the security council can call upon the united nations' members to serve it with their armies.

So much for the smaller nations. That's what the council can do to them. But it can't work that way against the Big Five. This is why:

The council will have 11 members, the Big Five as permanent members and six smaller nations elected to two-year terms each by the general assembly.

The most important single word to remember about the council is "veto." The Big Five have veto power to an extraordinary degree. The smaller nations have it, too.
(Continued on Page Two) (Column Five)

U. S. Plan—s Rip —Japs — —Valley

(AP)—Fifth —ack bomb—00 sorties a —zon, ripped —king their —Cagayan —ricans and —the kill. —mbing com—roons and —und. the —nd Thun—striking —in "death —division's —pushing —p bodies, —and shat—ring the —miles be—kao. —rom re—artillery

Toyoda —wn sky—nd mu—while —ll were —finally —od sur—dazed, —worth—

—erican —les of —cam—

—ntin—Aus—orted —New —ilities —total

Warfare Flares in Shangri-La Where 15 Yanks Marooned

HOLLANDIA, New Guinea, June 24 (Delayed) (AP)—A private war among the natives of Shangri-La and their belligerent neighbors added today to the complications of bringing a WAC and 14 escorts from this hidden valley of New Guinea.

About the time mechanical failures and lack of sufficient equipment arose to plague the work of the army air force rescuers, along came the battle among the Aborigines.

Not that the battle between the Shangri-Lalans and their unidentified native enemies is imperiling the party stranded in the mountain-locked valley, but the warfare is eddying uncomfortably close.

The natives of Shangri-La seem somewhat addicted to warfare. They have erected stockades —

Captain Cecil Walters, who heads the rescue party which parachuted into the valley, reported by walkie-talkie on the outbreak of native hostilities.

Unfriendly natives on the other side of the valley, he said, were warring on the natives of Shangri-La, and the fighting had spread close to the encampment.

Tests still are in progress to determine if glider rescue is practical. The suggestion has been made that little two-seater Cub artillery spotter planes might bring the 14 out one at a time. WAC Corporal Margaret Hastings, Owego, N. Y.; Lieutenant John R. McCollom, Trenton, Mo., and Sergeant Kenneth Decker, Kelso, Wash., are the only ones of 23 persons who emerged alive when an army transport on a sight-seeing tour crashed against a —

U. S. Warship Lost Off Borneo

WASHINGTON, June 26 (UP)— The navy today announced the loss of the minesweeper Salute as a result of enemy action in the Borneo area.

The 945-ton vessel, which carried a wartime crew of about 100, lost nine members—six killed and three missing.

Skipper of the vessel, Lieutenant John S. Nichols, Garden City, Long —

Diarrhea Kills Seven Infants in Nursery

NEW YORK, June 26 (UP)— Nurseries at the Misericordia hospital were closed today after an outbreak of diarrhea had killed seven of 31 infants there. Hospital officials said 11 other babie—

TRUMAN MAKES BRIEF STOP IN UTAH AFTER HAVING SIGNED THE U.N. CHARTER (Opposite) On June 26, 1945, the new president stopped briefly in Salt Lake City for a night's sleep in his return trip east from the San Francisco Security Conference where earlier in the day he had participated in the founding of the United Nations and the signing of the U.N. Charter. President George Albert Smith (left) and Governor Herbert B. Maw (right) met Truman at the airport that evening, and then Truman rode to the hotel with the Church president.

PRESIDENT SMITH SHARES STORY ABOUT TRUMAN'S GRANDFATHER'S RELATIONSHIP WITH BRIGHAM YOUNG During this brief ride, President Smith recalled the story of how Brigham Young helped save President Truman's grandfather from financial ruin. Solomon Young (below left), a "mule skinner," once drove a load of material to Salt Lake that the army was going to buy but, at the last minute, decided not to. Having come so far and now having no market for his goods, he sought out Brigham Young (right) for advice. Brigham helped him set up a place where he could sell the merchandise from the east and promised him he would not lose a penny—and he didn't. The president laughed at the story and said he recalled his grandfather telling it many times.[93]

PRESIDENT SMITH GIVES TRUMAN A PARTING GIFT Before parting, the prophet handed President Truman a personalized, leather-bound copy of A Voice of Warning—one of the Church's widely used proselyting pamphlets. In doing so, he informed the president that the Latter-day Saints regularly prayed for him. The chief executive promised to read the pamphlet, whose author, Parley P. Pratt, had been intimately involved in the Church's turbulent history in Mr. Truman's native Missouri.

THE FLYING WHITE HOUSE

TRUMAN WAVING FROM "THE SACRED COW" (Above and Right) The next morning, President Truman boarded his plane in Salt Lake for the continued journey eastward. The plane was the original Air Force One—a Douglas C-54 Skymaster that had been used to fly Franklin D. Roosevelt to the Yalta Conference in April 1945 and which was nicknamed "The Sacred Cow." Truman used this particular plane until 1947.

> *"Congressman Granger . . . told me that he had become so fond of me that when the Mormons moved back to Independence, he was going to let me stay."*

PRICE IS THE FIRST OF NUMEROUS STOPS IN UTAH *During his famous whistle stop tour of the country during the 1948 election, President Truman made several stops in Utah on September 21. At his first stop in Price (Price railroad station shown above), Truman (a native of Independence, Jackson County, Missouri) shared a funny story about a previous visit to Utah. "Congressman [Walter] Granger (shown top next to quote) paid me a very high compliment when I was out here as a Senator," Truman said. "He introduced me up at Bingham, and he told me that he had become so fond of me that when the Mormons moved back to Independence, he was going to let me stay. I thought that was the greatest compliment that could be paid to anybody."[94]*

TRUMAN SUPPORTS FIRST WOMAN TO REPRESENT UTAH IN CONGRESS

(Opposite) Truman went on to make brief speeches from the rear platform of the rail car in Helper, Springville, Provo (where he mentioned that he had been there on several occasions relating to the steel plant, Geneva Steel, (shown below) under construction from 1943–48), and American Fork

before arriving in Salt Lake City. In American Fork, Truman shared a laugh with American Fork native Reva Beck Bosone from the railcar as he plugged her Congressional campaign. Bosone won that fall, becoming the first woman to represent Utah in Congress.

TRUMAN DESCENDS FROM TRAIN PLATFORM IN SALT LAKE CITY

The Trumans arrived in Salt Lake late in the afternoon of September 21. They were in the midst of a thirty-five-day journey through the nation by train, traveling 31,700 miles and making as many as sixteen whistle-stop speeches per day. (Above) Daughter Margaret Truman, First Lady Bess Truman, President George Albert Smith,

and President Truman disembarked from the train to greet people. President Smith welcomed President Truman with two boxes of Utah peaches (one from Farmington and one from Cottonwood).[95] The two presidents had developed a good friendship from their several visits with each other, both in Utah and in Washington.

Belle S. Spafford, President of the Relief Society, and a group of RS sisters travelled to Washington D.C. to present a handcrafted lace tablecloth to First Lady Bess Truman on May 3, 1946. [96]

(Above) Relief Society sisters with Mrs. Truman at the White House in Washington, D.C. Mrs. Truman in center in dark dress. Belle Spafford to Mrs. Truman's left. (Below) Tablecloth & accompanying card.

Dear Mrs. Truman,

The Relief Society women of the Church of Jesus Christ of Latter-day Saints are honored to present to you, the First Lady of our great Nation, as an expression of our esteem, this lace tablecloth characteristic of the handwork of Latter-day Saint women.

We hope you will enjoy using it, and that it will serve to remind you that rare handwork skills are being perpetuated by our Society.

Sincerely,
Belle S. Spafford,
President.

May 2, 1946.

TRUMAN MOTORCADE   *Thousands of Utahns turned out to greet the thirty-third president as his convertible traveled the streets of Salt Lake City between the Rio Grande depot and Hotel Utah on September 21, 1948.*

PRESIDENTIAL BANQUET AT HOTEL UTAH   *At the Empire Room of Hotel Utah, state officials held a banquet to honor the presidential party. Seated left to right, Bess Truman, Governor Maw, President Truman, and President Smith enjoyed the banquet together. During the event, Governor Maw introduced Truman, and Truman began his remarks by saying: "Governor Maw, President Smith: I noticed very carefully that when the Governor addressed you, he said 'Fellow Democrats.' That included President Smith. [Laughter] That made me very happy."*[97] *George Albert Smith was long active as a Republican, although he personally greatly liked Truman.*[98]

TRUMAN SPEAKS AT THE TABERNACLE   *After dinner at Hotel Utah, President Truman spoke to an overflow crowd in the Tabernacle and left Salt Lake City at 9:58PM. President Truman, President Smith, and Governor Maw shared a light moment as the busy day drew to a close (Right). Truman then spoke briefly from his train car in Ogden at 11:15PM before concluding his whirlwind day through Utah. Marilyn Robinson of Ogden, "Miss Utah 1948," assumed the role of hostess to Mrs. Bess Truman and their daughter, Margaret Truman.*

THE OGDEN Standard Examiner

The United Press
The Associated Press

OGDEN CITY, UTAH, WEDNESDAY EVENING, SEPTEMBER 22, 1948

NEA Service
AP Service

18 PAGES—2 SECTIONS

Luster of Presidential Party's Visit Undimmed by Lateness of Hour

...cus Evans, captain of the Weber county sheriff's mounted posse, ...ws the honorary rank of captain on President Truman and enrolls as a member. "If the posse rides in jeeps, I'm all right," remarked ...the president.

President Truman continued his lambasting of the 80th congress and repeated earlier charges of "sabotaging the west" as he spoke briefly to a crowd estimated at more than 5000 gathered at Ogden's Union station last night.

Marilyn Robinson of Ogden, "Miss Utah of 1948," assumed the role of hostess to Mrs. Truman and Daughter Margaret. Here Miss Robinson pins an orchid corsage on Margaret after bestowing a similar favor on the nation's first lady.

...ds in Berlin ...wait Secret ...rley Friday

...LIN, Sept. 22 (AP)—West... today

'Propeller Jets' Are Slated for Commercial Use

VANCOUVER, B. C., Sept. 22 (UP)—Propeller-driven jets are feasible "within five years" for commercial airlines. Air Commodore Sir Frank Whittle said at the closing session of the Planning ...Dewey as he cut...

Dewey Drafts His Plan for Lasting Peace

EN ROUTE TO ALBUQUERQUE WITH DEWEY, Sept. 22 (AP) — A formula for preventing a new world war was promised today by Gov. ...

More Than 5,000 Persons Greet Truman at Ogden

By Bert O. Strand

Many Ogden area residents last night saw, heard and shook hands with 'a president of the United States for the first time in their lives.

Some of them gathered at the Union depot as much as one full hour before traintime to make sure they would catch a glimpse of the nation's chief executive as he spoke.

More than 5,000 persons were jammed against ropes when President Harry S. Truman did arrive, and heard him declare he was for prosperity in the west and would continue the fight against high prices.

"I want to keep the west prosperous," the chief executive declared as he took the stand. "Throughout my tour of the country I have seen prosperity. I have seen prosperity in the west."

"But I have a series of obstacles in the way," he grinned, naming the "blood sucking" Republican party, "whose interests never got past the Mississippi river, if even the Alleghany mountains." And the "awful" 80th congress, "the do-nothing congress," which, swayed by the Republican party, "failed to do anything about high prices, housing or reclamation."

Escorted by Mayor

Flanked by secret service men and local police, President Truman was escorted from the depot doorway to the speaker's platform by Mayor Harman W. Peery of Ogden. He was followed by his wife and daughter, Margaret, who were greeted with cheers as they were introduced by Roy C. Metcalf, chairman of the Weber county Democratic committee, and presented with orchid corsages by Miss ...

Utah, Ogden's own Marilyn Robinson.

Introduced by Rep. Walter K. Granger, (D-Utah), President Truman greeted the crowd with friendliness and enthusiasm, although his voice sounded tired and it seemed an effort for him to speak.

"If anyone stayed at home in Ogden tonight—I doubt it very much," he opened. "You know," he laughed, "these eastern papers won't believe you western people will stay up until eleven p. m. to see the president. You have proved they are wrong."

Reclamation Projects

In speaking about the west, Mr. Truman pointed to the various reclamation projects completed under the Democratic administration. He included the Ogden river project, "which has done much toward the prosperity of your state."

"Utah incomes on the average are six times higher than in 1932," he declared. This, he said was accomplished under a Democratic administration and not Republicans who "right now are selling out the best interests of the country by intention."

As the time drew near for the arrival of the special train, a buzz of nervous activity swept over the crowd. This changed to a stillness of expectation as newspaper men and photographers appeared at the depot doorway followed by secret service men. Truman waved his hand and paused for a moment in the doorway to be greeted by a

(Continued on Page Two-A)
(Column Four)

Bushnell Use as School Arouses Truman Interest

Rep. Walter K. Granger (D-Utah) said today that President Truman is interested in a proposal to use a part of army-abandoned Bushnell general hospital in Brigham City for a military school for men and women.

The congressman said he had outlined the proposal of Joseph A. Hill, of Portland, Ore., to direct such a school on the army hospital reservation to the president during Mr. Truman's Utah visit and was promised cooperation.

President Truman, according to Granger, said he would immediately request appropriate officials in Washington to inform him how facilities and equipment may be provided.

Some Surplus on Standby

The president told Granger that some surpluses are now set aside on a standby basis.

Granger said he found much interest in and support for the Hill proposal. He said the president is familiar with the Bushnell hospital situation and remembers the installation from his visit to it a few years ago when he headed the Truman committee.

Hill, who already operates two military schools, one at Portland, and one on the Puget Sound, visited Brigham City recently during the annual Peach days celebration, and conferred with Box Elder county commissioners, city officials and local educators.

Wants Place Equipped

While Hill was in Brigham City he said he was convinced he would be able to secure Bushnell, but said, "We want it equipped." He also said that he felt sure the war assets administration or the army had all surplus equipment needed to fit the hospital for adaptation as a military school.

Cooperation was pledged on the part of Box Elder county by Lewis S. Wight, commission chairman, on the part of the city by Lorenzo J. Bott, mayor, and J. D. Gunderson and Ezra B. Owen, chamber of commerce president and secretary, respectively.

Cites Reclamation Record

Observing that "we should stop quarreling about the means and achieve unified progress then will do the job," Mr. said:

"In all of these programs, I insist that so little superman from Washington be put in centralized control. The people in the areas whose lives are so deeply affected must have a full share in the planning, construction and in the operation of the projects."

In his Denver speech, he declared ...

Harries Case ... Jury Some Ti...

SALT LAKE CITY, Sept. 22 (UP)—The defense rested today in the bribery trial of Robert Harries after seven men testified favorably on the character of the former liquor commission law enforcement chief.

Harries is accused by the Salt Lake county grand jury of accepting a bribe from Cyrus Lack for assertedly promising to protect against raids the clubs where Lack was selling liquor from his agency at premium prices.

As soon as Defense Attorney Arthur Woolley rested his case, presentation of rebuttal witnesses began by District Attorney Brigham Roberts and Special Prosecutor Clifford Ashton.

District Judge Ray Van Cott, Jr., instructed jurors to return at ten a. m. tomorrow, then recessed the trial to prepare his instructions.

Character Witnesses

The character witnesses were led by John E. Harris, warden of the Utah state prison where Harries formerly served as deputy warden. Harris said that as far as he knew, Harries' reputation for honesty was good.

Similar testimony came from Gordon Taylor Hyde, gravel company president and former Utah state finance commissioner; Paul Beacher, veteran Granite district teacher; Dr. Morgan S. Coombs, physician; Arthur Gardiner, Salt Lake; L. D. S. temple worker; Charles Fogel, state highway patrolman, and William Caylas, Salt Lake City businessman.

The crowd in the small district court room laughed when Caylas admitted he was the bondsman for both Harris and Lack, who has been indicted on a charge of embezzlement.

Harries, who was on the stand all day Monday, ended his testimony yesterday with a denial that he had received a bribe from Cyrus V. Lack as charged by the Salt Lake county grand jury indictment. Lack who is under indictment for embezzlement, is a former operator of the Brigham Street Pharmacy package agency.

PRESIDENT HARRY TRUMAN

...e President of ...United States Speaks ...onight!!

The General Public is invited to attend this outstanding address by the nation's chief executive.

★ ★ ★
No Tickets Are Required!
★ ★ ★
Doors Open at 7:00 P.M.
★ ★ ★
See and Hear Your President in Person!
★ ★ ★
...ent Truman will have an important message for the people of Utah!
★ ★ ★
...President Truman Tonight in the Tabernacle

Salt Lake Tabernacle
★ ★ ★
7:45 P.M.
★ ★ ★

Parade Watcher Fatally Injured

SALT LAKE CITY, Sept. 22 (AP)—An elderly man was injured fatally last night as he walked across a Salt Lake police crowded with bystanders waiting to see President Truman drive by.

The victim was John Samuel Gordon, 74. He died this afternoon. Police said he was struck by a Salt Lake City lines bus at the Second South-Main street intersection.

Bus company officials said it was the first fatality in 15,600,000 miles of operations.

Baseball Today

By The Associated Press

National League

Pittsburgh ...	200 012 000—5 11 0
Brooklyn ...	000 000 601—1 6 1

Sewell and Kluttz; Taylor, Palica, Branca, Minner and Campanella.

St. Louis ...	012 401 000—8 17 2
Boston ...	001 000 100—2 6 1

Brazle and Rice; Spahn, Barrett, Hogue, Shoun, Lyons and Masi.

First:

Chicago ...	200 000 100—3 11 1
New York ...	000 100 001—2 5 0

Rush and Scheffing; Koslo, Trinkle and Yvars, Westrum.

Cincinnati at Philadelphia, night game.

American League

Philadelphia ...	000 010 000—1 7 0
Detroit ...	300 030 00x—5 9 0

Marchildon, Harris, Savage and Rosar; Newhouser and Ginsburg.

New York at Chicago, Boston at Cleveland and Washington at St. Louis, night games.

Blast Kills Nine In Jewish Sector

CAIRO, Egypt, Sept. 22 (AP)—Nine persons were killed and 12 injured when a heavy explosion damaged four buildings in the Jewish quarter of Cairo today. There may be other casualties. Several ambulances were rushed to the scene. Police threw a cordon around the area while investigators went to work. Rioting started after the explosion, but police stopped it.

President George Albert Smith traveled to Washington DC to unveil a statue of President Brigham Young in Statuary Hall of the Capitol on the pioneer's birthday, June 1. Arriving early, President Smith called at the White House to visit President Truman, giving him a specially bound copy of Preston Nibley's book, *Brigham Young, the Man and His Work.*

The dedicatory service took place in the rotunda of the Capitol, with a distinguished group of Church and government officials, civic leaders, and members of the family and press. The United States Marine Corps Band, the Utah Centennial Chorus, and the Manhattan Stake Choir furnished the music for the occasion. After a few speeches and the unveiling, President Smith offered the dedicatory prayer, and the statue was accepted by the United States Senate.

The ceremony seemed to go with silken smoothness, but weeks before the ceremony, the Arrangements Commission advised that the dedicatory prayer should not be too long and that a copy of it should be submitted in advance for editing of grammatical errors. When Senator Arthur V. Watkins advised him of these demands, President Smith showed an understandable irritation. He told Arthur to tell the commission that if they wanted someone to compose a prayer long before the event, without relying on the inspiration of the moment, they should get someone else to do it. The commission relented, and President Smith prayed extemporaneously at the dedication, as he always did. 99

Mahonri Young and President Smith greeting guests at the statue unveiling and dedication ceremony.

BRIGHAM YOUNG
THE MAN AND HIS WORK
PRESTON NIBLEY

DAVID O. McKAY AND TRUMAN TAKE A TRAIN RIDE TOGETHER

President David O. McKay visited President Truman in his railcar at the depot in Salt Lake, where they enjoyed breakfast together. President McKay recorded in his diary the events of the day: "President Truman then came in and said: 'Oh, President McKay, you honor me in coming down!' I thanked him for his invitation: The President then introduced me to his daughter Margaret. The President then invited me to come out to the platform with him to have pictures taken, stating that if having the picture taken would embarrass me for me not to do it. I, however, accepted his invitation." [100] *(Opposite: Presidents McKay and Truman behind microphones on the rear of the train.)*

The two presidents rode in the train together from Salt Lake to Provo. President McKay wrote in his diary of the event: "I had a very pleasant thirty minutes or so with the President, during which time, I saw the better Truman, and got a glimpse of his better nature—the cockiness was gone. He referred to the fact that this is his last official tour before retiring, saying, 'When I get through with this, it is my last.' He then told me what he wanted to do; viz. to spend his time instructing the youth of America in loyalty and American ideals. He mentioned some other men whom he would like to have join him in this project. I commended him for this desire, and told him that I think that is just what we need. I then gave him a few of my ideas on the subject, emphasizing the freedom of the individual; that that must be maintained at all cost. . . . On the train, President Truman made the remark to me that he did not have hatred in his heart for any man, and said: 'I am campaigning—that is politics.'" [101]

TRUMAN CAMPAIGNS FOR STEVENSON AND SPARKMAN

Rather than seek another term in 1952, President Truman campaigned for Democratic nominee Adlai Stevenson and his running mate John Sparkman. Truman arrived in Salt Lake City on October 6, 1952, for a campaign stop and a speech at BYU. This was Truman's third and final visit to Utah as president.

DEMOCRATIC PARTY FUNDRAISING DINNER PROGRAM FROM 1952

(Above Inset) Though Truman was not in attendance at this dinner, he was featured on the program as the current President of the United States. These fundraising dinners, named after Thomas Jefferson and Andrew Jackson as the founders of the Democratic Party, have been held as far back as 1900.

Tribune Telephone
To call any department of The Salt Lake Tribune dial 3-1511. For information service and sports scores, dial 5-7511.

The Salt Lake Tribune

Fair and Cooler
Salt Lake City and vicinity—Fair, some frost. Utah—Fair, frost. Idaho—Clear, little change in temperature. Wyoming—Fair, cooler west of Continental Divide.

VOL. 165, NO. 176
SALT LAKE CITY, UTAH, TUESDAY MORNING, OCTOBER 7, 1952
PRICE FIVE CENTS

Truman Chides 'Shortsighted' GOP

Yankee Win Extends Series to 7

Berra, Mantle Slam Homers to Give N. Y. 3-2 Victory

By DICK YOUNG
New York News Writer

NEW YORK, Oct. 6—Considered by some to be the most exciting championship struggle in baseball annals, the 1952 World Series Monday also became the most homer-packed of all classics as it buzzed into the deciding seventh game on the stomach-bubbling momentum of a 3-2 Yankee victory . . . on the power pokes of Yogi Berra and Mickey Mantle—and on the money-arm of Allie Reynolds.

A disappointing, but far from disappointed, crowd of 30,037 had seen Duke Snider blast another pair of circuits Monday to become the first National Leaguer ever to hit four in a series and edge the Brooks ahead in the sixth stanza by poling his first of the personal parley over Ebbets Fields' right screen. But Berra balanced that with his circuit sock in the next, and Mantle added an eighth-frame seat-smasher for the run that knotted the pulsating series at three games apiece.

Total of 14

Those four blasts boomed the series total to 14, with one game still remaining for additional target practice. The previous record was the 12 homers hammered in the 1925 series between the Washington Senators and Pittsburgh Pirates.

And yet, with all the long distance socking, this has been a pitcher series for the most part. The Brooks have received exceptionally strong jobs from Joe Black and Carl Erskine, and Preacher Roe. The Yankees have been kept breathing by the whipping arms of Allie Reynolds, Vic Raschi, and Allie Reynolds . . . and Allie Reynolds.

It was Reynolds who, with the one run Yankee edge threatening to be wiped out by the presence of a Brook runner on second base in the eighth, fired overpowering relief ball for the last four outs of the game. Reynolds had started the first game, and, with two days' rest, the fourth game.

One Day's Rest

Now, on one day's rest, he has been used as a desperation reliever in order for the Yanks to stay alive. So, the question is: Will Manager Casey Stengel be able to use the hardworking ace in Tuesday's vital tilt?

Reynolds fired just 22 pitches in his relief bit. He seemed to be as fast as ever. But an arm can stand only so much—especially a 34-year-old arm. To complicate matters, Allie stumbled off the mound while shooting one of Monday's bullets, and pulled a muscle in his back slightly.

If Casey Stengel starts him again Tuesday, in a third team-up with Brooklyn's Joe Black, how far can Allie go? Or, if Stengel starts another, and holds Allie in bullpen reserve for the possible clutch situation, will the over-extending right hander be able to stop the Brooks again?

(Complete details on Page 28.)

'WHOLE HOG IDEA'

Eisenhower Slashes Back at Truman

By W. H. LAWRENCE
New York Times Writer

SEATTLE, Oct. 6 — Gen. Dwight D. Eisenhower charged Monday night that the "sly apostles of Fair Dealism" believe in "whole-hog federal government" and promised that a Republican administration would expand the Western reclamation program by uniting the resources of private enterprise with those of local, state and federal governments.

Campaigning across Washington, where local politicians told him his chances of winning nine electoral votes are 50-50, the Republican nominee continued to reply to the rear-platform attacks made upon him by President Harry S Truman. The latter rolled through this area a few days ago attempting to win election for Gov. Adlai E. Stevenson of Illinois, the Democratic presidential nominee.

"You have been told by an expert in political demagoguery that I want to turn this great Northwest back to the prairie dogs and the sagebrush," Gen. Eisenhower said in a speech prepared for delivery at the Civic Ice Arena in Seattle.

Nonsense Fiction

"You have been told that these people, who are going to supplant the presnt shopworn administration, never will permit another dam in the reclamation program. You have been conducted through an underworld of imaginary devils. You have had a course in nonsense fiction."

Declaring that it was a Republican administration which started the reclamation program of the West, Eisenhower said the difference between the Republicans and the Democrats is that the party now in power believes in "whole-hog federal government."

"I have talked a good deal lately about corruption of the tax collector kind," he said, "and the kind that gives special privilege to political favorites. I speak now of a different kind of corruption, one that goes to the roots of our American system. The apostles of the whole-hog idea are interested not in money for themselves but in power for themselves. They thirst to govern. They are zealots. And in the long run they can do more harm to you and to your families than a hundred tax collectors dipping into the till."

Suggests First Step

While he opposed administration proposals for a Columbia Valley authority, similar to the Tennessee Valley Authority, as a "kind of super-government," the Republican nominee went on to say that he had "no pat and detailed answer for the mechanism we need to carry out river basin development." As a first step he said the planning, management and co-ordination of all present and future projects in the Columbia Basin should be vested not in a valley authority but in a new interstate body, with both state and federal members.

"I am convinced, out of my experience with some very big jobs, that the way to do it is by sharing of effort rather than by its concentration," the Republican nominee asserted.

"That means the full use of private resources, plus a local-state-federal partnership here in the state of Washington and the Northwest, rather than dependence upon a daily directive from Washington, D. C. . . . just as we would not remin perpetual vassals

See Page 2, Column 1

ALL PRESENT AS COURT OPENS TERM

WASHINGTON, Oct. 6—In a brief, 30-minute session, the Supreme Court Monday started on its new eight-month term.

All of the nine justices were present, including Willam O. Douglas, just returned from a two-month trip to the Far East and Southeast Asia.

A tribute to the memory of the late Charles Elmore Cropley, clerk of the court, was read from the bench by Chief Justice Fred M. Vinson. Cropley died last June.

Atty. Gen. McGranery was presented to the court by Robert L. Stern, acting solicitor general.

At the close of the short session, the justices adjourned until next Monday, when the tribunal will announce agreement or refusals to review many decisions of lower courts. A week later, arguments will begin.

Adlai to Doff Gloves in Final Round?

By JAMES RESTON
New York Times Writer

SPRINGFIELD, ILL., Oct. 6—Gov. Adlai E. Stevenson will start out Tuesday on a 4,350-mile campaign tour of eight states in the middlewest and south, and all indications are that he will take along a new and somewhat fiercer look.

The Democratic nominee feels that the "policy phase" of the campaign is over. He has covered the 13 policy fields he outlined late in August, and now he's going a-politicking.

The states to be visited, in the next five days, together with their electoral votes, are as follows:

Tuesday, Michigan (20); Wednesday, Wisconsin (12); Thursday, Missouri (13); and Illinois (27); Friday, Oklahoma (8); and Louisiana (10); and Saturday, Florida (10); and Tennessee (11). All of these states except Michigan and Louisiana voted Democratic in the 1948 presidential election. Michigan went Republican and Louisiana went for the States Right candidate.

To a reporter who has just switched back to the Stevenson camp after two weeks with the

See Page 2, Column 5

Two presidents confer at Brigham Young University. One, the President of the United States, Harry S Truman, seated, chats with the B Y U president, Dr. Ernest L. Wilkinson.

Taft Charges President Defies Truth

CINCINNATI, Oct. 6 (AP)—Sen. Robert A. Taft Monday night called Pres. Harry S Truman "a dangerous demagogue" who makes political speeches regardless of truth.

"His speeches must be taken apart," Taft told a Hamilton County Republican political dinner. "They are directed to personal units of each group and they exhibit complete recklessness of truth."

Taft, principal speaker at an "appreciation dinner" given 1,036 precinct workers, the county committee and the county and state tickets, said he has been studying the speeches made by the President on his current tour of the country.

'Not in the Bag'

And, in urging the Republican organization in his home county to continue to work to bring in a record vote, Taft warned:

"This election is not in the bag."

"Mr. Truman hasn't the slightest conception of the weight of taxes on the average person," said Taft. "Mr. Truman and Mr. Stevenson (Adlai E. Stevenson, Democratic nominee for president) haven't the slightest idea what that is about."

Taft, whom the Democratic leaders have called the boss of Gen. Dwight D. Eisenhower, Republican presidential candidate, also told approximately 1,400 persons:

Believes in Tax Cuts

"Gen. Eisenhower will end in November the threat against the very existence of the people of the United States. Eisenhower believes in the executive co-operating with the Congress and not in withholding secrets as has President Truman."

"Eisenhower believes in cutting down on spending and waste. He believes the budget can be cut for military needs and he believes in the cutting of taxes."

If Stevenson is elected, Taft asserted, "we will never have lower taxes: they might be higher."

Preceding Sen. Taft on the speaker's platform was Sen. John W. Bricker of Ohio.

Malenkov Uses 5½ Hours To Outline Red Defects

LONDON, Oct. 6 (AP)—The broadcast of Georgi M. Malenkov's keynote speech to the 19th All-Union Soviet Communist Party Congress in Moscow disclosed a wide range of defects in the Soviet economy.

In giving an exhaustive review of these defects, Malenkov, possibly the most powerful of the ruling Kremlin hierarchy after Stalin, plainly informed the Soviet Communists Sunday night they would bear future responsibility for their correction.

Replaced Stalin

He told them that the United States wields an ever-increasing threat of war over their heads and demanded strict supervision of all phases of Soviet life in an economic drive to raise the Soviet level closer to that of the United States.

The text of Malenkov's keynote address—the address heretofore given by Stalin himself—was broadcast by Moscow radio and monitored here. It took 5½ hours to read. In it Malenkov outlined an economic situation reflecting a considerable amount of confusion and a great many sore spots, such as these, in Malenkov's own words:

Industry: "Primarily there is great waste and unproductive expenditure in industry.

"At many enterprises, losses are admitted due to mismanagement and the uneconomical expenditure of material, fuel, electric power, instruments and other articles of value.

"Defective goods are still being produced. Losses and unproductive expenditure in enterprises of the union industry in 1951, for example, amounted to 4.9 billion rubles. This included losses connected with defective goods to the sum of three billion rubles. (The ruble is arbitrarily valued at 25 cents.)

Housing Shortage

Housing: "In spite of the big volume of housing construction, we still feel an acute housing shortage everywhere.

Transport and communications: "Inefficient and excessively long railway transportation of goods has not been liquidated. The work of road transport is still badly organized. Losses and unproductive expenditure are also large in transport.

Labor productivity: (This includes comment on the speed-up or "Socialist competition.") "Soviet ministries are lax in raising labor productivity in weak sections of their enterprises and are too content with over-all averages.

Low Productivity

Collective farms: The grain harvest was reported the best in years. The amalgamation of farms has reduced the number of collectives from 254,000 to 97,000 since Jan 1, 1950. But Malenkov said there was a tendency of collective farms "to place consumer and welfare arrangements ahead of the main production tasks." He said "timely measures" had to be taken.

Animal husbandry: "Through bad care of cattle, many collective farms have a high death rate among cattle and a low degree of livestock productivity.

The arts: There are serious shortcomings which must be remedied. There are not enough

See Page 2, Column 5

U. N. Repeats Plea For Delivery Of POW Parcels

TOKYO, Oct. 7 (UP)—The United Nations for the third time Monday asked the Communists to join in a plan to distribute winter parcels to Korean War prisoners of both sides.

Lt. Gen. William K. Harrison, chief U. N. delegate to the truce talks, sent a letter to the top Red delegate, Gen. Nam Il, asking that the Reds agree to deliver parcels to U. N. prisoners held by the Communists.

If the Reds would agree to deliver parcels from friends and relatives of U. N. personnel, Harrison said, the U. N. command would do the same for prisoners held by the Allies.

The first such U. N. offer, made on Aug. 5, was turned down. The second was made on Aug. 27 and Nam said he would "study" it. He has made no reply.

Red Push Hurled Back in Korea

SEOUL, Korea, Oct. 7 (AP)—Communist troops launched their greatest co-ordinated attack of the year Monday night and early Tuesday across two-thirds of the Korean battle front.

More than 12,000 Reds stormed Allied strongpoints in the western and central sectors.

But they were beaten back in savage, close-quarter fighting.

The heaviest weight of the assault—an attack by 4,000 Chinese troops—fell on White Horse Hill and another peak northwest of Chorwon near the old Communist iron triangle massing area.

Heavy barrages from both sides crashed down on the peaks and wild fighting swirled up and down the slopes and on the crest throughout the black night.

It was "like a human sea breaking up against a rock," a front line officer said of the battle on White Horse. First estimates placed the Chinese dead in this action alone at 900 troops.

Once the Chinese won the eastern nose of White Horse but were beaten off by a fierce Allied counter-attack.

The Reds even opened the floodgates of a reservoir to the north in an attempt to cut off and confuse the Allied defenders of the two hills.

Water in a river coursing around the two hills mounted only two feet, but the Chinese stormed up the slopes and fought it out at hand-to-hand range with fists, stones and grenades.

Allied defenders drove them back down the slopes.

Intense fighting carried on into the daylight hours for three or four minor hills in the extreme west.

But Allied troops repulsed the Reds at virtually every point along the western and central fronts.

In the extreme west, the Communists hit the Marines at 13 points. They seized a new hill north of Korangpo.

An Eighth Army staff officer said at least 12,000 troops joined in the biggest Communist operation of the year.

Red artillery battered the hills from noon Monday, Communist tanks rumbled into line in late afternoon and shelled Allied dug-outs. Between 6 and 7:30 p.m., 6,000 rounds of shellfire chewed up the slopes and crest of White Horse.

18,000 Utahns Hear President

By O. N. MALMQUIST
Tribune Political Writer

PROVO, Oct. 6—About 18,000 Utahns turned out Monday in three Utah cities to hear President Harry S Truman extol Democratic accomplishments and philosophy and to denounce the Republican opposition as a negative, short-sighted party "ruled by a little group of men who have calculating machines where their hearts ought to be."

In his major speech of the day in the Brigham Young University Stadium, the camaigning President aimed his appeal at youth by telling them that a return to Republican rule would mean a return to the philosophy of "each man for himself and the devil take the hindmost."

"If you were leaving college in a Republican world," he said, "some few of you might do very well. You might even get rich. But the devil would take an awful lot of you who happened to be the hindmost—or even in between."

Avoids Personalities

For his audience of between 12,000 and 13,000 in the B Y U Stadium, almost half of whom were students, Pres. Truman avoided personalities and emphasized issues.

But in his "whistle-stop" talks in Salt Lake City and Helper he fired some direct shots at the G O P presidential nominee—Dwight D. Eisenhower—by expressing the opinion that it would be a tragedy to elect him president of the United States because of his lack of political know-how and his "surrender to the most reactionary elements of the Republican party."

Despite the early hour of the presidential appearance in Salt Lake City, about 2,000 persons were at the Denver and Rio Grande-Western Pacific Station to give him a rousing welcome.

3,000 at Helper

At Helper, he addressed a crowd estimated at 3,000.

When the special train arrived in Provo, the streets were lined for blocks with school children along the parade route to the stadium.

The President rode in an open car with David O. McKay, president of the Church of Jesus Christ of Latter-day Saints, who boarded the train in Salt Lake City.

Ernest L. Wilkinson, president of B Y U, introduced Democratic party officials and Pres. McKay, remarking that the latter was there by special invitation as president of the church and president of the board of trustees of the university.

Reveals Merrill Appointment

He then presented Pres. Truman after explaining that the Republican case had been presented a week ago by Sen. Everett M. Dirksen of Illinois. He remarked that the G O P spokesman had not understated that party's case and invited Pres. Truman to state the "Fair Deal" case without restraint.

Pres. Truman opened his address by announcing the appointment of Eugene H. Merrill, a Utah resident, to the Federal Communications Commission and used this as a springboard to slash back at his critics who have accused him of selecting "cronies" for appointments.

"You know," he said, "I hear

See Page 6, Column 3

S. L. 'WHISTLE'

Truth's Best, Says HST, To Beat 'Em

In a brief speech from the rear platform of his special train, President Harry S Truman Monday morning told an audience of some 2,000 Salt Lake admirers that he doesn't strive for a reputation as a "give 'em hell" campaigner.

"I tell the truth on them," he declared, and that's a lot better for the country than giving them hell, because they can't stand the truth."

The President was in a jovial but political slugging mood when his train pulled into the Denver and Rio Grande-Western Pacific depot at 7:40 a.m. He confidently predicted that his party would win on a basis of "our record, our platform and our candidates."

He referred to the Democratic platform as the best any political party had ever adopted and the Republican platform' as "about the worst I have ever read."

He appealed for support of the Democratic congressional and state tickets, specifically mentioning and praising the records of Rep. Walter K. Granger, Senate candidate; Rep. Reva Beck Bosone and Ernest R. McKay, congressional candidates, and Mayor J. Glade, candidate for governor.

"The best thing, you know, for your own safety," he remarked, "is to just vote the Democratic ticket and send them all there."

In urging support of the Democratic presidential and vice pres-

See Page 6, Column 2

Drugged Tokoyite Nabbed in Theft

Reuters News Agency

TOKYO, Oct. 6—Police arrested a bank clerk Monday on charges of plotting with three men to drug himself and fake a robbery of four million yen (about $10,000).

Police said the 53-year-old clerk was carrying the bank's money in a train, gave it to his accomplices, and then dosed himself with ether to make it appear he had been drugged.

Police have arrested one of the accomplices and are searching for the other two, who made off with the loot.

CHALLENGE DEMOS

GOP Truth Squad in S. L. To Answer Truman Talk

A few hours after Pres. Harry S Truman had beaten a campaign trail through Utah Monday, the Republican senatorial "truth squad" flew into Salt Lake City by chartered plane to challenge and answer the presidential statements.

The "squad," made up of Senators Homer Ferguson of Michigan, Bourke B. Hickenlooper of Iowa and Francis Case of South Dakota, immediately went into a huddle with Utah G O P leaders to analyze transcripts of the President's Utah speeches. Sen. Case was scheduled to leave for his home state during the night but he will be replaced by Sen. Eugene S. Millikin of Colorado.

The G O P Senators will reply to the President at a press conference at 10 a.m. Tuesday and at a public meeting in the Brigham

8 p.m. But they offered an immediate reaction to one of the claims pressed by Pres. Truman during his B Y U assembly address—that the Democratic administration had greatly enlarged employment opportunities for your people.

"I agree with the President" said Sen. Ferguson, "that the administration has provided jobs for our young people—in the Army. The young men are being taken into military service and recruiting teams are out urging the young ladies to go to work in civilian branches of the government. They have provided jobs for some 2,800,000 up to date. And if the present trend continues it is only a matter of time until we will all be working for the government."

"That," chimed in Sen. Hicken-

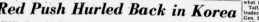

TRUMAN ARRIVING AT BYU (Left) Truman arrived to great cheers at Brigham Young University. He was the first president of the United States to speak at BYU. While addressing the student body, Truman announced that just that morning he had appointed Latter-day Saint Eugene H. Merrill as chairman of the Federal Communications Commission (FCC).[102] During his vigorous campaign speech, he also charged that the Republican Party was "ruled by a little group of men who have calculating machines where their hearts ought to be."[103] After he had delivered his harshly partisan speech, he sat down next to President McKay and asked innocently, "I wasn't so hard on them was I?" McKay seemed to appreciate Mr. Truman's friendliness and candor and recorded in his diary of the thirty-third president, "I had a higher opinion of him today."[104]

BYU PRESIDENT WILKINSON MEETS WITH TRUMAN (Above) Ernest L. Wilkinson had just been named president of BYU the year before Truman's visit and met with President Truman and President McKay as part of their BYU stop. Wilkinson led BYU from 1951–1971, growing the student body from 5,000 to 25,000.

Truman Flays GOP as 'Shortsighted'

Continued from Page One

a lot of talk about government by crony in Washington. That's sheer poppycock—and low politics. . .

"The truth is, of course, that I try to find the best qualified people I can for the many complicated jobs I have to fill. . . I couldn't possibly know all these people. . . . But I try in every case to find out all I can. . . .

"Most of the people I have brought into government have stood the test with flying colors —some few have broken under it."

Urges Public Service

Remarking that he had been deeply hurt in those few instances when appointees had failed, he emphatically defended government officials and employes and expressed the hope that many of the young people in the audience would make government service their career.

Turning to the Democratic administration of the past 20 years, Pres. Truman said that his predecessor — Pres. Franklin D. Roosevelt—had to start from scratch to determine the direction the government should take to meet the crisis of the 30s.

The task of the new president, he said, would be to perfect, to improve and to modify as the need arises. He expressed complete confidence in the character and ability of the Democratic nominee.

Lauds Stevenson

"Adlai Stevenson," he remarked, "is not only a wise and good man—he is a Democrat. That means that the basic spirit, the fundamental outlook of the Democratic Party will continue to guide our government in all its tasks as a servant of the people, and as a leader of the world."

After drawing a contrast between the Democratic Party as an organization "with a heart that cares about all people" and the Republican Party as an organization "which believes power of government should first be used to help the rich and privileged," President Truman declared that the Democrats had built up an economy in which the problem of college students was to decide which job to take.

"If there is one thing," he went on, "that the Democratic Party has proved, it is that we can have full employment in this country if we have wise government policies.

"We have shown that it's good economics to have protection for farmers, so they will have some assurance of good prices and a steady income.

'Good Economics'

"We have shown that it's good economics to have full employment at good wages.

"We have shown that it's good economics to help the small businessman, that cares about all the enterprise that is building up the country.

"We have shown that it's good economics to develop the great natural resources of the country, particularly the water resources of the western states."

Turning to foreign policy, the president declared that the United Nations, Marshall Plan and other aid programs had saved Western Europe from communism. He conceded that the administration received a lot of Republican help on these programs for a time but that the GOP had also offered a lot of opposition.

Hits GOP Opposition

"If the Republican opposition had prevailed," he said, "I have no doubt that France and Italy and almost all western Europe would be under the Communist yoke today.

"The fact is, the Republican Party just does not seem able to see or understand what it takes to meet the menace of Communist aggression and subversion."

As an example he cited GOP opposition to the Point Four program, which he declared offers the most return for the least money. He pointed out that Dr. Franklin S. Harris, former president of B Y U, was one of the pioneers in Point Four work and that 53 Utah men are now in Iran working on the program.

'Same Old Party'

His only reference to Gen. Eisenhower in the Provo address was a comment that the Republican Party had tried this year to clothe their "outworn and discredited philosophy" in "the shining armor of a national hero."

"But it's the same old party that has opposed every progressive step these past 20 years," he said.

"And you young men and women must realize," he concluded, "that you cannot make your way into a brave new world under the Republicans. The future does not lie with them. . . .

---

th's Best, s HST, Beat 'Em

Continued from Page One

candidates, President is said he thought it would be tragedy for the Republican te to be elected.

Great General

(Gen. Dwight D. Eisenhower) has been a great general, resident said. "But he has shown in this campaign cannot be depended upon ster the great political issues with which we are faced. He is not the kind of party elements of the Republican party. He is not the kind of we ought to have for president.

ow I like him. I made him f staff of the United States y. I sent him to Europe to mand the NATO military p, and I have every confidence in him as a military man, as president and politician, wouldn't know what to do. On the other hand, I am more ever impressed with what al Stevenson offers to the nation. He is talking sense to the American people. He is wise. He courageous. He is honest. He a man you can trust. And he n't be taken in by the special erests."

The presidential party was ined in Salt Lake City by party didates and state and county cials of the party organization.

Utahs Join Party

Among party officials who arded the train for the trip to royo and Helper were Calvin W. Rawlings and Mrs. Roxey omney, national committee members; Milton L. Wielenmann, state chairman; Mrs. George S. Ballif, state vice chairman; Gordon Weggeland, Democratic state treasurer; G. Hal Taylor, Democratic state secretary, and William T. Thurman, Salt Lake County chairman.

Margaret Truman, whom the President described as his "greatest asset," appeared on the platform to greet the early morning crowd. She was dressed in a tailored gray woolen suit with a spray of yellow daisies in a corsage arrangement.

t Truman . . . Capitol owd at Salt Lake step.

Huge crowd, made up of students and townspeople, turned out to hear President Harry S Truman, center, with back to camera, speak at Brigham Young University stadium. President delivered major address. In stadium after brief stop in Salt Lake City. He then boarded special train and went on to Helper.

President Harry S Truman, center, chats with Dr. Ernest L. Wilkinson, left, president of Brigham Young University, David O. McKay, president of LDS Church.

President Harry S Truman gestures with hands as he makes a point in address to huge crowd at B.Y. University stadium Monday. Democrats aid young, he said.

S. L. 'Whistle' man Monday

crowd. Lt. Stanley Butcher headed Salt Lake City's 25-man police detail, with Capt. C. W. Brady leading a contingent of eight bluecoats from the Salt Lake County force.

Samuel Mitchell, the 55-year-old "porter-messenger" who has served Herbert Hoover, Franklin D. Roosevelt and Harry S Truman as valet and attendant, termed President Truman "an especially easy man to work for."

A native of South Carolina, he "hopes to keep right on working in the White House and on trips like this no matter who wins in November."

President Truman was a symphony in blue for his Salt Lake City appearance. A neat blue handkerchief decorated his jacket pocket, his tie was blue-striped, his suit was a gray-blue hue. All of which matched the big curtain that hung between the observation platform and the inside of the private car—it was a deep, dull blue.

Margaret likewise appeared in a trim blue ensemble, but Salt Lake City's Mayor Earl J. Glade shattered the color scheme. He wore tan.

The biggest sign held aloft in the crowd seemed out of place among others that praised Truman, Stevenson, Granger and Bosone.

Despite the early air and almost chilly temperature, a good sized crowd greeted President Harry S Truman when he visited Salt Lake City Monday at 7:40 a.m. A few hecklers mixed with other Salt Lakers carrying pro Truman signs. President and daughter Margaret made brief rear platform appearance during

---

Truman declined three additional trips to Utah. President George Albert Smith invited President Truman to the fiftieth anniversary celebration of Utah's statehood on January 4, 1946,[105] a great Church-wide youth conference held in the summer of 1946,[106] and the pioneer centennial on July 24, 1947,[107] but the president was unable to make any of these events. President Truman did send a note of congratulations for Utah's fiftieth anniversary, saying "I like to believe that the hardy pioneer spirit survives in Utah."[108] He also sent a congratulatory telegram on the hundredth anniversary of the arrival of the pioneers, saying, "Through their labors was fulfilled the prophecy of scripture and the desert was made to blossom like the rose."[109] Truman made additional visits to the Beehive State as a former president four times: March 22, 1953; June 24, 1955 (shown above); December 29, 1959; and July 20, 1960.

He passed away on December 26, 1972.

Truman Sends Felicitations On Centennial

Tribute to Utah's Mormon pioneers and their influence upon this state are contained in a telegram sent by Pres. Harry S Truman to Gov. Herbert B. Maw and read by the governor at This Is the Place monument dedication rites Thursday.

The text follows:

One of the great states of the union had its beginning 100 years ago when Brigham Young looked out over the valley of the Great Salt lake and made his prophetic declaration: "This is the Place."

On that memorable day when the vanguard of Latter-day Saints beheld for the first time the promised land, there ended a 1400-mile trek across the western country which will always stand as one of the greatest migrations in American history.

The courage, sagacity and religious zeal of Brigham Young inspired his followers to endure hunger and thirst, disease and a hundred privations incident to the long march through a desolate and hostile country.

But the valiant band triumphed and was joined later by the main body of saints. Through their labors was fulfilled the prophecy of scripture, and the desert was made to blossom like the rose.

And now a hundred years later Utah stands in proud place among her sister commonwealths. Her rich agriculture, her business and industry, her pioneering in the social services, her zeal for education, and not the least, her men of wisdom and valiant women have given her a prestige unexcelled by any other state.

It gives me great pleasure to send hearty felicitations and warmest personal greetings to all who participate in this notable Centenary."

1947 UTAH CENTENNIAL Official Program

THIS IS THE PLACE

DWIGHT D. EISENHOWER

NATIONAL PORTRAIT GALLERY

DWIGHT D. EISENHOWER WAS PRESIDENT of the United States from 1953–1961 and served at the same time J. Bracken Lee and George Dewey Clyde were governors of Utah and David O. McKay was president of the Church. He came to Utah four times, including once as president for a brief stop in 1954.

UTAH STATE HISTORICAL SOCIETY

EISENHOWER CAMPS IN SKULL VALLEY *Lieutenant-Colonel Dwight Eisenhower was part of a 1919 army convoy that followed the Lincoln Highway from Washington DC to San Francisco to test the use of automobiles and trucks in moving troops and supplies. As he passed through Utah, the twenty-eight-year-old soldier and his group camped overnight at Orr's Ranch in Skull Valley (left), according to Dennis Andrus, former owner of the ranch.*[110]

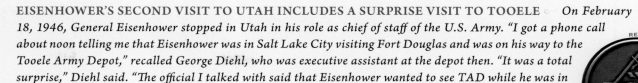

The Deseret News

Salt Lake City, Utah, Monday Evening, February 18, 1946

Vol. 241, No. 42, 96th Year

Weather Forecast

HOWER REACHES S. L.

Army Chief Will Inspect Local Bases

Gen. Dwight D. Eisenhower, chief of staff, U. S. Army, arrived at the Salt Lake Army Air Base today at 11:50 a.m. for an inspection of Utah army bases. There were no comments, no flashers and no officials other than army to greet the famous commander.

His arrival at the Salt Lake Army Air Base a few minutes after the scheduled time the officials reached the airport com-...

CHIEF OF STAFF ARRIVES—Five-star General Dwight D. Eisenhower, left, arrives at the Salt Lake Army air base for an inspection tour of Utah army stations. Maj. Gen. William E. Shedd, commanding general of the Ninth Service Command, center, and Col. A. P. Kitson, chief of staff, Ninth Service Command, right, greet the famous commander.

THE OGDEN Standard Examiner

OGDEN CITY, UTAH, MONDAY EVENING, FEBRUARY 18, 1946

Gen. Ike Begins Tour of Utah War Installations

Army Chief Arrives At Salt Lake Aboard Huge Plane

SALT LAKE CITY, Feb. 18 (AP) — Gen. Dwight D. Eisenhower, U. S. army chief of staff, arrived in Salt Lake City at eleven-fifty a. m. (MST) today for a tour of military installations in Utah.

The general's plane, the Sunflower Second, landed at the municipal airport, Eisenhower stepped briskly from the plane and was greeted by Maj. Gen. William E. Shedd, commanding general of the ninth service command.

Go to Fort Douglas

The two went immediately to Fort Douglas, command headquarters, where they planned to lunch. This afternoon Eisenhower arranged a visit to the Tooele ordnance depot, 25 miles west of Salt Lake City.

Eisenhower, making an inspection tour of western military installations, planned no press conference here.

The general was first off the huge C-54 transport. Just as he stepped from the landing steps the lower two steps of the ladder slipped and two staff members following him stumbled, and almost fell. None was hurt, however.

Eisenhower came here from Denver where he visited Fitzsimmons general hospital and Lowry field yesterday.

The general's itinerary here called for inspections of ninth service command headquarters at historic Fort Douglas and the Tooele ordnance depot.

Eisenhower is accompanied by Maj. Gen. Alexander D. Surles, of the general staff and Lt. Col. James Stack, aide-de-camp.

Will View A-Bomb Tests

The chief of staff told reporters at Denver he would be among those observing the atomic bomb tests in the Pacific this spring.

"If the bomb is as powerful and as cataclysmic as it has been said," Eisenhower commented, "I believe you will find the soldier more than anyone else yelling for international machinery to protect the peace and to make it work."

He told Lowry field soldiers that "you are not in the army to keep a lot of 'brass' in their jobs back in Washington. You are in...

UTAH VISITOR—Army Chief of Staff Gen. Dwight D. Eisenhower today began a tour of war installations...ed at Salt Lake City at eleven...

EISENHOWER'S SECOND VISIT TO UTAH INCLUDES A SURPRISE VISIT TO TOOELE *On February 18, 1946, General Eisenhower stopped in Utah in his role as chief of staff of the U.S. Army. "I got a phone call about noon telling me that Eisenhower was in Salt Lake City visiting Fort Douglas and was on his way to the Tooele Army Depot," recalled George Diehl, who was executive assistant at the depot then. "It was a total surprise," Diehl said. "The official I talked with said that Eisenhower wanted to see TAD while he was in Salt Lake because it was one of the military's largest operations. Back then we had about 5,000 people and things were really humming at the depot."*

After hearing the news, Diehl informed Sterling Harris, the superintendent of schools, who dismissed all the schools in the Tooele Valley so the children could glimpse the five-star hero of World War II. "The whole town turned out to see him," remembered George McKellar, who was a twelve-year-old student at the time. "The entire length of Main Street was lined with people. It was exciting. He was probably the most notable person to visit Tooele," McKellar said.

"Eisenhower wasn't aware of the crowd that had turned out to see him," Diehl said. "When he got to the edge of town and could see the people on the street, he got out of his sedan and rode in an open jeep so people could see him."

GEORGE DIEHL COLLECTION

Diehl was impressed with how personable Eisenhower was, his knowledge of military equipment, and his interest in details—from the number of tanks being repaired to the fluctuation in temperature and its effect on the storage life of ammunition.

The visit was so spontaneous that officials at the Pentagon were unaware and called depot officials afterward to make sure everything went all right. "I got phone calls asking me things like what did we show him, what did he ask, what were our answers," Diehl said. "I let them know that we were able to entertain such a high-ranking official at a moment's notice without any problem."[111] Eisenhower and his party stayed that night at Hotel Utah.[112]

HUNDREDS AWAIT GENERAL EISENHOWER'S ARRIVAL AT SALT LAKE MUNICIPAL AIRPORT *(Opposite & Above) On the evening of Friday, October 10, 1952, hundreds awaited the arrival of General Eisenhower at the Salt Lake Municipal Airport (which became Salt Lake City International Airport in 1968). Eisenhower arrived via Trans World Airlines just before 5:30PM, and Democratic Governor J. Bracken Lee greeted him in Salt Lake. "Welcome to Utah," the governor said. "Brack, come here and get your picture taken with me," Eisenhower warmly replied.[113] Governor Lee then helped Eisenhower into his convertible.*

SECURITY SCARE CHANGES PROCESSION *(Right) Salt Lake City police reports recorded that there was a man with a revolver who said the gun was for Eisenhower, which alarmed the candidate's security team, who made Eisenhower drive from the airport to the Church Administration Building earlier than planned.[114] His team whisked him through city streets that were far from filled up yet. Thousands were disappointed when they showed up on time and found out that the procession had already passed.*

IVY BAKER PRIEST ACCOMPANIES EISENHOWER *Ivy Baker Priest of Bountiful accompanied Eisenhower in the convertible. Priest was Utah's Republican National Committeewoman at the time and was also head of the GOP's women's auxiliary during Eisenhower's campaign. She was appointed U.S. Treasurer after Eisenhower won, and her signature appeared on all U.S. currency for the next eight years.[115]*

EISENHOWER SHARES A BIRTHDAY WITH A YOUNG POLIO SURVIVOR *(Below) After his visit at Church headquarters, General Eisenhower was introduced to Sharon Dartnell, a young polio survivor who shared Eisenhower's birthday, October 14. With their big day just four days away, the almost-eleven-year-old girl shared a birthday cake with the GOP nominee.*

IKE MEETS WITH UTAH DIGNITARIES *(Above & Right) Eisenhower, Utah Senator Arthur Watkins, LDS Church President David O. McKay, and Utah Governor Lee conversed in the Church Administration Building. After McKay welcomed Eisenhower to Utah, the general quipped, "Sorry to look so disheveled. Riding in these open cars does things to my hair."*[116]

Eisenhower and President McKay developed a strong friendship, and as president, Eisenhower would meet with the Church leader several times in the White House. J. Bracken Lee served as mayor of Price (1935–1947), governor of Utah (1949–1957), and mayor of Salt Lake City (1960–1971). Senator Arthur Watkins, a Republican, represented Utah in Washington from 1947–1959.

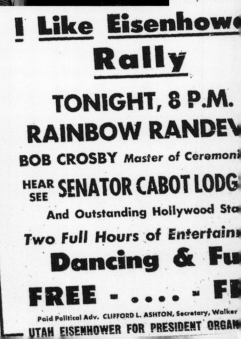

EISENHOWER SHARES HIS FAMOUS GRIN
Ike was famous for his big grin, which he shared liberally as he arrived at the Tabernacle on Temple Square, where he would deliver a speech.

IKE TAKES THE TIME TO SIGN AUTOGRAPHS FOR YOUNG BOYS   *Eisenhower was notable for taking time for the "little people" and signed autographs for a number of Boy Scouts and Cub Scouts before the Tabernacle program began.*

Dwight D Eisenhower

TABERNACLE SPEECH FOCUSES ON THE "MIDDLE WAY"

As General Eisenhower ascended the stand, Senator Watkins greeted him (above).

"I should like to express the deep sense of distinction I feel at the privilege to address this audience in a building of this character,"[117] General Eisenhower said as he began his remarks. He added, "I am extremely pleased that President McKay has found time to come out to hear me discuss what is on my mind."[118]

Ike then got into the meat of his speech and suggested that the middle way is the best option for the people. "Both extremes are wrong," he said. "Both are dangerous. One shackles man to the power of central government. The other strips him of the protection of his fellows and returns him to the law of the jungle."[119]

> *"We know that you folks pray for us every day and we wanted you to know that we feel of the strength that comes to us through those prayers."*

(Above) Senator Watkins, President McKay, General Eisenhower, and Governor Lee enjoyed a moment following Eisenhower's Tabernacle address.

Eisenhower hosted "stag" (all-male) dinners at the White House, and in May 1955, David O. McKay joined nineteen other invited guests for one of these events. President McKay was given the seat of honor directly across from Eisenhower, who called on McKay to say "grace" and who was very struck with the charm and wit of the eighty-one-year-old prophet.[120] Meeting with his Cabinet the following morning, President Eisenhower told of the event. "Among the group was President David O. McKay, head of the Mormon Church," Eisenhower said. "He was the life of the party."[121] First Lady Mamie Eisenhower telephoned Flora Benson (Elder Benson's wife) that day and said, "Flora, I just wanted to call you this morning to let you know that my husband was profoundly impressed by President McKay. After he returned last night, he spent most of the night talking to me about this singular and enjoyable experience." Then Mrs. Eisenhower said, "Flora, we know that you folks pray for us every day and we wanted you to know that we feel of the strength which comes to us through those prayers. In fact," she continued, "we frankly don't know what we would do without this strength."[122]

(Above) President Eisenhower invited President David O. McKay to attend one of his stag dinners. Eisenhower related the next day that President McKay was the life of the party.

President Eisenhower barely set foot in Utah as president of the United States when he made a brief touch down during a fly-by on September 4, 1954. As part of better understanding drought-ravaged areas of the West and the effects of reclamation projects, President Eisenhower undertook a 1,500-mile flight to survey key areas of Colorado, Wyoming, Utah, Nebraska, and Kansas. He had with him on the flight Secretary of the Interior Douglas McKay and Secretary of Agriculture Ezra Taft Benson and surveyed Utah on a stretch as he flew from Grand Junction, Colorado, to Casper, Wyoming.[123] Although not on the schedule to land in the Beehive State, the president remarked to reporters afterward in Casper that they "touched Utah" that day.[124] Having a

member of the Quorum of the Twelve Apostles in his cabinet (Secretary Benson), Ike did just fine electorally in Utah without

out ever having a more formal visit there as president. He was awarded 65 percent of the vote in 1956.

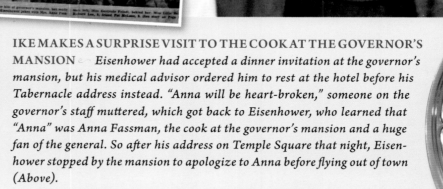

IKE MAKES A SURPRISE VISIT TO THE COOK AT THE GOVERNOR'S MANSION *Eisenhower had accepted a dinner invitation at the governor's mansion, but his medical advisor ordered him to rest at the hotel before his Tabernacle address instead. "Anna will be heart-broken," someone on the governor's staff muttered, which got back to Eisenhower, who learned that "Anna" was Anna Fassman, the cook at the governor's mansion and a huge fan of the general. So after his address on Temple Square that night, Eisenhower stopped by the mansion to apologize to Anna before flying out of town (Above).*

"I'm not in too much of a hurry to forget a little lady who cooked dinner for me," the general said to her.

"You are even better looking than on television," the beaming Anna replied. Photographers captured the tender scene, along with the governor's son Richard Lee, eight, and his friend Pat McKane, nine.[125]

ORIGINAL NEWSPAPER SL TRIB • PHOTO RON FOX COLLECTION

RONALD FOX COLLECTION

GOVERNOR'S MANSION *(Above & Left) Governor's Mansion where Eisenhower had been scheduled to have dinner. In the photo to the left, notice the grand stairway—this is where the photos of Eisenhower with Anna Fassman were taken.*

GOVERNOR'S MANSION SILVER *(Opposite Bottom) Had Eisenhower dined at the Governor's Mansion, he would have eaten off of the beautiful silver service in the home. The silver comes from the former battleship U.S.S. Utah and the Cruiser U.S.S. Salt Lake City, and it is only used when the governor formally entertains. The service came from the mansion's original owner, Senator Thomas Kearns, who was a silver magnate. When his wife gave the mansion to the state as a residence for the state's chief executive, she left the silver for future use in entertaining high-ranking officials and guests.*

JOHN F. KENNEDY

J OHN F. KENNEDY WAS PRESIDENT of the United States from 1961–1963 and served at the same time George Dewey Clyde was governor of Utah and David O. McKay was president of the Church. He came to Utah five times, including once as president.

SENATOR KENNEDY COMES TO SLC FOR "DOLLARS FOR DEMOCRATS" FUNDRAISER *(Above) Senator Kennedy stands*

with Cal Rawlins, the Democratic National Committeeman, and greets dignitaries upon their arrival in Salt Lake City. Senator Kennedy already had the reputation of "most likely to succeed" at the upcoming 1960 Democratic convention when he arrived in Salt Lake for his first visit on November 11, 1957. He headlined a "Dollars for Democrats" fundraising dinner Monday night, and Tuesday morning he addressed the Democratic State Central Committee meeting and met with local Catholic and LDS leaders.

The Salt Lake Tribune

Salt Lake City, Utah — Tuesday Morning — November 12, 1957

Senator Kennedy To Address Demos

SALT LAKE CITY (UP)— Senator John Kennedy (D-Mass) a leader in the labor racketeering hearings and a possible presidential candidate in 1960, will arrive here tomorrow to deliver a major address before Utah Democrats.

The Massachusetts leader will address the "Dollars for Democrats" dinner tomorrow night at the Rainbow Randevu.

The dinner is slated as the 1957 fund-raising drive for the party.

While in Salt Lake City he will confer with Catholic Church leaders and authorities of the Latter-day Saints Church.

The Tribune camera of Borge Andersen cap- | Kennedy in interview. Top, he li [...] of Sen. John F. | left, explains; bottom right, turn [...]

PRESIDENT McKAY MEETS JFK (*Below*) *President McKay met with Senator Kennedy in the Church Administration Building and said, "You are younger than I thought," when he was first introduced to the forty-year-old.*[126] *"I enjoyed my visit with him, although not too much impressed with him as a leader," President McKay wrote in his diary after the meeting.*[127]

KENNEDY AND McKAY ENGAGE IN WEIGHTY DISCUSSION ABOUT THE USSR (*Below*) *Senator Kennedy and President McKay engaged in a serious discussion about the previous month's launch of Sputnik and the future of the Soviet Union. President McKay prophetically predicted that the Soviet Union would eventually collapse from within. "They are fundamentally wrong. Free agency is inherent in every individual. Rule of force has been fought against by men throughout history." Kennedy disagreed and expressed his belief that the USSR would never break up on its own. "They have the power to continue. Their prospects for the immediate future are bright."*[128]

DESERET NEWS

DESERET NEWS

Biggest Indoor Rally

The senator spoke before what Utah Democratic leaders declared was the largest indoor rally in the history of the party. The manager of the Rainbow Randevu estimated the crowd at between 4,000 and 4,500. Seating provisions fell far short of the turnout and Warwick C. Lamoreaux, promotion chairman, said dinner was served to four times as many as planned. And some went unserved.

Sen. Kennedy said President Dwight D. Eisenhower's first report on the state of the nation's defense position was well-prepared and well thought-out. But the facts of our military position, he declared, are far more grim than the president indicated.

JACQUELINE KENNEDY JOINS HUSBAND ON 1959 CAMPAIGN VISIT TO UTAH *On March 6, 1959, Senator Kennedy and his wife Jacqueline made a stop in Salt Lake (see photos of arrival) to speak at a fund-raising dinner for the Utah Democratic Party. This was the only time Jacqueline Bouvier Kennedy came to Utah. While they were in Salt Lake, State Democratic Party Chair Milton L. Weilenmann brought Senator and Mrs. Kennedy to visit with the First Presidency. This time around, President McKay was more impressed. "Mr. Kennedy seems to be a very fine young man," the prophet recorded in his diary.*[129]

DESERET NEWS

THIRD CAMPAIGIN VISIT TO UTAH
(Above) Just two months before the first primary election, January 30, 1960, Senator Kennedy made another stop in Salt Lake City to garner support among local Democrats. His supporters showed high enthusiasm as they heartily welcomed Kennedy to the state.

DESERET NEWS

DESERET NEWS
STAFF PHOTO

DESERET NEWS

DESERET NEWS

MORE THAN MERE PLEASANTRIES

(Left) In the hour Kennedy and Mc-Kay talked, "they had a really significant conversation," said Oscar McConkie. "A lot more so than most political people, where you just bring them in and they kind of pass pleasantries, and this sort of thing. They had a serious talk about how it was going to be possible to bring democratic governments throughout the world. They discussed, for instance, such things as the fact that the difficulty the President would have in doing this was that there isn't any middle class in the rest of the world. The third world has extremely few very wealthy people, and then there is huge poverty. But President Kennedy was saying that it takes a middle class in order to make a democratic system work. It was a significant talk."[131] As McConkie was leading Senator Kennedy out of President McKay's office, the candidate said of McKay, "I have never met a man as ideally suited and qualified to be the spiritual leader of his people."[132]

> "I have never met a man as ideally suited and quali-fied to be the spiritual leader of his people."

KENNEDY VISITS CHURCH LEADERS

(Opposite) As was customary, Kennedy called again on Church headquarters. Oscar McConkie (left) introduced him to President Henry B. Moyle (center) and other General Authorities.

President McKay wrote about his third meeting with Kennedy in his diary: "We had a very pleasant interview with Senator Kennedy, talking on various domestic and international subjects. I was very much impressed with him, and think that the country will be in good hands if he is elected as he seems to be a man of high character. He comes from a home where he has received good training, and his father, a wealthy man, has seen to it that the children have had to work and take responsibility. Our interview lasted for nearly an hour."[130]

JFK SPEAKING AT FDR BIRTHDAY EVENT

In addition to his visit with Church leaders, Kennedy was the main speaker at the Utah Democratic Party's dinner event in honor of the late President Franklin D. Roosevelt's seventy-eighth birthday that day. Kennedy's father had been FDR's ambassador to Great Britain, and the senator had first-hand knowledge of the late president.

Post-War Utah Comes of Age 1946–1969 | 95

U.S. SENATOR

NNEDY ★ JOHNSON

PRESIDENT   FOR VICE PRESIDEN

KENNEDY 60

KENNEDY FOR PRESIDENT

KENNEDY GREETED BY EXUBERANT CROWDS *On September 23, 1960, hundreds of Utahns waited at the Salt Lake airport for a visit from the Democratic nominee for president. Mere weeks away from his historic election, Kennedy appeared to loud cheers and briefly spoke to the assembled fans. He was soon in his convertible, heading toward the city. (Opposite bottom) Shown riding in the back seat with Kennedy are: William T. Thurman, Chairman of the Utah Democratic Party; President Kennedy; and Utah Senator Ted Moss. Front seat: Cal Rawlings, Democrat National Committeeman.*

KENNEDY GIVES HIS FIRST SPEECH IN THE TABERNACLE

Once in Salt Lake, another crowd cheered Kennedy as he made his way from his car to the entrance of the Church Administration Building. President McKay was happy to welcome Kennedy once again for their fourth visit together, where they laughed like old friends. The week prior, the ninety-year-old leader told newspaper columnist Drew Pearson his latest opinion of Kennedy: "While he seemed to be a very brilliant and able young man," he said, "he was somewhat lacking in maturity."[133] After their visit, Kennedy gave his first speech in the Tabernacle.

The Inaugural Committee
requests the honor of your presence
to attend and participate in the Inauguration of

John Fitzgerald Kennedy
as President of the United States of America
and
Lyndon Baines Johnson
as Vice President of the United States of America
on Friday the twentieth of January
one thousand nine hundred and sixty one
in the City of Washington

Edward H. Foley
Chairman

NEW AIR FORCE ONE *(Above) On September 23–24, 1963, Kennedy made his historic presidential visit to Utah aboard the new Air Force One, a Boeing 707. He landed at 5:50PM, and the crowd cheered him.*

PRESIDENTIAL MOTORCADE MAKES ITS WAY THROUGH THE STREETS OF SALT LAKE CITY *(Left and Below) Between 6:00PM and 6:30PM, the presidential motorcade went from the airport to downtown Salt Lake, passing thousands along North Temple Street, State Street, 300 South, and finally Main Street as they made their way to Hotel Utah.*[134] *The car in which Kennedy is standing in this photo is the same car he used in Dallas when he lost his life.*

HOTEL UTAH WELCOMES ANOTHER PRESIDENTIAL GUEST *(Above) Hotel Utah rolled out the red carpet to welcome President Kennedy, the first overnight presidential guest Utah had hosted since Truman in 1945.*

PRESIDENT KENNEDY SPEAKS IN TABERNACLE (*Above*)
Hugh B. Brown, LDS President David O. McKay, and President Kennedy in the Tabernacle as Utah Senator Ted Moss (Right) speaks.

**KENNEDY HONORS EARLY MORMONS FOR ENDURANCE
AND FAITH** *"I take strength and hope in seeing this monument
[the Tabernacle], hearing its story retold by Ted Moss, and recalling
how this State was built, and what it started with, and what it has now,"
Kennedy said as he began his ninety-minute address in the Tabernacle.[135]
"Let us remember that the Mormons of a century ago were a persecuted
and prosecuted minority, harried from place to place, the victims of vio-
lence and occasionally murder, while today, in the short space of 100
years, their faith and works are known and respected the world around,
and their voices heard in the highest councils of this country. As the
Mormons succeeded, so America can succeed, if we will not give up or
turn back."[136] (Above) Ted Moss, Cal Rawlins, Kennedy.*

STANDING OVATION *Hugh B. Brown and President McKay congratulated the president on his speech as the audience gave him a standing ovation. Kennedy's speech in the Tabernacle was a major foreign policy address that Robert F. Kennedy later claimed his brother felt was "one of the best speeches he had ever given." He said that President Kennedy even played a tape of his speech for his mother and father.[137]*

BREAKFAST AT THE HOTEL UTAH *After a night at Hotel Utah, Kennedy enjoyed breakfast with President McKay there. "I asked the blessing on the food . . . . President Kennedy was the only one that had coffee," President McKay wrote of the breakfast. "The conversation was very pleasant, and in the words of the President, 'It was a refreshing hour.'"*[138] *The president flew out of Salt Lake at 9:45 AM. Later, when Robert Kennedy visited President McKay, he said, "My brother enjoyed the breakfast with you and Mrs. McKay, and admired all of the fine things you and your Church stand for."*[139]

(Below) Seated at the table are: Sen. Moss, and Mrs. Moss, President Kennedy, President McKay, Elder Hugh B. Brown, unidentified woman, and Secretary of the Interior Stewart Udall. In the background: waiter, US Secret Service, waitress, US Secret Service, reporters. (Far Below) Kennedy visiting with some of the staff of the Hotel Utah.

FLAMING GORGE DAM *Before leaving Utah, President Kennedy posed for a brief photo op at the airport, where he flipped the switch to start the first valve generator on the new Flaming Gorge Dam in Utah. (Inset: Artist rendering of the dam.)*

President Kennedy was killed in Dallas just eight weeks after his last Utah visit. The Church joined the nation and the world in mourning "the loss of a promising and dynamic young leader, . . . cut down in the prime of his manhood,"as President Harold B. Lee put it.[140] At a memorial service held at Brigham Young University, future Church President Gordon B. Hinckley spoke of "this young and wonderfully able leader" and added "I did not agree with President Kennedy on many things, but I had a great respect for the sense of dedication with which he pursued his ends and for the tremendous ability he brought to his task."[141]

LYNDON B. JOHNSON

LYNDON B. JOHNSON WAS PRESIDENT of the United States from 1963–1968 and served at the same time George Dewey Clyde and Calvin L. Rampton were governors of Utah and David O. McKay was president of the Church. He came to Utah seven times, including twice as president.

NATIONAL GALLERY

JOHNSON GIVES SPEECHES TO BOOST DEMO-CRATIC SUPPORT *(Above) During the heated midterm elections, Senate Minority Leader Lyndon B. Johnson (D-TX) stopped by Utah on October 18, 1954, for two campaign speeches. He spoke at Brigham Young University in the morning and at the Sandy Recreation Hall later in the day, confidently expressing his belief that Democrats would win big on Election Day and that Utah would be better served to support candidates of his party.*[142]

JOHNSON GREETED BY DEMOCRATIC PARTY OFFICERS AND WORKERS

(Right and Far Right) On November 1, 1958, Johnson again campaigned in Utah for congressional midterm elections, this time as Senate majority leader. A delegation of Democratic candidates, officers, and party workers greeted him at the airport after his 10:30AM arrival. Impressed with his airport welcome, Johnson then addressed a luncheon meeting at Hotel Utah.[143]

CAMPAIGNING FOR PARTY NOMINATION FOR PRESIDENT

(Left and Far Left) Campaigning now as a candidate for the Democratic nomination for president, Johnson came to Utah on April 23, 1960, to make his plea to local Democrats. Despite campaigning hard in Utah and other states, Senator Johnson came in a distant second to John F. Kennedy for the Democratic presidential nomination at their convention in Los Angeles that July. Kennedy then asked Johnson to be his running mate.

DEMOCRATIC VICE PRESIDENTIAL NOM-
INEE On October 27, 1960, Johnson came through Salt Lake again, this time as the Democratic vice presidential nominee. He held a campaign rally at the Salt Lake City and County Building. At the rally, Johnson told the assembled Utahns that the United States could not afford another four years of "status quo government" from a party that lacked "goals and unity" and that it was time to give the Democrats a chance.[144] He was heartened by a young Utah supporter (above) who did not seem to be a fan of Republican nominee Richard Nixon.

JOHNSON MEETS PRESIDENT DAVID O. McKAY (Below)

Johnson met David O. McKay in the Church Administration Building. Democrat National Committee Chairman Henry "Scoop" Jackson (left of Johnson), who was also a Senator from the state of Washington at the time, accompanied Johnson. They met with President McKay and his second counselor, President Henry D. Moyle (right of McKay), who told the visitors that he was "a lifelong Democrat."[145]

JOHNSON AND McKAY SHARE A LOVE OF HORSES (Above)

President McKay, seated between Senator Johnson and Senator Jackson, enjoyed discussing not only politics but also a shared love of horses, ranching, and cowboy hats.[146]

DESERET NEWS

DESERET NEWS

VICE PRESIDENT LYNDON B. JOHNSON PRAISES THE CHURCH'S MISSIONARY PROGRAM *As vice president of the United States, Johnson returned to Utah once again on October 19, 1962. The vice president drove to a meeting with President McKay and President Moyle, where he praised the Church's missionary program as a "wonderful supplement to furtherance of freedom in the world." Johnson praised President McKay for his "great contributions to humanity" and said, "I learn something every time I visit with President McKay."[147]*

DEMOCRATIC STATE COMMITTEE

Newhouse Hotel • Salt Lake City, Utah

CALVIN W. RAWLINGS
National Committeeman

LUCY REDD
National Committeewoman

STEPHEN F. SMOOT
State Chairman

SEVILLA REESE
State Vice Chairman

CARL H. TAYLOR
Treasurer

DONALD B. HOLBROOK
Secretary

J. LYNN DOUGAN
Executive Director

October 8, 1962

TO ALL VOTING DISTRICT VICE CHAIRMEN:

Our Vice President, Lyndon Johnson, will be in Salt Lake City on October 18th. He was persuaded to visit Utah because of the real need of the Democratic Party for funds to wage an effective campaign. These funds are needed to help us send David S. King, Bruce Jenkins and Blaine Peterson to Washington and to support Democrats running for various State and County offices.

To raise these funds, the Democratic party is sponsoring an "On to Victory Dinner" honoring Vice President Johnson at 7:30 P.M. on October 18th at the Terrace Ballroom in Salt Lake City. Tickets are $25 per plate.

We know the price is high, but the price was set at this figure because it is the only figure that will bring in the amount of money we need to campaign effectively. The Republican Party appears to have unlimited sources of funds which our Party hasn't been able to match. A successful Johnson Dinner will help to close the gap a bit.

While we know the $25 price tag is high, we also know it is going to be hard to find individual Democrats who can afford the $25. Therefore, each Voting District is being asked to conduct drawings to dispose of two tickets. We have sent to your Voting District Chairman the tickets and materials to help sell the tickets. Please contact your Chairman and give him any help necessary to sell the tickets.

It would be a great boost to our October 18th Johnson Dinner effort if more than two tickets can be sold in your District.

We urge your cooperation in this effort. It is vital to the Democratic Party in this 1962 election. We must elect Democrats who will move ahead with the Kennedy Administration in Washington and Democrats who will serve the best interests of the people in Utah and Salt Lake County. So please get out and push and get on the "On to Victory Dinner" bandwagon.

UTAH STATE EXECUTIVE OFFICERS

SALT LAKE COUNTY EXECUTIVE OFFICERS

Ed J. Flynn, Chairman
"ON TO VICTORY DINNER COMMITTEE"

UTAH STATE HISTORICAL SOCIETY

TOOELE HIGH SCHOOL MARCHING BAND WELCOMES VICE PRESIDENT JOHNSON TO FUND-RAISING DINNER *(Below) That evening, Johnson spoke at a Democratic fund-raising dinner, where he was welcomed by the Tooele High School marching band. At the event, Vice President Johnson and his wife sat at the head table with Utah Senator Frank "Ted" Moss and his wife (Opposite). He encouraged Utah to send more Democrats back to Congress in the upcoming midterm elections, saying President Kennedy needed support in Congress for his New Frontier programs.*

DESERET NEWS

**PRESIDENT JOHNSON MAKES A SPONTANE-
OUS STOP IN SALT LAKE CITY TO VISIT PRES-
IDENT McKAY** *(Below) He had been to Utah as
Senate minority leader, Senate majority leader, candidate for president, candidate for vice president, and
as vice president; but on September 17, 1964, Johnson
came to Utah as president of the United States. Johnson, who was returning from a trip to Sacramento,
California, spontaneously asked the pilot of Air Force
One to land in Salt Lake City so he could visit President David O. McKay. "I could not fly over Utah without stopping to see President McKay," Johnson said. "I
always feel better after I have been in his presence."*[148]

**SCRAMBLE TO GREET THE UNEXPECTED
PRESIDENT** *(Right) President Johnson waves to
the crowd of 1,000 at the Utah Air National Guard
hanger at the airport as he drives away, accompanied
by President N. Eldon Tanner of the First Presidency
and Senator Frank Moss. With only a three-hour notice, the Church and civic officials had scrambled to be
there to greet the president.*[149]

DESERET NEWS

THOUSANDS GATHER WITH ONLY THREE HOURS' NOTICE

Despite only a three-hour notice, more than 20,000 Utahns gathered along the streets of Salt Lake City to welcome the president of the United States.[150] The enormous spontaneous crowds of well-wishers underscored the fact that Lyndon B. Johnson had the highest average approval rating in his first term of any modern president in their first term.[151]

JOHNSON GREETED BY ANOTHER CROWD IN THE LOBBY OF HOTEL UTAH *A large crowd also greeted the president in the lobby of the Hotel Utah. President Johnson waves at the press before disappearing into an elevator that took him up to President McKay's Hotel Utah apartment, where he spent thirty minutes visiting the Church president. "I wanted to see you and wish you well," he told McKay. Johnson also extended an invitation to the prophet to come stay a few days at the White House during the inaugural festivities in January, which President McKay accepted but was unable to do because of poor health.*[153] *A large crowd was still gathered outside Hotel Utah when the president left that evening to return to Air Force One.*

The Mormon Tabernacle Choir performed "Battle Hymn of the Republic" at Lyndon B. Johnson's Presidential Inauguration on January 20, 1965. The Choir has sung for every president of the United States since President Taft and has performed in five presidential inaugurations, the first of which was for Lyndon B. Johnson. Dense fog at the Salt Lake Airport forced 251 members of the 363-strong choir to board buses for a nine-hour ride to Las Vegas, Nevada, where they caught a subsequent flight and arrived just three hours before they were scheduled to assemble on the Capitol's east side.[152]

The Inaugural Committee
requests the honor of your presence
to attend and participate in the Inauguration of
Lyndon Baines Johnson
as President of the United States of America
and
Hubert Horatio Humphrey
as Vice President of the United States of America
on Wednesday the twentieth of January
one thousand nine hundred and sixty five
in the City of Washington

JOHNSON CALLS ON THE MCKAYS PRIOR TO HIS TABERNACLE SPEECH *(Below) Before going to the Tabernacle for his address, the president called once again on President McKay and posed for a picture op with (from left to right) Emma Ray McKay, President McKay, President Johnson, First Lady Lady Bird Johnson, and Senator Moss. Johnson once commented, "I don't know just what it is about President McKay. I talk to Billy Graham and all of the others but somehow it seems as though President McKay is something like a father to me."*[154]

OFFICIAL PRESIDENTIAL VISIT *(Opposite) Unlike the spontaneous visit of September, Johnson made a proper presidential visit to Salt Lake City on October 28, 1964—just eleven days before Election Day.*

JOHNSON GIRLS *(Above) The president appeared amused by the little girls in matching costumes who were waving pennants that said "We're Johnson Girls."*

President Johnson did not bring the usual presidential car to Utah in 1964.

In March 1961, President Kennedy was presented with a new presidential limousine—a 1961 Lincoln Continental 74A that had been modified to Secret Service specifications by Ford Motor Company's Advanced Vehicle Group and Hess & Eisenhardt of Cincinnati, Ohio. After Kennedy's assassination in Dallas in November 1963, the presidential limousine was impounded for evidence and then underwent major enhancements, including titanium armor plating, bullet-resistant glass, a bullet-proof permanent roof, and solid aluminum rims inside the tires to make them flat-proof. However,

while the Lincoln was being rebuilt, President Johnson still needed a secure vehicle to travel in, including during his September 1964 visit to Salt Lake. The best alternative available was the armored Cadillac that Hess & Eisenhardt had specially modified for the director of the Federal Bureau of Investigation, J. Edgar Hoover. So President Johnson borrowed the FBI director's Cadillac for a few months and used it on his trip to Utah.

President David O. McKay and President Lyndon B. Johnson had the closest friendship of any LDS president and American president to date. Two months after assuming the presidency, Johnson called and asked Pres. McKay if he would come for a visit to the White House. "... I just need a little strength I think that would come from visiting with you an hour or so," said Johnson. Though still re-

LDS CHURCH HISTORY LIBRARY

covering from a mild stroke he'd suffered just a few months earlier, McKay said he would come, making him the first religious leader invited to the Johnson White House. Upon his arrival, McKay received a tour of the historic mansion, introductions to Johnson's staff, and then proceeded to have lunch with Johnson. While dining, Johnson said to McKay, "I feel that the spiritual and moral fiber of this country needs strengthening, and we need it badly. I would like to ask you, President McKay, if you can tell me how we can get it." McKay's reply was, "Let your conscience be your guide, and go forward and let the people see that you are sincere, that this is the problem that you have before you, and one that should be met, and lead out in it and let the people follow."

SPEECH AT THE TABERNACLE GETS VIGOROUS APPLAUSE *(Right) In an animated campaign speech responding to recent charges by the Soviet Union and Republican Barry Goldwater's campaign, Johnson said, "We will always keep our guard up but we will always keep our hand out. We intend to bury no one. But we do not intend to be buried, either." The crowd in the Tabernacle responded with vigorous applause.*[155]

DESERET NEWS

MIKE WINDER COLLECTION

MIKE WINDER COLLECTION

JOHNSON'S VISIT SECURED UTAH'S ELECTORAL VOTES ON ELECTION DAY *(Opposite) A large number of people gathered to see President Johnson depart Temple Square. People were even perched on the gates of Temple Square to get a glimpse of the president. As President and Mrs. Johnson ascended the steps of Air Force One, the November elections fast approached. Although Utah had gone Republican four years prior, Johnson would win in Utah in 1964, 55 percent to Goldwater's 45 percent. Davis County and northernmost Utah went for Goldwater, as did southern Utah, which bordered Goldwater's home state of Arizona. However, the bulk of the populated Wasatch Front carried the day for the Democratic president, guaranteeing Utah's four electoral votes.*[156]

JOHNSON
HUMPHREY
1964

BECOMING REAGAN COUNTRY

1970–1988

RICHARD M. NIXON

LIBRARY OF CONGRESS

SALT LAKE CITY, UTAH, SUNDAY MORNING, JUNE 5, 1949

Prominent figures at the National Editorial Assn. | of Utah Press Assn.; Orrin R. Taylor, preside convention. Left to right, Hal G. MacKnight, head | of N.E.A.; Rep. Richard M. Nixon, a guest speake

R ICHARD M. NIXON WAS PRESIDENT of the United States from 1969–1974 and served at the same time Calvin L. Rampton was governor of Utah and David O. McKay, Joseph Fielding Smith, Harold B. Lee, and Spencer W. Kimball were presidents of the Church. He came to Utah ten times, including twice as president.

CONGRESSMAN NIXON MAKES BRIEF COMMENTS DURING AIRPORT LAYOVER *Nixon's first stop in Utah was as a college debate student in 1932. His Whittier College debate team traveled to BYU for a tournament and lost to the Cougars. (Right) Nixon returned to Utah on June 4, 1949, as a thirty-six-year-old congressman from California, who had recently begun his second term. He spoke to the press at the airport about the threat of communism before flying on to his next destination.*

Fascism Draws Fire At Editorial Confab

Dictatorships of the right and the left were the chief targets of speakers at the opening functions of the National Editorial Assn. convention in Salt Lake City Saturday.

Dr. Kenneth McFarland, superintendent of schools in Topeka, Kan. told the nations editors of weeklies and small dailies that a man cannot be a dictator in the modern world unless he is a liar, a traitor and a murderer.

"cannot align themselves with such governments without compromising both Christianity and democracy."

Guest Speaker

Dr. McFarland was guest speaker at a banquet in Newhouse hotel sponsored by the Carpenter Paper Co. He appeared under the auspices of General Motors Corp., which entertained delegates at a reception.

At the opening luncheon in Hotel Utah Saturday, Richard M. Nixon (R. Cal.), former chairman and now a minority party member of the un-American activities committee, defended the committee's emphasis on Communist front organizations as the greatest threat because it is part of an international conspiracy. He declared that the committee has, and will continue, to investigate subversive rightist organizations. He invited criticism from the press but asserted that some of the critical reaction to the committee's activities has in the past been inconsistent or predicated upon misinformation or misunderstanding.

Other Highlights

Other highlights of the opening day activities included:
Appearance of Virginia Mayo, movie actress, and her husband, Michael O'Shea, at a fashion show given by ZCMI for wives and daughters of the newspaper publishers.
A welcome program for a special trainload of delegates from

the east at the Denver and Rio Grande Western station.
Announcement of awards in the organization's "national Better Newspaper Contests" at the evening banquet.
Sightseeing tours around the city and distribution of maps and information by the convention courtesy committee.
Dr. McFarland criticized sharply the nation's foreign policy in his banquet speech and called for development of a policy based upon "everlasting principles of right and wrong" instead of expediency.
"Our policy," he said, "apparently is based upon an old Balkan proverb which says: 'In time of great peril, my son, you may walk
See Page 14, Column 2

Senate Prober May Request A-Bomb Total

WASHINGTON, June 4 UP—The size of America's atomic stockpile may have to be disclosed to get a proper assessment of the work of the Atomic energy commission, Sen. Brien McMahon (D., Conn.) said Saturday.

McMahon is chairman of the senate-house atomic energy committee which is investigating charges of "incredible mismanagement" leveled by Sen. Bourke B. Hickenlooper (R., Ia.) at AEC chairman David E. Lilienthal.

'Not Safe'

The current investigation, McMahon said, "gives point and meaning" to his earlier suggestion for a study of the effects of lifting the secrecy ban on the number of bombs.

However, Hickenlooper told reporters he doesn't think that is "a safe area for publicity."

McMahon noted he had pointed out in a February speech "that it would be impossible to properly assess the conduct of the atomic energy commission's affairs un-

NEA'S CHOICES
East Papers Win Top Meet Prizes

A daily and weekly news in New Jersey and a wee New York state won top in the general excellence sponsored by the Nationa torial Assn.

The awards in nine d were announced at a dinn

Ten intermountain news won one or more awards orable mention. They w Lusk, Wyo. Herald; Spri Utah Herald; Casa Ariz. Dispatch; Price, Ut Advocate; Jerome, Ida. Side News; Thermopolis, Independent Record; Wyo. Tribune-Herald; Rock Falls, Mont. Hungry Horse News; Taos, N. M. Star.

urday night in the Newhouse hotel, part of the association's national convention.

In each instance, first, second and third place awards were made for the daily division and two for the weekly divisions, depending upon the circulation.

Winners Listed

The winners follow:
First in general excellence: Daily Journal at Elizabeth, N. J., daily; The Schoharie County Journal of Cobbleskill, N. Y., and The Times of Montclair, N. J., weekly divisions.
Second in general excellence: The Salinas, Cal., Californian, daily; Lusk, Wyo., Herald and Lapeer, Mich., Lapeer County Press, weeklies.
Third in general excellence: Hastings, Neb., Daily Tribune, daily; Laurens, Ia., Sun, and weekly:
See Page 14, Column 1

PROGRAM AT A GLANCE
Editorial Conventi

Program for National Editorial Assn. convention:
SUNDAY
9:30 a.m.—Concert by Taber

NIXON COMES TO UTAH TO CAMPAIGN AS EISENHOWER'S RUNNING MATE *As a thirty-nine year-old U.S. senator from California, Nixon visited Utah for the second time on September 26, 1952, when he was campaigning for the vice presidency as Eisenhower's running mate. Utah Senator Arthur V. Watkins rode with Nixon and his wife, Pat, (Above) to call on Church President David O. McKay and other Church leaders at Church headquarters.*[157] *(Top Right) Congressional Candidate William A. Dawson, Senator Arthur V. Watkins, Stephen L. Richards, David O. McKay, Richard Nixon, J. Reuben Clark, and George Dewey Clyde. Apostle Marion G. Romney heard Nixon and was not impressed: "I listened to some of it, as much as I could swallow. He seems to be a nice boy, but for the life of me I can't discover anything which would qualify him to be Vice President."*[158] *(Bottom Right) After visiting with President McKay, Nixon spoke at a Republican rally.*

VICE PRESIDENT NIXON GREETED BY "IKE GIRLS" *(Left and Far Left) Although President Eisenhower barely touched down in Utah during his eight years as president, Nixon came three times during those years as his vice president. A group of enthusiastic Utah women awaited Nixon's arrival on September 24, 1956, as he campaigned for Eisenhower's reelection. The "Ike Girls" greeted Vice President Nixon, Pat Nixon, and Utah Senator Wallace Bennett (shown R to L).*

IKE DICK

NIXON SPEAKS AT THE RAINBOW RANDEVU *(Above) After a parade with Republican candidates, Vice President and Mrs. Nixon were given a hearty welcome at the Rainbow Randevu, a downtown Salt Lake City dance hall, where Nixon gave the Utahns a pep talk for the 1956 election. While they were at the Rainbow Randevu (left), U.S. Treasurer Ivy Baker Priest introduced Pat Nixon but botched her words in the process, saying, "I now give you the next wife of the vice president." BYU President Ernest Wilkinson later quipped, "Ivy was probably just showing her Mormon background."*

DESERET NEWS

CAMPAIGNING FOR SENATOR WATKINS (Above) On October 17, 1958, Vice President Nixon stopped in Salt Lake to help campaign for his friend from the Senate, Arthur Watkins. Watkins was in a three-way battle for reelection with Democrat Frank "Ted" Moss and with former Utah Governor J. Bracken Lee, who was running as an independent after failing to get the Republican nomination. Despite Nixon's help, Moss defeated Watkins. (Governor George Dewey Clyde standing behind Nixon in the crowd.)

DESERET NEWS

NIXON SIGNS THE GUEST REGISTER (Below) Nixon signed the guest register at Church headquarters while visiting with the First Presidency (David O. McKay, Stephen L Richards, J. Reuben Clark). It was a long-standing tradition for prominent visitors to sign the book.

Sidelights of Nixons' Visit Show Human As Well as Official Traits

By JOAN GEYER

Little incidents will linger in the minds of Provoans long after the visit of Vice President Richard Nixon Friday.

They are impressions of the Nixons as people rather than political leaders.

As the blue and silver United Air Line plane touched down at Provo Airport Friday a few minutes earlier than scheduled, a small crowd moved forward, waving bright colored banners.

"Welcome Pat and Dick," said posters of the Young California Club and Young Republicans of Brigham Young University.

Impression of Vitality

The vice president is of athletic build and gives a first impression of unusual vitality. He was dressed conservatively in oxford grey suit, white shirt and blue tie.

His wife Pat has a fine-boned patrician quality, together with a gracious dignity, which we usually call lady-like.

The Nixons, like all members of the president's official family, are closely guarded, but they are not withdrawn. The vice president, flanked by Governor George D. Clyde, Senator Arthur Watkins, Charles Peterson, Utah County Republican chairman, and Congressman William A. Dawson, moved at a leisurely pace to where a grey convertible was waiting.

He shook hands, pausing to say a word or two to people as individuals. Press present included such VIPS as two Life Magazine correspondents, New York Times and Washington Post, but Mr. Nixon took time for a pleasant word with a Provo High School student reporter.

Stops For Students

As the vice presidential procession reached Provo High School, students surged out onto the highway islands on University Avenue, and Mr. Nixon's car slowed.

He told the hundreds of students he must meet his schedule at the fieldhouse, but nevertheless got out and shook hands with nearby teenagers, remarking on beauty of the weather.

His handclasp is firm.

The vice president continued to give an impression of pleasant deliberativeness with perhaps a special liking for young people.

More youngsters were waiting at the fieldhouse, trim blue-uniformed AFROTC cadets and sponsors in honor lines, and a fieldhouse packed with university students from every state in the union and from 44 foreign countries.

Quality of Humor

Another quality appeared as Mr. Nixon began his address — slow humor. Informed by Dr. Ernest Wilkinson, BYU president, that the audience included 1700 Californians, he indicated he could well believe it. "Every place I appeared in California," he said, "parents came up and asked me to 'say hello' to a son or daughter at BYU, so hello."

Mr. Nixon said he was impressed at the turnout, and joked about a "captive audience." He recalled that he had last appeared at BYU in 1933 as member of the Whittier, Calif., College debating team, and at that time had been amazed at debate turnout—until he learned students got credit for it.

Audience Not Captive

The vice president was assured by Dr. Wilkinson that Friday's audience was not captive. "If you knew these students as I do, you would know they are never captive," he said. "Neither is this a partisan turnout," said Dr. Wilkinson and young Democrats among students cheered.

The BYU president explained he had been shocked some years ago at "indifference and ignorance" of most American college students about national affairs, and, when he became BYU president had instituted regular forums to which national leaders in various fields were invited.

Students are not required to attend and get no credit, but attendance is always high, said Dr. Wilkinson. He said he had been trying to get Mr. Nixon for two years to talk on foreign policy

Before introducing Mr. Nixon, Dr. Wilkinson briefly sketched his biography to explain why the respect accorded the Nixons is personal as well as that due his office.

At Whittier College, Mr. Nixon was president of the student body and second scholastically in the graduating class.

He was student body president again at Duke University law school and third in the graduating class.

Mr. Nixon served two terms in Congress, where he was a member of the House un-American activities committee, which uncovered evidence leading to conviction of Alger Hiss on perjury. Mr. Nixon served a term also in the U.S. Senate before becoming vice president.

Student of Government

He was described by Dr. Wilkinson as a "great student of government, who due to ability not position greatly magnified his calling." Next to President Eisenhower, Mr. Nixon is regarded as a leading exponent of national policy, Mr. Eisenhower has called Mr. Nixon a "most valuable member on any team."

As a college debater, Mr. Nixon became a California champion, but

although the Whittier team won plaudits of the crowd at BYU in 1933, for delivery and polish, the debate judges, Senator Watkins, Worthen and District Judge A. H. Worthen and District Judge A. K. Christenson, ruled in favor of BYU's negative team, Wendell Jacob and Weldon J. Taylor, now dean of BYU business college.

Mr. Christenson was father of Utah Federal Judge Sherman Christenson.

The topic, "Resolved United States Should Cancel International Allied War Debts," indicated that even as a student Mr. Nixon had a keen interest in world affairs.

Three-Minute Ovation

Mr. Nixon's terse simplified description of American foreign policy, its current dangers and aims today brought a three-minute standing ovation from his audience.

Mr. Nixon recalled another visit to Utah in 1952 when Mrs. Nixon was introduced at the Rainbow Rendezvu in Salt Lake City by Utah's Ivy Baker Priest, now U.S. treasurer. In a flurry of introductions, Mrs. Priest said "I now give you the next wife of the vice president."

"Ivy was probably just showing her Mormon background," said Dr. Wilkinson.

At Kiwanis Meet
GOP Head Stumps for Party Issues

"When it comes to sizing up the issues of the 1958 campaign, the voters of Utah are fortunate," said Tom G. Judd, Salt Lake City, Republican state chairman in a talk to the Provo Kiwanis Club.

"The choice is a simple one. It is either to continue the solid record of growth and development accomplished by Utah's experienced Congressional delegation, or to experiment with the negative proposals of the Third party candidate and the untried promises of the other candidates."

Mr. Judd outlined the accomplishments of the Republican delegation in Congress in the fields of reclamation, agriculture, mining, peace and defense, highways, economy, education and labor. He also cited in his talk the long-term record of previous Republican national administrations as compared with Democratic administrations.

Cites G. O. P. Record

Mr. Judd who was introduced by Charles E. Peterson, Republican county chairman, cited the record on peace and war as follows: "In this country Democrats have controlled the executive branch of the government for 28 years, the Republicans for 30. Three times during this period we have become involved in international war—three times under Democratic administrations, never under the Republicans.

Turning to fiscal integrity he said: During the same period there have been 25 balanced federal budgets, 34 unbalanced budgets. Nineteen of the 25 balanced budgets were under Republican administrations, only six under the Democrats. Twenty-two of the 34 unbalanced budgets were under Democrats."

In regard to tax reduction he said there have been 15 increases in individual income tax rates since 1913, Democrats were responsible for 14 of them, Republicans, one. There were 10 reductions during the same period, Republicans made seven of these cuts, Democrats, three.

"Stifling government controls have been lifted from the backs of the Nation's business community," continued Mr. Judd. "An era of business-building and punitive legislation came to an end when the Eisenhower administration took office. In the eyes of the federal government it is once more respectable to be a businessman."

New Members Initiated

Guests of the club at the meeting were most of the Republican candidates on the county ticket who were introduced to the club members.

George S. Ballif had charge of the initiation of Joseph L. Oliver,

NEW MOTORBIKE FOR TRAFFIC ... Jess Evans, left, checks the newly-purchased which Patrolman John J. Tracy will downtown traffic during business ho the first time in several years that Provo time traffic officer assigned specifically district.

NIXON STOPS MOTORCADE TO VISIT WITH PROVO STUDENTS *After meeting with the Church leaders, the Nixons then traveled to Provo for a speech to 12,000 students at the Brigham Young University fieldhouse (Opposite). While driving through Provo, Vice President Nixon stopped the motorcade in front of Provo High School to spontaneously visit with some of the surprised students (Right and below).*[159]

The Daily Herald

EIGHTY-SIXTH YEAR, NO. 56 — PROVO, UTAH COUNTY, UTAH, FRIDAY, OCTOBER 17, 1958 — PRICE FIVE CENTS

MOSTLY CLEAR

Firmness Means Peace, Weakness War -- Nixon

WELCOME TO PROVO, MR. VICE PRESIDENT! — Vice President and Mrs. Richard Nixon are welcomed as they arrive at Provo Airport today, by Mayor G. Marion Hinckley, right. Sen. Arthur V. Watkins, immediately behind the Nixons, and Utah Gov. George D. Clyde are shown coming down ramp. Mr. Nixon addressed a throng at BYU Fieldhouse after motorcade from airport. (Herald staff photo by M. Grant Bartholomew)

U.S. Policy Outlined in Provo Talk

13,000 Pack BYU Fieldhouse to Set All-Time Indoor Record

By JOAN GEYER

Vice President Richard Nixon, addressing a capacity crowd of 13,000 in Brigham Young University Fieldhouse, today set forth American foreign policy with simplicity the youngest student could understand — declaring a firm policy means peace, a weak diplomacy means war.

He outlined America's aims: To wage peace against an agressive, dedicated and powerful enemy, to win over one billion uncommitted world citizens, and to build America from within to the image we want of her abroad.

The vice president, looking vigorous and fit despite his tight packed schedule; Mrs. Nixon, beautiful in a tailored grey suit, Governor George D. Clyde, BYU President Ernest L. Wilkinson, and other members of the cavalcade drove from the airport past thousands of school children recessed to watch the procession.

See Page 10 for interview with Mrs. Richard (Pat) Nixon by Phyllis Phillips, Herald society editor.

Sets Forth Principles

Principles set forth in the Nixon speech were these:

Why is American foreign policy the single greatest issue before the nation—and on a non partisan base? Because good jobs, social security and other benefits avail little if we aren't alive to enjoy them.

What dangers do we face? Only the communists at Moscow and Peiping would wage war on us. They represent one billion people; one third of the earth's surface. They have many times announced their dedicated goal to conquer the world—if necessary by force, but preferably by other means. United States and her allies represent another one billion people. A third billion in South America, Asia, Africa and the Near East are as yet uncommitted.

Firm Policy Needed

Is American foreign policy vacilating? We have experimented with conciliation and even of disarmament to convince the communists we are people of good will and not a threat to them. United States now believes only a firm policy will keep us safe.

Are we weakening America by "give – away programs abroad which is failing to buy us friendship?" We aren't trying to "buy" friends. Of our four billion spent for mutual security, three billion goes for arming allies ringing
(Continued on Page Nine)

RESCUE MISSING MEN

MOBILE, Ala. (UPI) — Three men missing for five days in the Gulf of Mexico were taken aboard a motorship Thursday and were reported in "perfect health." The three—J. B. Self, Tommy Baker and John McGaughan — had left Clearwater, Fla., early Sunday in an outboard motorboat.

Utah Lineman Electrocuted

MONTICELLO (UPI) — A lineman was electrocuted in the Anth Oil Field Thursday while connecting a "hot" line on a power pole.

He was David W. Whitehead, 32, a native of Livingston, Tex. He had been living with his wife and two children in Blanding for the past four months while in the employe of the R. S. Goodman Co.

The firm was doing sub-contracting work for the Utah Power & Light Co. in the field.

...P DRIVE
...s 5300-Mile
...ng Expedition

his most ambitious for an off-year election since he took office. His major speeches will be regional in nature, but he will visit a lot of places and see a lot of Republicans.

Simple Battle Plan

Eisenhower's plan of battle is fairly simple, but not without difficulty. His chief aim is to encourage and inspire GOP workers to greater action and greater effort. (Continued on Page Two)

Sunday Supplement

...shing Names of Juvenile
...Help Curb Delinquency

...article, "Does Publicity Curb Delinquency?"

Provo Host to Nation's Vice President

Townspeople, Students Hear Address

(Continued from Page One)

communist. If we sent our own troops abroad to defend this perimeter, cost would be five times as great, and we would have to up our draft. Example: It costs $125 to $200 to equip an army soldier; $2500 to equip one of our own.

Formosa, Islands Vital

Why can't we give away the two barren islands off Formosa or Formosa itself to keep peace? Because the Quemoy islands are aimed at Formosa, and loss of Formosa crumbles an entire line of defense from Formosa to the Philippines. The communists wage aggression on a 25 to 50 years basis. We intervened in Korea because it was a dagger pointed at Japan, weak militarily in 1950 but a rich prize industrially. A firm policy is a peace policy; a weak diplomacy means war.

How can we win the support of the one billion who are not yet committed? We must avoid the mistakes of the British who were harsh in regarded their colonies as inferior human beings. We must think in terms, not of the Voice of America, but the Voice of India, and other countries—in so far as they too have legitimate objectives.

People Want Dignity

What are these objectives? Very much the same as those for which we waged the American Revolution. They want independence and economic security but their poverty is so great—is some nations 1/20th of Mississippi standards—that they must place economics first. But even more, these people want—just as we do—the right to be recognized as individuals of human dignity.

What can college students do—in either party—to help American foreign policy? They can recognize their responsibility as one in 10 with university training to help Americans to a mature, dedicated understanding of long range objectives; that one defeat does not mean a policy is not good; that must be expected. College students can get into politics; they can help in their own communities to see best leaders are picked in both parties; for we cannot survive with second rate chiefs. They can dedicate themselves to helping to build America at home where...

as closely as possible to the high ideal we want of our nation abroad.

Speak Out For Right

They can use their influence when they see injustice or prejudice to speak out for right, knowing that any small incidence in United States will be magnified by many times abroad.

Dr. Wilkinson who introduced Vice President Nixon said when he came to head Brigham Young University he was shocked at the difference and ignorance of American college students and international about national and international issues. He set about to change things at Brigham Young University by arranging for top speakers in every field at weekly forums. These forums are not compulsory, but are always packed, Dr. Wilkinson said.

Cosmopolitan Audience

He told Vice President Nixon that his audience of 9900 BYU students was cosmopolitan, including men from Mr. Nixon's home state of California; students from every state and territory of United States and from 44 foreign countries.

It was Mr. Nixon's second visit to BYU. He was at Provo in 1932 as a member of Whittier College debating team, and although a California champion, lost to BYU. Although Provo was smallest city on Mr. Nixon's agenda, turnout of 13,000 at the fieldhouse and thousands along the route was higher than at Salt Lake City. Among several thousand along the route were 8,000 school children, recessed to see the vice president pass.

GUARD OF HONOR FOR NATION'S VEEP—Vice President Richard M. Nixon and Dr. Ernest L. Wilkinson, his official host as president of Brigham Young University, walk past the Air Force ROTC guard of honor as they enter the BYU Fieldhouse for the vice president's talk. To the left and rear is Mrs. Nixon. (Photo by Herald staff photographer Lenore Carter)

"Soaring," the art of embossing, is a term used in the work of a goldsmith, according to the Encyclopedia Britannica.

TV SERVICE
any make
Low . . . low rates
daily service on RCA Victor TV
WAKEFIELD'S
Phone FR3-1263

SEE THIS NEW ABC TV SHOW
Live From New York Daily

WHO DO YOU TRUST

Johnny Carson masterminds the quiz show that'll keep you guessing — and laughing — all the way!
2:30 – 3 p.m.
KUTV, CH. 2

4TH WEST PHARMACY
IVAN SORENSEN
Registered Pharmacist
PRESCRIPTIONS
SICK ROOM SUPPLIES
DRUG SUNDRIES
Prompt Free Delivery

"Every place I appeared in California parents came up and asked me to 'say hello' to a son or daughter at BYU, so 'Hello.'"

DESERET NEWS

1960 ELECTION *(Above) Nixon's Utah visit was just one month before the presidential election. Senator Watkins, V.P. Richard Nixon, Governor Clyde walking with Church office building in background. (Left) This hot pot holder was a very popular campaign item amongst housewives, since it was "good for something" other than the election. Nixon, however, did not win the election. He was the GOP nominee again in 1968.*

KEEP THINGS COOKING
FOR
VICTORY
IN '60
VOTE NIXON - LODGE
NOV. 8

RONALD FOX COLLECTION

PRESIDENT McKAY OFFERS NIXON PERSONAL WISH FOR SUCCESS
(Above) On October 10, 1960, GOP presidential nominee Richard Nixon spoke in the Tabernacle and met with President McKay. On that occasion, the prophet said to Nixon, "I sat by your competitor [Kennedy] in this office a few weeks ago and told him that if he were successful we would support him. In your case I'll say we hope you are successful."[160] The media picked up this comment around the country and interpreted it as a Church endorsement for Nixon, but President McKay clarified he was speaking as an individual and not for the Church.[161]

NIXON JOKES WITH McKAY ABOUT IMPROVING HIS GOLF GAME (Above) Nixon made a brief visit to Salt Lake City on September 15, 1966, to speak at a Republican rally at The Terrace Ballroom. But first he called on his "old friend," President McKay. Noting that Billy Casper had just won the U.S. Open Championship after being baptized a member of the Church, Nixon asked, "If I become a convert, would it improve my golf?" Mrs. McKay interjected, "Of course, it would!"[162]

BACK ON THE CAMPAIGN ROAD AS GOP PRESIDENTIAL NOMINEE (Right) Once again the GOP nominee, Nixon made a campaign stop in Utah on September 18, 1968. With President McKay ill in Huntsville, Nixon met with President Joseph Fielding Smith and Elder N. Eldon Tanner before addressing an enthusiastic audience in the Tabernacle. His former opponent for the Republican nomination, Michigan Governor (and Latter-day Saint) George Romney, was present, along with Senator Wallace Bennett. (L to R) George Romney, unidentified, Wallace Bennett, Richard Nixon and Congressman Sherman P. Lloyd.

Tooele High School marching band represented Utah in Nixon's 1969 Inaugural Parade. A band from each state performs in the order in which their state was admitted to the union. Utah being the 45th state admitted meant the THS band performed near the end. They were dropped off at 9AM and left in the bitter cold until the parade ended around 4PM. "It's a different kind of cold than here because of the humidity," said Richard Downey, who played the trumpet. "I remember a lot of us going into tents . . . and getting Styrofoam cups of coffee just to hold to keep our hands warm." Scott Dunn, a freshman tuba player, recalls his lips freezing to the mouth of his instrument and bleeding during the parade. Band director C. Roy Ferrin asked the Army colonel in charge of the military band what they did to keep their instruments from freezing. The colonel said they dipped the valves of the brass instruments in diesel fuel.[163]

TOOELE HIGH SCHOOL 1969 YEARBOOK

RONALD FOX COLLECTION

DESERET NEWS

The Mormon Tabernacle Choir was asked by the Nixon administration to sing "This is My Country" at the Inauguration Ceremony. This was the Choir's second inaugural performance. The director of ceremonies named the Choir, "The world's greatest and most celebrated singing unit."[164]

(Left) Shown on stand are: Mrs. Nixon, Chief Justice Earl Warren, President Johnson, President Nixon, V.P. Spiro T. Agnew, Hubert H. Humphrey, Senators Mike Mansfield and Everett McKinley Dirksen, Representative Gerald Ford, and Speaker John McCormick.

DESERET NEWS

DESERET NEWS

DESERET NEWS

DESERET NEWS

PRESIDENTIAL MOTORCADE WELCOMED BY THOUSANDS OF UTAHNS

On July 24, 1970, Richard Nixon made his first of two visits to Utah as president. He was invited to participate in the Days of '47 festivities, celebrating the anniversary of the arrival of the pioneers to Utah, and stopped by for three hours in between meetings with Midwestern governors in Fargo, North Dakota, and his ten-day working vacation at his "Western White House" in San Clemente, California. President Nixon; his wife, Pat; and his daughter Tricia enjoyed Salt Lake City's warm welcome as they drove from the airport to the Church Administration Building. A section of South Temple Street in front of the Church Administration Building was closed off to vehicles, and 10,000–15,000 people gathered there to greet the First Family.

NIXON INTRODUCES HIS FAMILY TO THE FIRST PRESIDENCY *(Above) President Joseph Fielding Smith and his counselors, Presidents Harold B. Lee and N. Eldon Tanner, met First Lady Pat Nixon. President Nixon then introduced his daughter, Tricia. The two women were then taken via underground tunnel beneath Main Street to Temple Square, where they enjoyed a tour of the world-famous Tabernacle while the president stayed inside to visit with Church leaders for an hour.*

NIXON PRAISES LDS CHURCH FOR IMPRESSION MADE DURING EXPO '70 IN TOKYO, JAPAN *(Below) The president shares a laugh while visiting with Church leaders in the Church Administration Building (L to R: Harold B. Lee, Richard Nixon, and Joseph Fielding Smith). In that discussion, Nixon lauded the Church and its members, specifically mentioning the favorable impression the missionaries had made at the Mormon exhibit at Expo '70 in Tokyo. He said that according to his daughter, Julie, and her husband, David Eisenhower, the LDS missionaries were the finest American ambassadors in Japan.[165]*

(Left) Expo '70 was the World's Fair held in Suita, Osaka, Japan, from March 15 to September 13, 1970. Its theme was "Progress and Harmony for Mankind."

NIXON ADDRESSES THE CROWD GATHERED OUTSIDE CHURCH ADMINISTRATION BUILDING

After his visit at Church headquarters, President Nixon came out to address the gathered crowd along South Temple Street. "I want you to know that we always have found our visits to Salt Lake City to be extremely heartwarming," Nixon said. He called the Church "a

great institution that has played a part in this administration," and went on to thank the Church publicly for providing the Tabernacle Choir to sing at his inauguration and "for providing for the Cabinet two of the outstanding Americans of our time, two of the most selfless public servants I know—the Secretary of the Treasury, Mr. [David] Kennedy, and the Secretary of Housing and Urban Development, George Romney."[166] After his remarks, President Nixon greeted well-wishers gathered on the steps of the Church Administration Building.

DAYS of '47   OFFICIAL PROGRAM JULY 1970

Nixon attended the Days of '47 Rodeo at the Salt Palace when he was here on Pioneer Day—July 24, 1970. He said it was his first rodeo in thirty years. In his remarks earlier in the day, he said, "Pioneer Day means something to the people of Utah but it also means something to the people of America, because the pioneers who came here taught other pioneers who went on through the balance of the West. And it is that kind of spirit . . . that doesn't blame adversity on somebody else but tries to do something about it himself. That is what built this State; that is what built America. . . . Thank you for giving America such a fine lesson."[167]   *(Below) Nixon at rodeo with hand under chin, George Romney (behind Nixon), Pat Nixon, and Richard Richards (behind Pat).*

"We always have found our visits to Salt Lake City to be extremely heartwarming."

FOND FAREWELL   *Nixon appeared somewhat amused with the crowd's eagerness to shake his hand. As the president entered his car to leave, he emerged from the sun roof to bid farewell to the crowd and enjoy the Utah enthusiasm.*

PRESIDENT RETURNS FOR FOUR-STATE MIDTERM CAMPAIGN (Below) President Nixon made his second and final presidential visit to Utah on Halloween—October 31, 1970—to speak in the Tabernacle as part of a four-state swing to campaign for the midterm congressional elections. Despite cooler weather, well-wishers greeted him as he drove into town from the airport.

MIKE WINDER COLLECTION

DESERET NEWS

NIXON SPEAKS IN TABERNACLE (Right) The famed Tabernacle organ bellowed "Hail to the Chief" as the president entered. Senator Wallace Bennett, Secretary of the Treasury David Kennedy, President Nixon, and President Joseph Fielding Smith stood in respect while the presidential anthem was played. In his remarks, Nixon said, "I do not know of any group in America . . . who have contributed more to that strong, moral leadership and high moral standards—the spirit that has kept America going through bad times as well as good times; no group has done more than those who are members of this Church. I want to thank you for what you've done for the spirit of America. . . . If you can continue those spiritual values, I'm sure America is going to go ahead and do very well."[168] With the midterm elections just days away, Nixon ended his remarks with an enthusiastic finish and with his trademark victory signs. The crowd roared as he blasted "those who carry a peace sign in one hand and a bomb in the other" as the "super-hypocrites of our time," noting that Utah Senator Frank Moss and other Democrats were part of the problem and that Republican Congressman Laurence Burton needed to be elected to the Senate.[169]

MIKE WINDER COLLECTION

DESERET NEWS

DESERET NEWS

A MOVING PERFORMANCE (Right bottom) Nixon was visibly moved by the Choir and closed his eyes while they sang "God Be With You Till We Meet Again." Several times during the performance, he leaned over to Isaac M. Stewart, choir president, and said "This is the world's greatest choir."[170] During his remarks, the presidential seal fell off the podium, clanking noisily to the ground and gaining the laughter of the crowd. By the closing musical number, someone had picked it up and set it on the pulpit again.

DESERET NEWS

NATIONAL PORTRAIT GALLERY

DESERET NEWS

GERALD R. FORD

G ERALD R. FORD WAS PRESIDENT of the United States from 1974–1977 and served at the same time Calvin L. Rampton and Scott Matheson (only for 14 days or so) were governors of Utah and Spencer W. Kimball was president of the Church. He came to Utah at least eighteen times, including once as president.

DESERET NEWS

CAMPAIGNING FOR REPRESENTATIVE BURTON *(Top Right) President Gerald Ford's first visit to Utah was on September 22, 1965, when, as House minority leader, he stopped by to campaign for Representative Laurence J. Burton, who represented Utah's first congressional district from 1963–1971.*

CAMPAIGNING FOR CONGRESSMAN LLOYD *(Bottom Right) Minority Leader Ford stopped by Utah again on May 10, 1968, to stump for the reelection of Congressman Sherman P. Lloyd of Utah's second congressional district. Representative Lloyd represented Utah in the U.S. House of Representatives from 1963–1965 and 1967–1973.*

Ogden Standard-Examiner

B-Section | OGDEN, UTAH | MONDAY EVENING | OCTOBER 15, 1973 | 1B

Ford Appears Confident On Northern Utah Visit

Fails, at First, to Recognize Student Son With Full Beard

By CLIFF THOMPSON

Rep. Gerald Ford, R-Mich., spent almost five hours in Northern Utah Sunday, appearing confident of winning congressional approval of his vice presidential nomination.

However, he told newsmen during visits to Tremonton and Logan that he "doesn't want a hurry up nomination.

"I want Congress to be sure," Rep. Ford said as he arrived in Tremonton about 6 p.m. to dine with Mr. and Mrs. James E. Brown, long time friends of the Fords and host for his Utah visit.

Rep. Ford said he "wouldn't dare speculate" on the outcome of his nomination by President Nixon to succeed Spiro T. Agnew in the nation's second highest office.

At the same time, he said "my colleagues know me pretty well", referring to his 25 years in the House where he now is minority leader.

Later in Logan, Rep. Ford said that as vice president he "could work well with both the legislative and executive" branches of the federal government.

Sunday's visit to Utah was played in a low key and was one of several, Rep. Ford has made here in the past decade to visit Mr. Brown, a Thiokol Chemical Corp. executive.

Rep. Ford flew into Hill Air Force Base a few minutes after 5 p.m. Sunday and departed again shortly before 10 p.m.

He arrived in a blue and white Air Force 707 carrying the insigna "United States of America" and a U.S. flag on its fuselage.

Greeting the vice presidential nominee were Mr. Brown, Brig. Gen. James P. Mullins, vice commander of the Ogden Air Materiel Area, Hill AFB commander Col. James Hall, including former Rep. Sherman P. Lloyd who served with Rep. who served with Rep. Ford in the House for a number of terms.

Waving and smiling broadly, Rep. Ford followed a contigent of newsmen and Secret Service men off the plane.

TALKS BRIEFLY

He talked briefly with the welcoming delegation and then got into the rear seat of a waiting car with Mr. and Mrs. Brown.

The party then headed north in a motorcade escorted by the Utah Highway Patrol where dinner was waiting at the Brown home in Tremonton.

Almost 100 Tremonton residents had gathered on the lawns around the Brown home to welcome the man they believe will be the next vice president.

Rep. Ford said that while he had never been to Tremonton before "I've heard so much about it from my good friends Jim and Gloria Brown that I felt I knew it as we drove in."

He thanks the Tremonton crowd for "your warm and gracious welcome" and then went inside the Brown home for dinner.

One of the lighter moments came when Rep. Ford was shaking hands with the crowd greeting him at the Brown home.

"How are you? Good to see you," Rep. Ford was saying as he shook hands with several people in the crowd.

FULL BEARD

A tall young man with a full beard and mustache stepped up and held out his hand.

"Hello. How are you," Rep. Ford asked the young man.

"I'm fine," replied John Gardner Ford.

"Oh . . . I hardly recognized you," said his father after a double take. "How are you, big boy?"

Ford's son had grown the beard since they saw each other last.

Also joining the group at dinner were three of young Ford's roommates at Utah State and a girlfriend of one of the roommates.

The 21-year-old John is a forestry student at Utah State.

One of his roommates is David Carpenter, son of Mr. and Mrs. Duane C. Carpenter of 2651 Brinker. His girlfriend, who was at the dinner, is Kathy Goodwin, a daughter of Mr. and Mrs. Linden B. Goodwin of 2156 W. 3950 S. Roy.

After dinner, Rep. Ford and the Browns drove to Logan where the congressman met with USU President Glen Taggart during an informal reception in the USU University

VICE PRESIDENTIAL nominee Rep. Gerald R. Ford, R-Mich., is greeted on arrival at Hill AFB Sunday by former colleague Sherman P. Lloyd (left) and James E. Brown (right background), host for the congressman during his five-hour visit here.

SOCIETY SETS SPORTS SPREE

DEFENSE DEPOT OGDEN—LaVar Hurst, president of the Ogden Chapter of the American Logistics Society is announcing Wednesday at 7 p.m. as this years Sports Spree night in conjunction with Browning Arms.

There will be prizes galore. Top prize will be a Browning Automatic Shotgun (winner need not be present).

Other prizes include: Hunting clothes, gun cases, Bag Boy golf cart and a wheelbarrow of groceries. A top flight sports film will be shown. Tickets will be available from members of the association and at the Public Affairs Office.

Eight Injured In Various Area Mishaps

Eight persons have been reported injured in various area accidents.

A collision at the intersection of 28th and Harrison late Saturday night has left two persons hospitalized.

Mrs. Lawrence Palletti, 44, of 776 Taylor, was in "serious" condition this morning at St. Benedict's Hospital.

Jeffrey Kirkbride, 17, son of Mr. and Mrs. Ronald Kirkbride, 1543 Binford, was "satisfactory" at McKay-Dee Hospital.

An occupant of the Kirkbride vehicle, Randon Burr, 15, son of Mr. and Mrs. Larry Burr, 1543 Binford, was treated and released at McKay-Dee.

BIKE HITS VEHICLE

Another accident at 28th and Wall left Ellis L. Watkins, 50, of 341 Grant, injured. He was reported "good" at St. Benedict's. His motorcycle reportedly struck a vehicle in the intersection.

Four persons were treated and released at McKay-Dee in a third traffic mishap. Dale Briggs, 8, son of Mr. and Mrs. Ted D. Briggs, 4871 S. 5500 W., Hooper and Mr. and Mrs. Wayne Fowers and their 1-year-old son, Brett, were all injured.

Paul A. Jones, Box 175, Morgan was reported in "satisfactory" condition at McKay-Dee after a horse fell on him Sunday.

SPANISH CLUB OFFERS FILM

The Weber State College Spanish Club will show a motion picture at 7 tonight in the WSC Union Theater.

The films are "El Inreible Professor Zobek," and "Acompaname." The public is invited.

INVITED TO DINNER

Buddies Say Ford 'Just Jack's Dad'

Although Rep. Gerald Ford will very likely become the next vice president of the United States, to his son's roommates, he's just "Jack's dad."

Of course according to one roommate, Dave Carpenter, 22, son of Mr. and Mrs. Duane C. Carpenter of 2651 Brinker, a bit of excitement was generated by President Nixon's announcement of Rep. Ford as his choice for vice president on Friday.

Gathered around the television set, none of his roommates, or even John Ford himself, (his friends call him Jack) had any idea that the President would be announcing "Jack's dad."

PRETTY EXCITING

"It was pretty exciting," said Dave who was at work when the announcement was made. "They called me to give me the news and everyone seemed pretty surprised and happy."

Originally Rep. Ford had been planning a weekend visit to Utah to see his son who is a junior forestry major at Utah State University.

Because of his recently increased commitments, the visit was necessarily shortened to a few hours on Sunday.

A dinner was planned and Jack's roommates were invited, but to make the entire event official — plans also called for a motorcade.

Lacking any other means of transportation, Dave and his girl friend Kathy Goodwin, daughter of Mr. and Mrs. Linden B. Goodwin of 2156 W. 3950 S., Roy, joined the line of shiny new cars in Dave's somewhat less sparkling 1966 station wagon.

To Dave, both the meal and the experience of eating with a future U.S. vice president was "fantastic."

"It was kind of unbelievable really," he said. "I just had to keep my mind on eating my steak."

The evening, however, did not afford much of a chance for the future vice president to talk with his son.

According to Dave, "there were just too many people around for them to talk."

While this may be a sign of things to come — for now, life for Jack Ford and his three roommates has just about returned to normal.

Asked this morning, how Rep. Ford's new position had affected Jack, Dave said, "Not at all — he just got up today, like always, and went to school."

BACKYARD VISIT — Vice presidential nominee Gerald R. Ford and his son, John, 21, talk on back lawn of friend's home at Tremonton. Ford stopped in Utah to visit the Utah State University student en route from Washington to Portland, Ore.

Cities Repo[…] Candidate […]

With the filing deadline only a week away, candidate activity is still at a relatively slow pace in most of Weber County's third class cities.

Contests have shaped up for the mayor's seat in six of the 10 cities but there are contests for City Council seats in only three of them.

The filing deadline is Friday at 5 p.m. Candidates must file with the clerk or recorder in each of the cities.

Ogden City's filing deadline has already past with an Oct. 23 primary contest on tap for mayor and in the First and Second Municipal Wards.

In the other cities, mayoralty contests have shaped up in South Ogden, Roy, Harrisville, Washington Terrace, Pleasant View and Riverdale.

Contests for city council seats are assured so far in only South Ogden, Roy and Riverdale.

The general election is scheduled in all 11 communities on Nov. 6.

With the exception of Ogden, each city will elect a mayor and two council members. Ogden will elect a mayor and its entire six-member city council.

The largest field of candidates for mayor is in Washington Terrace where four men have announced bids to succeed Mayor Owen Burrell who isn't seeking reelection.

They are Ronald Stephens, R. Gene Allphin, E. Larry Neves and Donald W. Aunspaugh.

However, there are but two candidates announced for the two City Council seats up for election in Washington Terrace. They are Mrs. Bernell Jensen and Darnel L. Haney.

South Ogden, Riverdale and Roy have two candidates for mayor and four each for the two Council seats.

In South Ogden, two incumbent councilmen have announc-

[…]

City Council candidates in Riverdale are Howard Coleman, Norman Farr, Grant D. Bendixson and John D'Agnillo.

Harrisville has a race for mayor between Richard Larsen and Dr. William Shurtleff but only two candidates for the two City Council seats. They are Duane Poulsen and William W. Smith.

TWO SEATS

In Pleasant View, Deloy J. Spencer and Richard G. Diamond have announced their candidacy for mayor but no one has filed for the two City Council seats.

North Ogden Mayor William A. Bailey has no opponent so far in his bid for reelection and only Councilman Brent Van Wagoner and Eldon D. McColley have filed for the two City Council seats.

No candidates have announced so far in Plain City, Huntsville and Uintah.

Public Works Director For Ogden Will Retire

Rulon H. Sorensen, public works director since July 1966 and city engineer, announced Thursday he will retire from public service no later than Jan. 15, 1974.

Mr. Sorensen said he submitted a letter announcing his retirement to City Manager Richard L. Larsen on Oct. 3.

A successor has not been announced, but the public works director said he feels his 3½-month notice will allow the manager "time to replace me with the person of your choice."

Mr. Sorensen, who became assistant city engineer in 1963, was boosted to his present post when the former public works director, Charles R. Kelley, was named city manager in 1966.

CONSTRUCTION ENGINEER

Prior to going to work for the city, he had spent 13 years as a construction engineer and superintendent for M. Morrin & Sons Inc., of Ogden.

Mr. Sorensen also has worked for the Utah Construction Co., Utah Water and Power Board and the U.S. Bureau of Reclamation.

A native of Fielding, Box Elder County, he spent his boyhood at Bothwell and Logan and in 1941 was graduated from degree in professional engineering.

During World War II, he served with the U.S. Army Engineers in the Pacific theater, coming to Ogden in 1950.

He and his wife, Alliene, have two children, Louis Sorensen who is city engineer at Kingman, Ariz., and a daughter, Mrs. Sandra Griffin of Salt Lake City.

They plan to continue making their home in Ogden at

RULON H. SORENSEN
To Retire in '74

Page 16—THE HERALD, Provo, Utah, Monday, December 24, 1973

Veep on Skiing Vacation

VAIL, Colo. (UPI) — Vice President Gerald Ford watched football on television this weekend waiting for a swirling storm that dumped three inches of snow on the ski resort to end and then took his family out on the ski slopes.

The vice president was accompanied by a ski patrolman, an instructor and four Secret Service agents.

"He hasn't asked for any special treatment," said Pam Conklin, a spokesman for the ski resort where Ford has a $50,000 condominium. "He's just another skier. This is strictly family-type vacation for him as far as we're concerned."

Ford went virtually unnoticed Sunday while he waited five minutes in line at a small shop to buy a pair of ski gloves.

"It's not that people don't care," Miss Conklin said. "They are impressed with the idea of having a resident vice president here. But they also are nice about letting people alone."

Dennie Hoeger, a former ski instructor and a personal friend, said Ford is a good skier and has little trouble with Vail's slopes, regarded by many professionals as being pretty tricky.

Ford's skiing party was held up for eight minutes Saturday by a gondola lift that stalled partway up the mountain. Miss Conklin said the gondola was being repaired and she had assured the vice president the trouble would not happen again.

Ford, accompanied by his wife, Elizabeth, a son and a daughter, arrived in Vail by car Saturday morning. The party had driven from Denver following a flight from Washington to Buckley Air National Guard Base.

Ford watched three periods of the Minnesota Vikings-Washington Redskins playoff game on television Saturday before donning blue ski pants, a dark blue parka and a red, white and blue ski cap and heading off for four hours on the slopes.

Secret Service agents checked out the resort two weeks ago when it was learned the Vice President's family planned to spend the holidays here.

Miss Conklin said few social functions were planned for the Fords. One exception is a New Year's Eve tour of six homes in the community followed by a $100-a-ticket champagne dinner and dance to benefit the Vail Hospital.

SHOWING PRETTY FAIR FORM, Vice President Gerald Ford makes a turn down Vail Mountain in Colorado with ski instructor Dennis Hoeger in pursuit. The vice president and his family are Christmas vacationing at Vail.

Energy Shortage Around Globe

Energy Bill Too Loaded, Solon Says

Oil-Starved Japan Needs Huge Imports

TOKYO (UPI) — Oil-starved

Venezuela To Boost Oil Prices

VICE PRESIDENTIAL NOMINEE VISITS SON AND FRIENDS IN TREMONTON AND LOGAN *(Below and Left) On October 14, 1973, Ford made a brief stop in northern Utah to visit his friends Mr. and Mrs. James Brown and his son Jack Ford, who was attending Utah State University at the time. Ford had just been nominated by President Nixon two days prior to replace Vice President Spiro T. Agnew, who had resigned. As vice president designee, Ford's entourage of Secret Service and national press was much larger than he had expected when he first planned the visit to the Brown home in Tremonton. The Fords and Browns enjoyed ski vacations during the holidays together, including trips to Park City. Ford also spoke at a brief reception in Logan.*[171]

DESERET NEWS

FORD AWARDS MEDAL TO SCOUT *(Above) After having his nomination confirmed by Congress, Gerald Ford was sworn in as vice president on December 6, 1973. As vice president, he spent a busy three days in Utah on June 7–9, 1974. He presented a life saving medal to an Eagle Scout, visited his friend James Brown in Tremonton and went horseback riding with him on Promontory Mountain, delivered the commencement address at Utah State, met with the First Presidency, and enjoyed a few numbers from the Tabernacle Choir.*

VP FORD WALKING IN GRADUATION PROCESSION AT UTAH STATE UNIVERSITY *(Right) The vice president not only gave the commencement speech at Utah State, but he also received an honorary doctorate of laws degree from Utah State University President Glenn L. Taggart.*

FORD'S COMMENCEMENT ADDRESS *(Opposite) "It was Horace Greeley," Ford said in his remarks, "who said 'Go West, young man,' but it was Brigham Young who knew where to stop."[172]*

"One of the differences I sense about Utah State," Vice President Ford said in his commencement remarks, "is that here you can still feel the exciting challenge of the American West, the magnificent harmony between God and man, between nature and civilization, which exists among your rugged mountains and fertile valleys and between your bustling cities and your silent skies."[173]

"It was Horace Greeley who said 'Go West, young man,' but it was Brigham Young who knew where to stop."

President Ford spoke at three Utah universities. He was the commencement speaker at Utah State University when his son John graduated in 1974; he spoke at Brigham Young University in 1987 and lectured in several classes in both 1978 and 1987; and he spoke at the University of Utah, where he addressed the student body in Kingsbury Hall, spoke at the Hinckley Institute of Politics in 1982, and spoke to students in the Special Events Center in 1974.

PRESIDENT KIMBALL SHARES A BOOK WITH VICE PRESIDENT FORD *(Above) First Presidency members Spencer W. Kimball, Marion G. Romney, and N. Eldon Tanner share a copy of the book* Meet the Mormons *with Vice President Ford in the Church Administration Building. Ford said he and Mrs. Ford felt a "nice closeness to people of the Mormon faith" because of their "many, many" LDS friends in Washington.*[174]

A POSITIVE IMPRESSION *(Right) During President Ford's one-time visit to Utah as president of the United States on November 1–2, 1974, he and President Kimball hit it off well, and Ford thanked President Kimball for the Church's loyalty and patriotism. "You should be proud of the high moral principles which in many respects are an example to all of us who live in the other 49 states," Ford said. "We look forward to returning because we like people from Utah, we like your country, and we like what you stand for."*[175]

"We look forward to returning because we like people from Utah . . . and we like what you stand for."

JAKE GARN

**announcement of
candidacy
United States Senate**

JON MOORE

**CAMPAIGNING FOR JAKE
GARN** *(Left and above) Ford's
visit to Utah as president was specifically to campaign for Salt Lake
Mayor Jake Garn, who was running for the U.S. Senate against
Wayne Owens.*[176] *He arrived at
10:30AM and left at 2:30PM the
next day on the last lap of a twen-
ty-one state tour to head off Democratic gains in Congress.*

PRESIDENT SPEAKS AT U OF U *(Right) Ford's final
event in Utah during his 1974 swing was a speaking event
at the Special Events Center at the University of Utah. His
efforts helped propel Jake Garn into the United States Senate on Election Day, but nationally, the Republicans lost
three seats in the Senate and forty-nine seats in the House
of Representatives in the first election since Watergate and
Nixon's resignation.*

**FORD MAKES A STOP AT CO-
LUMBUS COMMUNITY CEN-
TER WITH MAYOR GARN**
*(Left and below) In his brief stop in
Utah, President Ford toured the Columbus Community Center in South
Salt Lake with Mayor Garn and
was impressed with "one of the two
best centers for the mentally, physi-
cally and socially handicapped in the
country."* [177] *Students of the school
showed the president how they refur-
bished telephone cords, among other
projects.*

UNIVERSITY OF UTAH – SPECIAL EVENTS CENTER

- ADMIT ONE -

President Gerald R. Ford
addresses the people of Utah

SATURDAY NOVEMBER 2, 1974 — 12:00 NOON

Doors open at 11:00 a.m. — Limited seating · first come first serve

FORDS ATTEND BANQUET HONORING J. WILLARD MARRIOTT *On November 29, 1977, former President and Mrs. Ford traveled by private plane to Utah to pay tribute to their friends the Marriotts, who were being honored at a banquet in the Grand Ballroom of Hotel Utah on the occasion of the debut of J. Willard Marriott's biography. Elder Marvin J. Ashton of the Twelve and chairman of the board of Deseret Book, which published the book, introduced the guests. (Above L–R) Gerald Ford, Betty Ford, J. Willard Marriott, Alice Marriott, Marion G. Romney of the First Presidency (who offered the invocation for the event), and Ida Romney.[178]*

FORD CAMPAIGNS FOR DAN MARRIOTT *(Right) Former President Ford came to Utah again on October 23, 1978, to headline a fund raiser for Representative Dan Marriott's reelection. Marriott represented Utah's second congressional district from 1977–1985.*

FORD LECTURING AT BYU *(Above and Left top) On December 4–6, 1978, former President Ford visited BYU. Ford spoke to political science classes at the J. Reuben Clark Law School and addressed a forum assembly as an Enterprise Institute fellow. "Let's take away the hate from the hearts of our citizens," Ford instructed the audience at BYU. He also encouraged them to maximize their talents, efforts and prayers to make the United States a more perfect union.*[179] *(Left bottom) The J. Reuben Clark Law School Building had been completed and dedicated in 1975— only a few years earlier than Ford's visit—and the school graduated its first class in 1976.*

DALLIN H. OAKS HOSTS FORD DURING VISIT *(Left) Ford spent considerable time on the campus of Brigham Young University as the guest of BYU President (and future Apostle) Dallin H. Oaks. Ford even enjoyed a family home evening with the Oaks family.*

FORD SPEAKS AT UTAH REPUBLICAN PARTY FUNDRAISER *(Right) Former President Ford headlined a fund-raising event for the Utah Republican party on February 5, 1980. At this point, Ford was seriously considering a run for the presidency and was frequently making appearances like this around the country. There were advantages in winning the White House in his own right and shrugging off the burden of being an "accidental president"; but Ford also had some concerns that if the Republicans nominated Ronald Reagan, he might be too conservative for the country and it would ensure a second term for Carter. However, on March 15, he announced that he would forgo seeking the GOP nomination and would support whomever the party chose.*

FORD PARTICIPATES IN FORUM AT HINCKLEY INSTITUTE OF POLITICS *(Right) Ford visited the campus of the University of Utah on February 11, 1982, where he spoke at a forum at the Hinckley Institute of Politics. He defended newly inaugurated President Ronald Reagan and said that his proposed cuts were the shock therapy the federal budget needed.*[180]

CHALLENGE LECTURE IN KINGSBURY HALL *(Opposite) He also delivered a Challenge Lecture in Kingsbury Hall (right) at the university. The associated students of the University of Utah paid Ford $12,000— the highest they had ever paid anyone up to that point—to deliver the address. Ford stressed the need for a strong national defense and defended his decision to pardon Nixon to get the Watergate era behind the country.*[181]

CAMPAIGNING FOR PARTY CANDIDATES

(Above) Ford stopped in Utah again on July 30, 1982, to attend a private fund-raising event for the reelection campaign of Representative Dan Marriott at the home of business magnate Earl Holding. (L to R: Mrs. Marilyn and Rep. Dan Marriott, Gerald Ford) He made twenty-five to thirty campaign appearances around the country to help Republican congressional candidates in the 1982 midterm elections.[182]

JEREMY RANCH
GOLF COURSE

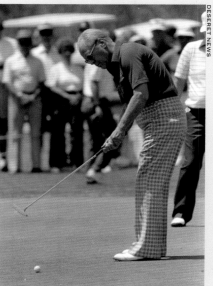

GERALD FORD AND BOB HOPE PARTICIPATE IN THE GREAT AMERICAN INDIAN GOLF SHOOTOUT *On June 1, 1986, Ford stopped in Utah to join Bob Hope for the Great American Indian Shootout—a charity golf event at Jeremy Ranch in Parley's Canyon—to raise money for Indian programs in the United States, Mexico, and Canada.*[183] *Afterward, Ford quipped, "I would like to deny all allegations by Bob Hope that during my last game of golf, I hit an eagle, a birdie, an elk and a moose."*[184]

FORD CONTINUES CAMPAIGNING FOR REPUBLICAN PARTY *(Left) Ford continued to come to Utah to campaign for Republican congressional candidates, like he did on October 13, 1986, for Salt Lake County Commissioner Tom Shimizu, who ran unsuccessfully for the U.S. House of Representatives.*

FORD VISITS BRIGHAM YOUNG UNIVERSITY FOR THE SECOND TIME *(Right) Ford made another visit to the Brigham Young University campus on March 19, 1987, where he lectured at an event in the Wilkinson Center (above) Ballroom on the problems with the Iran-Contra affair and then held an hour-long question-and-answer session with students and faculty at the David M. Kennedy Center.*

FORD SPEAKS AT E-CENTER *(Above) On September 9, 1989, Ford spoke again in Utah. He came for a number of paid speaking engagements in his later years, including at a motivational seminar at the E-Center in West Valley City in 2003.*

JIMMY CARTER

◦——

J IMMY CARTER WAS PRESIDENT of the United States from 1977–1981 and served at the same time Scott M. Matheson was governor of Utah and Spencer W. Kimball was president of the Church. He came to Utah seven times, including once as president.

CARTER SPEAKS AT UEA CONFERENCE AT THE SALT PALACE *Utah Governor Cal Rampton applauded Georgia Governor Jimmy Carter (Opposite top center), who stopped by Salt Lake City for three hours on October 7, 1976, as he campaigned for president. Carter spoke to 12,000 people in the Salt Palace (Opposite bottom and top left), who were gathered there for the annual conference of the UEA (Utah Education Association).*

POLITICAL LEADERS JOIN CARTER *(Left) Joining Carter on the stand at the UEA event were (L–R) Elizabeth Vance (Utah's Democratic national committeewoman), gubernatorial candidate Scott Matheson, Daryl McCarty (Utah's Democratic national committeeman and executive secretary of the UEA), and Senator Frank Moss (D-UT).*

DESERET NEWS

> "The family home evening program [is] especially helpful for parents and children to face the future in confidence with a spirit of truth and honor."

CARTER MEETS THE FIRST PRESIDENCY *(Above and right inset) During his October 1976 visit, Carter also spent a half hour with the First Presidency. President Kimball instructed Governor Carter about the Church's missionary program and presented him with his genealogy, a leather-bound volume of the book* Meet the Mormons, *and a leather-bound family home evening manual.[185] President Kimball discussed their visit with the media before turning the microphone over to Carter for a few remarks. Jimmy Carter praised the Church for its commitment to the integrity of the family. He said that the family home evening program was especially helpful for parents and children to face the future in confidence with a spirit of truth and honor.[186]*

DESERET NEWS

DESERET NEWS

DESPITE WARM WELCOME, CARTER CARRIES ONLY TWO COUNTIES IN UTAH ON ELECTION DAY

(Opposite and below) Carter greeted many Utahns outside the Church Office Building after his meeting with Church leaders. Despite the warm welcome Utah gave candidate Carter in 1976, on Election Day, Ford-Dole had more than 62 percent of the vote, while Carter-Mondale had less than 34 percent of the vote, losing in every Utah county but Carbon and Emery.[187]

PRESIDENT CARTER COMES TO CELEBRATE NEWLY PRO-CLAIMED "NATIONAL FAM-ILY WEEK" IN UTAH *As president, Jimmy Carter made just one visit to Utah on November 27, 1978. The president had proclaimed the week of Thanksgiving as National Family Week and felt an address in the Tabernacle at the headquarters of the pro-family LDS Church was fitting. President Carter arrived in Salt Lake City at 1:30PM, where a welcoming party consisting of President Spencer W. Kimball, Governor Scott M. Matheson and other state officials, awaited him. Members of Utah's congressional delegation, including Congressman Gunn McKay, (left—following President Carter out of the plane), arrived with the president on Air Force One.[188]*

PRESIDENTIAL MOTORCADE DRIVING AWAY FROM AF1 *(Right and above right) Carter waves before climbing into the presidential limousine. President Carter used a twenty-two-foot-long 1972 Lincoln Continental that was outfitted with armor plating and bullet-resistant glass and was powered by a 460-cubic-inch (7.5 liter) V8 engine mated to a C-6 three-speed automatic transmission.[189]*

PRESIDENT CARTER AND PRESIDENT KIMBALL HAP-PILY REUNITED *The audience in the Tabernacle applauded Presidents Carter and Kimball as they walked across the stage to their seats. On the front row (seen above President Kimball's head) was Utah industrialist Jon M. Huntsman and his eighteen-year-old son Jon Jr. (future U.S. ambassador to China and governor of Utah). Two rows behind the Huntsmans (upper right corner) was Bruce Hough, future state Republican Party chair and national committeeman. (Below) A special Primary children's chorus of forty-one ten-and eleven-year-olds sang "I Am a Child of God" at the Tabernacle event.*

President Carter's 1978 Utah visit skipped traditional protocol of working with the governor or congressional delegation to schedule the visit and instead worked directly with the Church. Although this was somewhat awkward, it was the president's preference. "Jimmy Carter really liked President Kimball and felt very comfortable going directly to him," Jim Jardine, a regional representative of the Twelve who was a White House Fellow during the Carter administration noted.[190] The event marked the first time a president of the United States traveled to Salt Lake City solely to participate in a Church-sponsored event.

(Above) President Carter, President Kimball and Governor Scott Matheson gather briefly outside the Tabernacle with President Marion G. Romney and other Church leaders before the event inside.

THE OSMONDS PERFORM FOR THE PRESIDENT *(Left) The Osmonds—who sold 102 million records worldwide, produced a hit television show, continued success as solo performers, and were always known for being faithful Latter-day Saints—sang "Love at Home" as part of the program in the Tabernacle. Jay, Alan, Donny, Jimmy, Marie, Merrill, and Wayne Osmond also presented Carter with a leather-bound volume of* The Story of a Family, *a book about themselves, which he said he would pass on to his daughter, Amy.*[194]

PRESIDENT KIMBALL SPEAKS *(Left) A rare view of a Church president speaking behind the podium designated for the American president. President Kimball emphasized that Mormons love their country and are loyal to it in his remarks. He said that the family is "the very foundation upon which the nation is built."*[191]

NAUVOO STATUE REPLICA GIVEN TO CARTER *(Right and Below) President Kimball presented President Carter with a replica of a statue that stands in Nauvoo of a mother and father helping a child learn to walk. "The family is our chief source of physical, emotional, and moral strength, our protection against adversity," President Kimball said. "It is the only institution that guarantees an environment that can insure the perpetuation of the principles that have made us strong."*[192] *President Carter was quite pleased with the statue. As he was getting into his limousine to leave Temple Square, he said "Where's my statue? I want to show that to Rosalynn tonight." Although it had originally been planned to ship it to the White House the following day, he sent an aide back into the Tabernacle to retrieve it, and Carter hand-carried it back to Washington aboard Air Force One.*[193]

HOMEFRONT VIDEO CLIPS FEATURED IN PROGRAM (Above) A packed Tabernacle joined President Carter in his celebration of the family. The program included viewing several video clips from the Church's award-winning Homefront series of public service messages encouraging stronger family ties.[195] (Below) One of the Homefront series clips, "I'll Always Make Time for You:"

I'll always make time for you.
Cause there's nothin' that I'd rather do.
Than to sit down beside you and hear all
about you.
No, there's nothin' that I'd rather do.
I promise, I'll always be there for you.
No, there's nothin' that you and I can't
get through.
As long as we sit down together and hear
out each other.
Oh, I'll always make time for you.
Families grow closer . . .
One conversation at a time.

"Your great church epitomizes to me what a family ought to be."

CARTER FEELS A KINSHIP WITH THE CHURCH'S PURPOSE (Below Left) "I know how much less difficult my own duties would be as president if your mammoth crusade for stable and strong families should be successful," President Carter said. "That is why I feel a close kinship with you in achieving this noble purpose. Your great church epitomizes to me what a family ought to be."[196]

REVERENCE IN PRAYER (Below) Jimmy Carter was an especially religious man and was not shy about showing his reverence during the benediction offered by Barbara B. Smith (Left), general president of the Relief Society. The Secret Service, of course, kept their eyes wide open during the prayers.

CARTER DEEMS VISIT TO UTAH A GREAT SUCCESS

(Left) President Carter took time to greet well-wishers following the program in the Tabernacle. "I felt I was among friends," the president said to the Utah Congressional delegation as Air Force One left Salt Lake (Below). He felt the event was a great success to conclude his National Family Week.[197]

"I felt I was among friends."

MR. AND MRS. CARTER VISIT TEMPLE SQUARE *(Right) On July 19, 1990, Jimmy and Rosalynn Carter had a layover in Salt Lake City and made a quick trip to Temple Square. Pam Misbach, a sister missionary from California, showed them around. "He was very nice, very personable," Sister Misbach reported. During the tour, the thirty-ninth president asked about the significance of temple marriage. Rosalynn asked some questions about the Book of Mormon. They paused for a photo near the Christus statue in the Visitor's Center (see above). As they were leaving, Jimmy Carter politely thanked Sister Misbach for the tour and kissed her on the cheek.*[198]

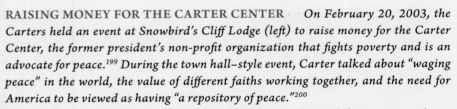

RAISING MONEY FOR THE CARTER CENTER On February 20, 2003, the Carters held an event at Snowbird's Cliff Lodge (left) to raise money for the Carter Center, the former president's non-profit organization that fights poverty and is an advocate for peace.[199] During the town hall–style event, Carter talked about "waging peace" in the world, the value of different faiths working together, and the need for America to be viewed as having "a repository of peace."[200]

The Carter Center, founded in 1982, strives to give the world's poorest people access to skills and knowledge they can use to identify solutions that will improve their own lives. It also houses a number of peace programs that strengthen election processes and advance human rights and different health programs that combat illnesses others often ignore.

In 2002, President Carter received the Nobel Peace Prize for his work in finding peaceful solutions to international conflicts, advancing democracy and human rights, and promoting economic and social development through The Carter Center.

CARTER SPEAKS AT SUNDANCE TREE ROOM AUTHOR SERIES

On September 5, 2004, the Carters came to Utah's mountains again—this time to speak at the Sundance resort's Tree Room Author Series.[201] Carter spoke about his latest book and first work of fiction, *The Hornet's Nest, a historical novel set in the Deep South during the Revolutionary War.*[202]

CARTER CREDITS ROBERT REDFORD FOR HIS PRESIDENTIAL VICTORY

(Left) "I was probably president because of Bob Redford," Carter said. "You can imagine the feeling of a Georgia peanut farmer who is scheduled to have three televised debates with the incumbent president of the United States: I didn't know what in the world I was going to do. And here came Robert Redford to Georgia, and he had a 16 mm film of the Nixon-Kennedy debates, and he sat on our living room floor and we played the debate over and over, and he gave me advice." Carter said that advice gave him the confidence he needed to defeat Ford.

"So since I won by a fairly narrow margin, I think it's fair to say that all the things that I did as president, good or bad, Bob Redford has a share in them," he joked.[203]

BOOK SIGNING IN SUGAR HOUSE *(Below) On November 29, 2005, Carter stopped by the Sugar House Barnes & Noble bookstore to sign copies of his new book,* Our Endangered Values: America's Moral Crisis. *More than 3,000 lined up to greet the former president.*[204]

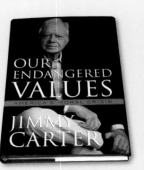

DESERET NEWS

DESERET NEWS

BOOK SIGNING AT THE KING'S ENGLISH BOOKSTORE *(Left and Above)* On October 28, 2010, Carter made his first stop in Utah in five years. He signed copies of his latest book, *The White House Diary,* for thousands who came by The King's English Bookshop.[205] The former president also spoke with the local media on his seventh Utah visit *(Above Right).*

WHITE HOUSE DIARY

JIMMY CARTER

RONALD REAGAN

OFFICIAL WHITE HOUSE PHOTO

Ronald W. Reagan was president of the United States from 1981–1989 and served at the same time Scott M. Matheson and Norman H. Bangerter were governors of Utah and Spencer W. Kimball and Ezra Taft Benson were presidents of the Church. He came to Utah at least fifteen times, including three times as president.

REAGAN HONORED BY UTAH STATE UNIVERSITY *Reagan came to Utah with Sen. Barry Goldwater on April 28, 1962, to receive the Robins Award "for outstanding inspiration to America's youth" from Utah State University. This was during the time that Reagan was in transition from actor to politician.*

REAGAN SPEAKING TO CROWD AT SALT LAKE AIRPORT *He was back June 15, 1968, but this time as California's governor, for a brief airport visit. But it was on July 12, 1968 that Governor Reagan came to Utah for his first substantive visit and spoke to a huge crowd at the Salt Lake International Airport (Right). Many wanted Reagan to be the Republican nominee, and he remained coy up until the August convention.*

GOVERNOR REAGAN MAKING THE ROUNDS IN SALT LAKE CITY

Reagan arrived at the airport at 4:30PM and, after his brief speech to the crowd there, went on to a courtesy call at Church headquarters, a speech at a fundraising dinner, and then a trip to The Terrace ballroom to rouse the delegates at the Utah Republican convention with a keynote address.[206] *Reagan received numerous ovations from the delegates at the state convention (Above) as he blasted the Democrats. "What we face today is a choice—a choice of placing faith in a government which has lost faith in the people or of rediscovering the ability*

to govern ourselves," he said.[207] *LaMar Rawlings, an unsuccessful candidate for governor, had signs near where Reagan spoke.*

REAGAN MEETS PRESIDENT JOSEPH FIELDING SMITH & WIFE *Reagan stopped at the Church Administration Building for a courtesy call on Church leaders, where President Joseph Fielding Smith and his wife, Jessie, enjoyed meeting him (Below left). President Smith was president of the Quorum of the Twelve Apostles at the time and a counselor to President David O. McKay, whose health prohibited him from meeting with Governor Reagan. (Below right - shown walking up the steps of the Church Administration Building.)*

OGDEN STANDARD EXAMINER

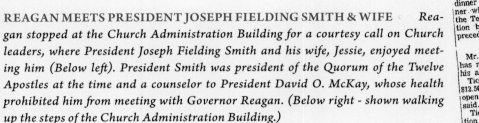

Reagan Dates Address At GOP Dinner in S.L.

SALT LAKE CITY—California Gov. Ronald Reagan will be featured speaker at the annual Lincoln Day dinner here Feb. 13, sponsored by Weber and Salt Lake County Republicans.

Frank S. Blair of Marriott, dinner chairman, said the dinner will be held at 7 p.m. in the Terrace Ballroom. A reception by special invitation will precede the dinner at 6 p.m.

HASN'T SAID

Mr. Blair said Gov. Reagan has not announced the topic of his address.

Tickets for the dinner are $12.50 per person. The dinner is open to the public, Mr. Blair said.

Ticket sales are under direction of Grant Bingham and may be obtained through any legislative district chairmen. Con-firmation on ticket sales should be made by Feb. 9, said Mr. Blair.

GOV. RONALD REAGAN
Lincoln Day Speaker

DESERET NEWS

DESERET NEWS

DESERET NEWS

REAGAN SPEAKS AT LINCOLN DAY BANQUET
(Above and Opposite) On February 13, 1974, Reagan returned to Salt Lake City to speak at a Lincoln Day banquet at The Terrace, which gave him a chance to greet some local girl scouts and Senator Wallace Bennett (R-UT).

California's Gov. Ronald Reagan and Republican
Party Chairman George Bush cross trails for few

minutes while here for separate appearances to
raise money and boost enthusiasm for Utah GOP.

Watergate's Fading

Gov. Reagan Urges GOP Action

By Douglas L. Parker
Tribune Political Editor

Gov. Ronald Reagan told Utah Republicans Wednesday night to leave the
doomsaying behind in approaching this
year's elections — "cast out the Chicken
Littles of our society.

The Californian was part of a double-
barrelled speaking fare for the Utah GOP
to mark traditional activities connected
with Lincoln Day observances.

National party chairman George Bush,
preceding the governor in a noontime appearance, declared that Watergate should
take a backseat to the rising fortunes of
Republicans in the congressional elections.

Speaking to more than 800 diners at a
$25-per-couple fund raiser in The Ter-
race, 464 S. Main, Gov. Reagan said Re-

publicans must make it plain that no one
is more disappointed or indignant at the
part of Watergate cast over the victory of
1972.

'Looms Before Bar'

"Watergate looms before the bar of
justice," he said, "and that should be
looked upon with pride because there are
not many countries that wouldn't have
swept it under the rug."

"But let justice be done . . . . let the
innocent be cleared, and let us get on
with the business of running the United
States of America," the governor said to
applause of the partisans, including most
GOP elected state officials and party officers. Sen. Wallace F. Bennett introduced Gov. Reagan.

On the basis of philosophy, the party
still represents the majority in the coun-

try, Gov. Reagan contended. Democrats
are still in the grips of the "shop-worn
welfarism" of their party leaders, he
added.

Cites Immoral Acts

The illegal and immoral acts of a few
in connection with Watergate must be
balanced with an administration philosophy of easing foreign tensions, that must
cope with inflation and bureaucracy built
up by previous Democratic administrations, and the fact that "there are no
young" Americans dying in rice paddies
over there" . . . Gov. Reagan said.

Republicans, it must be remembered,
are the "OUT PARTY" IN Congress,
and not responsible for policy, he said.
He decried what he called people in high

See Page B-10, Column 1

REAGAN SPEAKS AT 1976 REPUBLICAN BICENTENNIAL DINNER AT THE SALT PALACE *(Right) Reagan wowed 750 Republicans at a Bicentennial dinner in the Salt Palace on April 7, 1976, and he was heartily welcomed when he keynoted the state convention on July 16 of that year. He was aggressively wooing supporters that year as he made a solid—but unsuccessful—challenge to President Ford for the GOP nomination.*

"I CAME PREPARED TO GIVE A SPEECH" *(Right) Senator Jake Garn spoke at the state convention to plead the case for Utah to send delegates supportive of President Ford to the national convention, but it was Reagan's speech that won over the crowd. During his speech, Reagan was notified that he had only two minutes left, and he replied, "I came prepared to make a speech." State Party Chairman Richard Richards allowed Reagan to continue and apologized to the delegates for not informing Reagan in advance of the time limit.[209]*

Reagan brought his wife, Nancy, with him to Utah for the 1976 state convention on her first visit to the state.

REAGAN MEETS WITH CHURCH PRESIDENCY COUNSELORS *(Above) Reagan met briefly with the two counselors of President Spencer W. Kimball— Marion G. Romney and N. Eldon Tanner—who presented the governor with some books about the Church. Reagan expressed his admiration to them about the Church's welfare program as a means of rehabilitating people and helping them escape the cycle of poverty.[208]*

REAGAN CAMPAIGNS FOR HATCH *(Above) Reagan came a third time to Utah in that bicentennial year, this time on October 27, 1976, to campaign for a little-known forty-two-year-old lawyer named Orrin Hatch. Elaine and Orrin Hatch listen to Reagan at an event, which helped Hatch win his U.S. Senate seat.*

REAGAN'S CITIZENS FOR THE REPUBLIC POLITICAL ACTION COMMITTEE

(Below) In 1977 Reagan visited twice, first on June 25 to kick off a series of nationwide seminars with a luncheon at Hotel Utah and again in October to speak at a governor's conference. Reagan's Citizens for the Republic political action committee kept him involved with various events around the country throughout the Carter years.

STATE REPUBLICAN CONVENTION IN SALT LAKE GETS BIG SURPRISE *(Far Left) Reagan made a stop in St. George on July 7, 1978, to stump for Representative Dan Marriott's re-election, but it was his appearance at the state Republican convention on June 27, 1980, that journalist LaVarr Webb described as "among the biggest political extravaganzas ever staged in Utah."[210] The entire Osmond family and a brass band whipped up the 2,500 delegates into a patriotic frenzy , and then Reagan appeared with the drop of thousands of red, white, and blue balloons. After Reagan spoke, a live circus elephant was paraded through the hall, adding to the razzle-dazzle of the convention scene.*

Senators Hatch and Garn relished the moment of the Republican presidential nominee interacting with a live symbol of the party. "Ronald Reagan wooed, wowed and won Utah Republicans Saturday," LaVarr Webb wrote of the convention in the Deseret News, "arousing waves of applause, cheers, and even tears of joy as he promised tax cuts, less government, more energy, a tougher defense, a turnover of public lands, and more prosperity for all."[211]

When Reagan quit smoking in the 1960s, he began eating jellybeans. On his first day as governor of California, Reagan received a big bowl of jellybeans from candy-maker Henry Rowland that he continually filled and passed around at cabinet meetings. At the inauguration parties in 1981, more than 40 million jellybeans were consumed. Once in the White House, Reagan shared jellybeans in cabinet meetings, with senior staff, and with guests as he passed around a crystal jar filled with the treat. When he traveled, Reagan had jellybeans in Air Force One and in his presidential limo. He had jellybeans present in each of his three presidential visits to Utah. Sometimes on his visits, the president would hand out small packages of the candy.

In the summer of 1988, Richard Snelgrove, a part owner of Salt Lake City–based Snelgrove Ice Cream Co., Inc. and a candidate for Congress, met Reagan in the White House. He was introduced to the president as an ice cream–maker, and Reagan asked him if he had ever made jellybean ice cream. Snelgrove replied that he had not, nor had he ever thought to, but that he was open to the idea. The president was apparently very serious about the inquiry because on July 13, Snelgrove received a call from Judy Butler of the White House political office, requesting a shipment of jellybean ice cream. Before a week had transpired, the Utah ice cream–maker had customized the new flavor and had shipped six gallons to 1600 Pennsylvania Avenue.[212]

RONALD FOX

DESERET NEWS

President Reagan, shaking hands in a multitude of well-wishers, makes his way back to his limousine after speaking at the Hooper picnic Sept. 10.

A presidential visit

Reagan's overnight stop refuels fires of support

By DANIEL GOLD
Standard-Examiner Staff

Beyond all else, The Day The President Came To Town may be remembered as the day Ogden came of age.

Surely the city had never seen anything like Sept. 9, 1982 before: the long motorcade speeding across the 24th Street overpass, the press buses, the hum of excitement in the lobby of the Hilton, the feeling that the town had, indeed, gone Big League.

As the president renewed political ties, area residents — regardless of persuasion — felt a thrill common to those "close to the source." After all, the President was here.

The attraction was as understandable as it was irresistable: President Reagan is news, and wherever he stays he becomes the eye of a news hurricane.

So it was for Ogden. The carnival began about 4 p.m. courtesy of "The National Press."

The "Zoo Plane" carrying a horde of some 115 reporters, sound technicians and cameramen arrived minutes before Air Force One landed at 4:07 p.m. at Hill Air Force Base.

Hill employees looking out windows or mingling near the airstrip could see the pack of journalists raring near where the president's aircraft would unload its precious cargo.

As President Reagan — accompanied by Sen. Orrin Hatch and GOP national chairman Richard Richards — descended the airplane stairway, cameramen ignored press boundaries and jostled for position about 25 feet away. "getting video" for the nightly news broadcast.

While Gov. and Mrs. Scott M. Matheson and Maj. Gen. Leo Marquez, commander of the Ogden Air Logistics Center, greeted the president, reporters called questions to him about the day's hot news, the congressional override of his appropriations veto.

If spectators had hoped for a closer look, they were disappointed. Massive presidential limousines were driven out

and whisked him away at the head of a 35-car motorcade which stopped traffic on Interstate 15 — delaying hundreds of unwary motorists — before exiting into Ogden.

The national press, following in three chartered buses, seemed to embody the frenzy of the trip — which had begun in Washington and had stopped over in Kansas for several hours. Indeed, the clamor was infectious.

Attention focused on the Hilton, where Reagan held a brief question-and-answer session.

Reporters excluded from the session groaned in the lobby while curiosity seekers nervously fingered their cameras, hoping to steal a glimpse and snap a picture of the president, who remained hidden from view.

The president then met for an hour with Republican party chairmen from 11 Western states.

Meanwhile, the mood remained lively and playful, with interplay between reporters and such Republican luminaries as Richards and Hatch resembling that at a political convention.

Because of the influx of people at the hotel, security remained extremely tight well after the president retired for the evening about 9 p.m. Even registered Hilton guests had to identify themselves before they were allowed to return to their rooms.

Yet the festive air continued through the night.

White House advance staffers arranged to take interested out-of-state journalists to Bigfoot's, a country-western bar at 31st and Wall.

Other reporters were found Friday morning still talking with GOP officials at the Hilton bar or across the street at a drinking club.

In his first night in Ogden, Reagan didn't need to make any appearance to spark interest and excitement. Knowing he was here, along with the trappings and glamor of his entourage, was somehow enough.

Enroute to the Ogden Hilton from Hill AFB Thursday afternoon, the presidential motorcade cruises over the 24th Street viaduct into the city.

DESERET NEWS

AIR FORCE ONE LANDS AT HILL AIR FORCE BASE

(Above) President Reagan made his first of three visits to Utah as president on September 10, 1982. Senator Orrin Hatch (R-UT) accompanied him on his flight in Air Force One (shown descending behind Reagan), which landed at Hill Air Force Base in Ogden.

DESERET NEWS

REAGAN TOURS THE OGDEN WELFARE CANNERY *The president enjoyed a tour of the Ogden Welfare Cannery on September 10, 1982. The tour was led by President Gordon B. Hinckley of the First Presidency, along with Elder Thomas S. Monson of the Twelve. Reagan appointed Thomas S. Monson to the Presidential Private Initiatives Task Force to encourage volunteer activity and private charity in helping the needy. Reagan was always greatly impressed with the Church welfare system, had toured a similar facility in Sacramento while governor, and said to the media that day, "What I think is that if more people had this idea back when the Great Depression hit, there wouldn't be any government welfare today, or need for it."*[213]

(Right) President Reagan was especially touched that volunteers from all walks of life came to volunteer at the cannery to help their neighbors in need. "It's an idea that once characterized our nation," he said after the tour. "It's an idea that should be reborn nationwide. It holds the key to the renewal of America in the years ahead."[214]

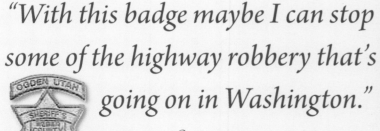

THE BUCKAROO STOPS HERE

With Best Wishes
Ronald Reagan
40th PRESIDENT
OF THE
UNITED STATES

REPUBLICAN VOLUNTEER PICNIC IN HOOPER

(Below) After his tour of the cannery, President Reagan attended an old-fashioned Republican picnic at a park in Hooper. Amid bales of hay, wagon wheels, and the scent of nearby pastures, Reagan wowed the thousands who had waited patiently in the rain to hear the president. In fact, some had driven from St. George for the event, starting their journey at 3AM.[215]

"It's always a pleasure to come here to your state," Reagan said. "This is almost as big a crowd as an Osmond family reunion!" He spoke about being made an honorary member of the Weber County Sheriff's Mounted Posse moments before. The audience laughed when he told them that as the posse rode up he thought that he was "going to get put up in the slammer." But, he said, as he held up his posse badge, "now with this badge maybe I can stop some of the highway robbery that's going on in Washington."[216]

(Right) Unidentified, Congressmen Dan Marriott, Jim Hansen, President Ronald Reagan, National Party Chairman Dick Richards (behind the President), Elaine Hatch, Republican State Party Chairman Chuck Akerlow.

"With this badge maybe I can stop some of the highway robbery that's going on in Washington."

UTAH REPUBLICAN
VOLUNTEER PICNIC

"This is almost as big a crowd as an Osmond family reunion!"

The handiwork of five Utah women became the focus of attention at the Ladies of the Senate luncheon in 1983. The luncheon, held in Washington DC, was held in honor of First Lady Nancy Reagan. Kathleen Garn, wife of Sen. Jake Garn (R-Utah), organized the presentation of a gift for Mrs. Reagan, and felt

DESERET NEWS

it was important for her to receive something distinctive that would represent the industrious women of the Beehive State. The Ladies of the Senate is a National Red Cross service organization made up of wives of U.S. Senators.

DESERET NEWS

PRESIDENT REAGAN RETURNS JUST A FEW WEEKS LATER TO SPEAK AT REPUBLICAN RALLY *(Right) Reagan's second visit as president to Utah came just a few weeks after his first, on October 29, 1982. The president spoke to 6,000 in the Salt Palace for a Republican rally days before the midterm election. (L to R) Senator Orrin Hatch, Senator Jake Garn, and Congressman Jim Hansen applauded Reagan, who said that with their help "we can give the American people something brand new, a recovery meant to last."* [217]

DESERET NEWS

DESERET NEWS

(Above) The crowd in the Salt Palace roared their approval of Reagan, and one man even interrupted the president's speech by yelling, "We love you!" The rest of the crowd met the statement with a wild standing ovation. Reagan replied, "I love you, too." [218]

(Left) Twice in his remarks Reagan referred to Hatch as his friend, and the president stressed the need to keep conservatives in the Senate. His pleas worked, and Hatch was successful in his reelection over Salt Lake City Mayor Ted Wilson. Additionally, Republicans nationally maintained control of the Senate. [219]

PRESIDENT REAGAN RETURNS TO UTAH IN 1984 *(Right) Reagan's third and final visit to Utah as president was on September 3–4, 1984. He spoke at the American Legion convention, met with Church leaders, and attended a midmorning reception for the Republican Party's Elephant Club of significant donors.*[220]

REAGAN SPEAKS AT AMERICAN LEGION CONVENTION *(Right) President Reagan brought 12,000 Legionnaires to their feet in the Salt Palace with a powerful address that weaved together economic and patriotic themes. "Keeping alive the hope of human freedom is America's mission," he said, "and we cannot shrink from the task or falter in the call of duty."*[221]

President Hinckley read some of the Book of Mormon to President Reagan, and it launched a twenty-minute discussion. Church leaders gave Reagan his own copy of the scriptures during his 1984 visit with Church officials, and President Hinckley read to him some of Ether chapter 2, concerning the divine destiny of America. President Reagan said he had "the same sense of the destiny of the United States" as expressed in those verses. He said that "those who came to this country for religious freedom were much more successful than those who came for gold." The president also shared his feeling that "without God and the help of a Supreme Being," the burdens he carried "would be impossible to face."[222]

REAGAN AND HINCKLEY SHARE A LAUGH

(Above) Reagan had a twenty-minute meeting in the Church Administration Building led by second counselor in the First Presidency Gordon B. Hinckley, with whom he got along especially well. All members of the Quorum of the Twelve attended, along with Primary General President Dwan J. Young, Young Women General President Ardeth G. Kapp, and Relief Society General President Barbara W. Winder.[223]

(Left) Former Eisenhower cabinet member Ezra Taft Benson, then president of the Twelve, had a good discussion with President Reagan. President Benson would visit Reagan in the White House in 1986 after becoming president of the Church.

REAGAN'S LAST VISIT TO UTAH

(Right) Reagan came to Utah only once after leaving the White House, on February 15, 1991, to speak at Brigham Young University. Utah's Lieutenant Governor Val Oveson and Salt Lake City Mayor Palmer DePaulis greeted him as he deplaned. Reagan also spent forty-five minutes visiting with Presidents Gordon B. Hinckley and Thomas S. Monson at Church headquarters before going south to Provo.[224]

REX LEE PERSONALLY INVITED FORMER PRESIDENT REAGAN TO SPEAK AT BYU

(Right) Reagan and BYU President Rex Lee sang the national anthem with hands over hearts at the beginning of the program in Provo. Lee, father of future U.S. Senator Mike Lee and Utah Supreme Court Justice Tom Lee, had served as Solicitor General of the United States under Reagan from 1981–1985. It was his personal invitation that brought the former president to BYU. In his address, Reagan spoke about service and valuing freedom. "As you climb the ladder of success, do not skip over the rung labeled humanity. Stop to think what you are giving to society," Reagan said in his speech. "Think about those whose lives may not be as blessed as yours. As you enter the real world, do not take freedom for granted," Reagan counseled. "It is a precious gift which we must constantly seek to preserve. It's so easy to take things for granted at your age, but none of us will be here forever. Make every day count."[225]

REAGAN RECEIVES A BYU SWEATSHIRT

(Left) "I am honored to be here today at BYU, speaking to the students and faculty," Reagan said. "All of you should be very proud of your university, founded in 1875. BYU is strong, a birthplace of many talented leaders and athletes. As students you've made all of us very proud and also very optimistic about what this country will accomplish in the years ahead. A whole new world is opening up to you students." Before he left, Reagan added, "I have great admiration for your school here. I know how great it is and know how successful you are in so many ways."[226]

REAGAN RECEIVES THANKS FOR VISITING UTAH ONE LAST TIME *(Above) Senator Garn, Senator Hatch, and Governor Norm Bangerter thanked Reagan for making one last visit to Utah after a career filled with memorable stops in the Beehive State.*

DEPARTING WITH LOVE
(Right and Opposite) Reagan bid farewell to Utah before departing for the last time. Fewer than three years later, he would announce to the nation his struggles with Alzheimer's and declare, "I now begin the journey that will lead me into the sunset of my life. I know that for America there will always be a bright dawn ahead. Thank you, my friends. May God always bless you."[227]

O.J. cop Mark Fuhrman • The world's richest little girl fu

FEBRUARY 27, 1995 $2.45

People weekly

Courageous families tell their storie

ALZHEIMER

Mike Myers
• Dad was 'terrified'

She
• N

Jay Rockefeller
• A mother's agony

Ronald Reagan
• 'Fading slowly'

Nov. 5, 1994

My Fellow Americans,

In opening our hearts, we hope this might promote greater awareness of this condition. Perhaps it will encourage a clearer understanding of the individuals and families who are affected by it.

I have recently been told that I am one of the Americans who will be afflicted with Alzheimer's Disease.

Upon learning this news, Nancy & I had to decide whether as private citizens we would keep this a private matter or whether we would make this news known in a public way.

In the past Nancy suffered from breast cancer and I had my cancer surgeries. We found through our open disclosures we were able to raise public awareness. We were happy that as a result many more people underwent testing. They were treated in early stages and able to return to normal, healthy lives.

So now, we feel it is important to share it with you. In opening our hearts, we hope this might promote greater awareness of this condition. Perhaps it will encourage a clearer understanding of the individuals and families who are affected by it.

At the moment I feel just fine. I intend to live the remainder of the years God gives me on this earth doing the things I have always done. I will continue to share life's journey with my beloved Nancy and my family. I plan to enjoy the great outdoors and stay in touch with my friends and supporters.

Unfortunately, as Alzheimer's Disease progresses, the family often bears a heavy burden. I only wish there was some way I could spare Nancy from this painful experience. When the time comes I am confident that with your help she will face it with faith and courage.

In closing let me thank you, the American people for giving me the great honor of allowing me to serve as your President. When the Lord calls me home, (sic) whenever that may be I will face it with the greatest love for this country of ours and eternal optimism for its future.

I now begin the journey that will lead me into the sunset of my life. I know that for America there will always be a bright dawn ahead.

Thank you, my friends. May God always bless you.

Sincerely,

Ronald Reagan

Ronald Reagan

[The above letter is reproduced exactly as written and was obtained through the archives at the Ronald W. Reagan Presidential Library & Museum.]

DESERET NEWS

GONE BUT NOT FORGOTTEN *(Above) HeeHaw Farms in Layton, Utah etched the likeness of U.S. president Ronald Reagan in a corn maze Monday, September 20, 2004 (just two months after Reagan's death). The 600-foot image covered eight acres and contained nearly three miles of twists and turns.*

Ronald Wilson Reagan died on June 5, 2004, after his battle with Alzheimer's. In response, President Hinckley and his counselors released a statement that lauded Reagan "as a man of uncommon decency and dignity."[228] President Hinckley continued to personally mourn Reagan's passing. In New York City's Radio City Music Hall, he shared with Church members, "This is a very sober time in the history our nation. Buried yesterday [June 11] was President Ronald Reagan. I do not care whether you are a Democrat or a Republican. He was a man who left his mark upon the world. He was a good friend of the Church." After sharing his many experiences with the U.S. president, President Hinckley said, "I counted

DESERET NEWS

him as a friend. I have tonight in my shirt these cuff links which he gave me, which have on their face the seal of the President of the United States of America, and on the reverse side the name of Ronald Reagan."[229]

(Above) President Hinckley wearing his Reagan cufflinks while speaking at BYU graduation.

RONALD FOX COLLECTION

AMERICA'S REDDEST STATE

GEORGE BUSH

NATIONAL PORTRAIT GALLERY

GEORGE HERBERT WALKER BUSH WAS PRESIDENT of the United States from 1989–1993 and served at the same time Norm Bangerter was governor of Utah and Ezra Taft Benson was president of the Church. Bush came to Utah at least eight times, including three times as president.

BUSH SPEAKS AT LINCOLN DAY DINNER *(Opposite) George Bush made his first visit to Utah on February 13, 1974. He was chairman of the Republican National Committee at the time and was speaking at an annual Lincoln Day dinner fundraiser for the party. Bush had served as a congressman from Texas and as U.S. ambassador to the United Nations, so he was able to speak on a wide range of topics. A few months after Bush's visit to Salt Lake, President Ford appointed him to represent the country in the People's Republic of China.*

BUSH AT REPUBLICAN RECEPTION AT THE LION HOUSE

(Below) After representing the United States in China and then serving as director of the Central Intelligence Agency for a year, Bush was among seven candidates seeking the 1980 Republican nomination. On May 14, 1979, he stopped in Salt Lake City to call on Church leaders and to speak at a reception of Republicans at the Lion House (Left). Although he was down in the opinion polls, at the gathering he quipped, "I'm way up in qualifications and background for the job of president."[230]

VICE PRESIDENT BUSH ADVOCATES FOR REAGAN'S ECONOMIC PLAN IN THE UTAH LEGISLATURE *(Right) Ronald Reagan chose Bush to be his running mate, and they were successful in 1980. Bush made his first visit to Utah as the nation's vice president on January 29, 1982, where he advocated for Reagan's economic plan in the Utah Legislature (with Senate President Miles "Cap" Ferry behind him). Later that trip, he raised $50,000 at a Republican fundraiser, campaigning for Senator Orrin Hatch's reelection.*[231]

To N. Eldon Tanner
With best wishes — highest personal regard
Cap Bush

FIRST PRESIDENCY COUNSELORS PRESENT BUSHES WITH STATUE REPLICA *(Left) While in town in 1982, Vice President and Barbara Bush called on Church headquarters. With Church President Spencer W. Kimball ill, they met with his counselors: (L to R) President N. Eldon Tanner, Barbara Bush, George Bush, Marion G. Romney, and Gordon B. Hinckley. The First Presidency members presented the vice president with a replica of the Monument to Women statue.*[232]

VICE PRESIDENT BUSH CALLS ON NEW CHURCH PRESIDENT EZRA TAFT BENSON *(Above and Opposite) On March 1, 1986, Air Force Two landed in Salt Lake City again as Vice President and Mrs. Bush stopped in for a visit. They called on new Church President Ezra Taft Benson, who, along with first counselor Gordon B. Hinckley, presented the Bushes with a ceramic sculpture of a seagull. President Benson explained to them the account of the seagulls saving the pioneer crop from crickets.*[233] *The Bushes also talked with the leaders about world affairs. "I am not a member of your Church, but I have great respect for the Mormon people," Bush said. Vice President Bush kept calling President Benson "Mr. Secretary" and would then correct himself. "All my life the name Ezra Taft Benson has been associated with the post of Secretary of Agriculture," he said, "and I have a hard time calling Ezra Taft Benson anything but 'Mr. Secretary.'"*[234]

The honor of your presence
is requested at the ceremonies attending the
Inauguration of the
President and Vice President
of the United States
January twentieth
Nineteen hundred eighty-nine

Wendell H. Ford, Chairman,
George J. Mitchell, Ted Stevens,
Jim Wright, Thomas S. Foley,
Robert H. Michel

Joint Congressional
Committee on Inaugural Ceremonies.

Please present the enclosed   11:30 A.M.
card of admission

> *"The nation still marvels at the courage of Utah's settlers more than a century ago, harnessing faith and muscle and technological ingenuity to build a civilization."*

DESERET NEWS

Metro edition

139TH YEAR — No. 220   SALT LAKE CITY, UTAH   FRIDAY, JANUARY 20, 1989

Bush takes nation's helm in 'new breeze of freedom'

By Lee Davidson
Deseret News Washington Bureau chief

WASHINGTON — Saying a new breeze of freedom is blowing in the world, George Herbert Walker Bush began his push for a kinder, gentler nation Friday as he took the oath of office as the 41st president of the United States.

His wife, Barbara, held two Bibles for him to swear the oath upon, their family Bible and the same Bible that George Washington used in the first inauguration 200 years ago. Chief Justice William Rhenquist administered the oath.

Bush shunned the formal, black-tie clothing that most of his recent predecessors wore at inaugurations and appeared in a simple business suit — a move that Steve Studdert, the Utahn who headed Bush's inaugural committee, said was a gesture to reinforce his "common man" ideals.

His inaugural speech also stressed such themes, and called for a more moral America to use strong will to overcome problems with poverty, drugs and the budget deficit — but to still remain strong to defend freedom worldwide. (See excerpts on A2.)

"I do not mistrust the future; I do not fear what is ahead. For our problems are large, but our heart is larger. Our challenges are great, but our will is greater. And if our laws are endless, God's love is truly boundless," he said.

His first act as president was to offer a prayer at the opening of his speech. "Make us strong to do your work," he prayed to God.

"If the man you have chosen to lead this government can help to make a difference; if he can celebrate the quieter, deeper successes that are made not of gold and silk, but of better hearts and finer souls; if he can do these things, then he must.

"America is never wholly herself unless she is engaged in high moral purpose. We as a people have such a purpose today. It is to make kinder the face of the nation and gentler the face of the world," he said.

"We will turn to the only resource we have that in times of need always

Please see BUSH on A3

Justice Rehnquist swears in Pres. Bush as Barbara Bush holds Bibles. Ex-Pres. Reagan is at right.   UPI photo

George Bush took the oath of office as 41st president.   AP photo

THE UTAH VISIT OF
THE PRESIDENT OF
THE UNITED STATES OF AMERICA

GEORGE BUSH

WEDNESDAY, SEPTEMBER 18, 1991
SALT LAKE CITY INTERNATIONAL AIRPORT
Gates open at noon for 1:00 p.m. arrival

Follow signs   Outdoor event

PRESIDENT BUSH PRAISES UTAH *President Bush made his first visit to Utah as president of the United States on September 18–19, 1991, when he swung through to help garner support for domestic programs. He arrived at the Salt Lake airport and spoke to the cheering of thousands, with Utah Governor Norm Bangerter and U.S. Senator Jake Garn at his side. Bush praised Utah for its commitment to family and applauded the state's high public education test scores, even though Utahns spend less per pupil than any other state. "You've clearly shown that 'tax and spend' is not the formula in a quality education," he said. Bush also said that Utah stands for courage. "The nation still marvels at the courage of Utah's settlers more than a century ago, harnessing faith and muscle and technological ingenuity to build a civilization and make the desert blossom." After the airport rally, the president went to the downtown Marriott to speak at a $1,000-a-person Republican Party fundraiser.*[235]

BUSH VISITS PRIMARY CHILDREN'S HOSPITAL *In his 1991 visit, President Bush's motorcade passed the typical protesters (Right top) and drove to Primary Children's Hospital (Right bottom). There, the president visited with young patients, gave them high-fives, and even played catch. He also spoke briefly to patients, hospital officials, and staff (Above), stating that the hospital is "a monument to America's volunteer spirit." He concluded his remarks saying, "I'm confident you will remain one of the finest pediatric care centers in the entire world."[236]*

BUSH HAS MOVING VISIT WITH CHURCH LEADERS *(Inset) President Bush made a second visit to Utah as president on July 17–18, 1992, where he held a briefing Friday afternoon with Governor Bangerter and other Utah Republican leaders and then called on President Hinckley, President Monson, and eleven members of the Quorum of the Twelve (Right).*

When asked afterward in the Administration Building's lobby what was discussed, Bush replied, "It was a total tour of the whole world. I learned a great deal from them." When the media asked a political question, the president said he was not going to answer the question "in this hallowed setting. It would be most inappropriate."[237] President Hinckley recorded in his journal of the incident, "I felt it was a classic answer, and the expression of a gentleman who carries respect for that which is good and sacred."[238] President Hinckley also recorded Bush's genuine interest in the missionary program: "We talked about our missionary work in various parts of the world. He asked how we go about opening a new country. He seemed sincerely curious. We told him the procedures we follow. We talked about our program to strengthen families. He was deeply interested. We were free to ask anything, and he did not hesitate to respond. He talked openly and freely and in a very friendly way."

President Bush said to President Hinckley: "The fact that your church has an active mission program around the world is a wonderful thing. Not only does the program project commitment by the individual missionaries, but it also shows the church's concern for this wonderful but troubled world in which we live. You do care and that comes through loud and clear."[239]

BUSH
QUAYLE 92

BYU & Utah Families
Welcome President Bush

MARRIOTT CENTER SPEECH LACED WITH UTAH HUMOR *The morning of Saturday, July 18, 1992, Bush spoke to more than 15,000 fans in the Marriott Center at Brigham Young University. His election year rhetoric was laced with humor and Utah references, much to the delight of BYU President Rex Lee (seen laughing behind the president in above photo) and all in attendance. The president promised that if given a Republican Congress and a line-item veto, for example, he would do with federal government waste what Utah Jazz forward Karl Malone will do to opponents' basketball shots in the Barcelona Olympics—"swat it into the front row." He spoke about family values and said, "We need to restore the special values that have carried this nation for 200 years . . . Americans need to understand something that you all know very, very well—no other success can compensate for failure in the home." The crowd jumped to a standing ovation in approval of President Bush quoting this famous line from past Church President David O. McKay.*[240] *(Middle right) As Bush waved good-bye at the end of his remarks, prominent leaders were his backdrop, including Senate candidate Joe Cannon, Senator Jake Garn, Provo Mayor Lewis Billings, and Utah industrialist Jon Huntsman Sr.*

E · PLURIBUS · UNUM

The Utah Visit of
THE PRESIDENT OF
THE UNITED STATES OF AMERICA
GEORGE BUSH
Saturday, July 18, 1992 — 10:00 a.m.
Brigham Young University Marriott Center, Provo, Utah
Doors open at 8 a.m.; program begins at 10 a.m.
Seating on first-come, first-seated basis

Paid for by Bush/Quayle Primary, Inc.

BUSH
QUAYLE
92

PRESIDENT BUSH SPEAKS TO OUT-DOORSMEN AT RED BUTTE GAR-DEN *After speaking at BYU, President Bush returned to Salt Lake City for a visit with outdoorsmen at a gathering at Red Butte Garden (Above). The president, who went from business to wilderness in a matter of hours, changed from his suit to outdoor clothing in large RVs that were brought to the site. Bush, a member of Ducks Unlimited, shared with the audience his lifelong enthusiasm for hunting and fishing. The meeting was filmed for a commercial for the fall campaign and focused on hunting and fishing. During the event and filming, Bush sat between Utah Lt. Governor Val Oveson (left) and Bountiful resident and founder of Sportsmen for Fish and Wildlife Don Peay (right).*

Bush made a spontaneous visit to the Tabernacle Choir's pre-tour concert on Temple Square during his July 1992 visit. Choir president Wendell M. Smoot (Inset) received word at 6:30PM that the president would like to attend the 7:30PM concert. Smoot said he did not know how President Bush learned of the concert or what prompted him to attend. Smoot said, "He came unobtrusively and unannounced to be in our audience. When the crowd realized he was in the Tabernacle, they all arose to their feet and gave thunderous applause. He shook hands with people and waved as he walked across the front part of the Tabernacle. I greeted him, and thanked him for coming. I reminded him of the marvelous experience the choir had in singing at his inauguration in 1989. President Bush said he was delighted to attend. He added that he just wanted to enjoy the concert." The President sat on the twelfth row of the Tabernacle's main floor and promptly took off his jacket to abate the heat he felt in the Tabernacle. As President Smoot welcomed the audience to the concert, he said, "If there are any of you that would care to take your coats off, please follow the example of the president of the United States."[241] President Bush stayed for the first half of the concert,

leaving at intermission. "We were greatly honored to have President Bush attend the concert," Smoot said. "He added a great dimension to it. His presence was a great send-off for our tour, which is to commemorate the 500th anniversary of Columbus coming to America. Having the President of the United States attend this send-off concert made it a unique, exciting evening."[242]

DESERET NEWS

BUSH AND CLINTON ADDRESS THE NATIONAL GUARD

DESERET NEWS

On September 14–15, 1992, President Bush visited Utah for his third and final time as president, this time to address a national gathering of the National Guard. Just seven weeks before the November election, Bush pledged his support to keeping America's military strong and obliquely referred to Clinton's draft record by pointing out that a president must lead the military and bear the "awful authority" of sending America's sons and daughters into harm's way. Bush shared the same podium and the same audience as his opponent, Bill Clinton (who spoke later)—the first time in Utah history that two presidential nominees were at the same event together.[243]

The Visit
Salt La

September

BUSH RECEIVES HONORARY DEGREE FROM SOUTHERN UTAH UNIVERSITY *(Below)*
Bush made his first post-presidency visit to Utah on May 2, 1997, when he went to Cedar City to speak and receive an honorary doctorate at Southern Utah University. It was a special Centennial Convocation for the university, and Bush was seated next to Church President Gordon B. Hinckley. "Any passion for freedom must include service to others," Bush said in his remarks, mentioning the Church's missionaries as an example. "All you have to do is get off the sidelines."[244]

BUSH TAKES A MINUTE TO GREET THE CROWD
(Left) After former President Bush stepped off the plane at the Salt Lake airport, he took a minute to greet members of the crowd. Bush enjoyed a moment with one of the younger members of the group as his Secret Service agent advised photographers and reporters to back away.

BUSH HELPS KICK OFF SENATOR BOB BENNETT'S REELECTION CAMPAIGN *(Above) Bush made a second post-presidency visit on April 21, 1998, when he helped kick off Senator Bob Bennett's reelection campaign at an event at the Utah State Fair Grounds. He was in town for a paid speaking engagement at the Peter Lowe International Success event.*[245]

BILL CLINTON

LIBRARY OF CONGRESS

HINCKLEY INSTITUTE OF POLITICS

BILL CLINTON WAS PRESIDENT of the United States from 1993–2001 and served at the same time Mike Leavitt was governor of Utah and Ezra Taft Benson, Howard W. Hunter, and Gordon B. Hinckley were presidents of the Church. He came to Utah five times, including twice as president.

1991 CLINTON SPEAKING AT HINCKLEY INSTITUTE OF POLITICS   *(Right) Arkansas Governor Bill Clinton was invited to speak at the Hinckley Institute of Politics at the University of Utah and did so on May 3, 1991. It was his first visit to Utah, and because he was a former head of the National Governor's Association, there was already speculation that Clinton would run for president in 1992.*

DESERET NEWS

CLINTON COMES CAMPAIGNING FOR PRESIDENT *Bill Clinton came to Utah a second time on September 14–15, 1992, to speak to members of the National Guard from all fifty states who had gathered for meetings in Utah. Democrat activist Terry Rushton and party leaders greeted him at the airport when he arrived Monday night. His opponent, President Bush, was also in Salt Lake City that day. Because of the thousands in town for the National Guard convention, all the downtown hotels were booked, and Clinton had to stay in Little Cottonwood Canyon at Snowbird.*

DESERET NEWS

Clinton Gore

CLINTON SPEAKS AT NATIONAL GUARD EVENT *(Below)*
President Bush spoke first, and later in the day Governor Clinton addressed the National Guard. He was running about twenty minutes late and was making last-minute changes to his speech. Unlike Bush, Clinton did not spend as much time discussing military issues and instead shared his plans for the economy. During his remarks, his microphone went dead twice. Clinton quipped that "this is another reason why we shouldn't cut the Guard budget too much."[246]

DESERET NEWS

PRESIDENT HINCKLEY MEETING GOVERNOR CLINTON *(Left)
After speaking to the National Guard, Governor Clinton called on Church leaders at the Church Administration Building for a twenty-minute visit. Congressman Wayne Owens (D-UT) introduced Clinton to President Gordon B. Hinckley, then first counselor in the First Presidency, and Democratic candidates for lieutenant governor (Paula Julander) and governor (Ron Holt) accompanied them. Clinton thanked the Church for helping victims of Hurricane Andrew, which had just clobbered Florida the month prior. President Hinckley used that opportunity to explain to Clinton the practice of fasting for two meals each month and offering at least the value of the two meals for relief of the poor.*[247] *"The Church," President Hinckley stated, "uses that money to assist the needy of the Church as well as to help those in serious distress in various parts of the world."*[248]

Deseret News

METRO EDITION

SALT LAKE CITY, UTAH

WEDNESDAY, JANUARY 20, 1993

143RD YEAR / No. 220

WEDNESDAY

Clinton takes oath of office as nation's
42nd president

Oath of office

I, William Jefferson Clinton, do solemnly swear that I will faithfully execute the office of president of the United States, and will to the best of my ability, preserve, protect and defend the Constitution of the United States, so help me God.

New U.S. leader calls on Americans to embrace change and end deadlock.

By Lee Davidson
Deseret News Washington correspondent

WASHINGTON — After placing his hand on a family Bible and taking the oath of office Wednesday as the nation's 42nd president, William Jefferson Clinton proclaimed an end to deadlock and drift and the start of a new season of American renewal.

Clinton — who won the White House with a theme of bringing change to the government — also made change the central theme of his jubilant but brief, 1,500-word inaugural speech.

"Today we pledge that the era of deadlock and drift is over. A new season of American renewal has begun," he said.

"Profound and powerful forces are shaking and remaking our world, and the urgent question of our age is whether we can make change our friend and not our enemy," he told a crowd of 250,000 at the Capitol, plus billions watching on television worldwide.

"To renew America, we must be bold. We must do what no generation has had to do before. We must invest more in our people and in our own future, and at the same time cut our massive debt," he said.

As former President George Bush looked on a few feet away at the peaceful transition of power, Clinton — at age 46 the third-youngest president ever — also reveled in becoming the first baby-boom

freedom but threatened still by ancient hatreds and new plagues.

He urged a focus on America's problems first but also said America must continue to lead the world

health care devastates millions and threatens to bankrupt many of our enterprises, great and small, when fear of crime robs law-abiding citizens of their freedom, we have

government or from each other. Let us take more responsibility, not only for ourselves and our families but for our communities and our country."

Clinton added that America must also meet challenges abroad

the people. Let us put aside personal advantage so that we can feel the pain and see the promise of America."

With his daughter and wife at his side, William Jefferson Clinton is sworn in by Chief Justice Rehnquist on the west steps of the Capitol.

Elk 'soup kitchen'

Cache Valley's Hardware Ranch began feeding the elk in 1948 to keep them off farmers' lands. The 25,000-acre ranch is a prime spot to watch wildlife, conduct research or just enjoy a sleigh ride. **D1**

INSIDE

World/nation

MOODY KIDS: Why is life so unhappy for many adolescents? One reason is that they get hit with an emotional double whammy, a study suggests. Often, they not only face a pileup of distressing events, but they also react to those events more strongly than younger kids do, researchers find. **A3**

PEACE PLAN: The self-proclaimed parliament of Bosnia's Serbs approves a peace plan to end fighting and deny the Serb minority an independent state. But the decision might be a tactic to buy time. **A3**

Utah

ON THE GO: Metro area residents are more likely than ever to commute to work outside the county where they live. According to recently released 1990 Census numbers, out-of-county commuting increased slightly during the 1980s. **B1**

TAXATION: In another effort to change the Democratic Party's public image, House Democrats

This Household Supports

CLINTON GORE '96

THE FIRST FAMILY SPENDS FOUR DAYS IN UTAH FOR A BIRTHDAY CELEBRATION   *(Below and Opposite) Bill Clinton's first visit to Utah as president came February 26–March 1, 1998. He arrived in Salt Lake from California on a Thursday evening for a four-day celebration for his daughter, Chelsea's, eighteenth birthday (February 27). Hillary and Chelsea Clinton had arrived two days earlier, and the First Family stayed at the mountain mansion of Hollywood producer (and CEO of DreamWorks) Jeffrey Katzenberg in the exclusive Bald Eagle Club at Deer Valley. Salt Lake City Mayor Deedee Corradini greeted the president at the airport, and then Clinton set out on a white-knuckle ride through a blizzard in icy Parley's Canyon.*[249]

UNITED STATES OF AMERICA

CLINTON GIRLS AT DEER VALLEY SKI RE-SORT *(Above)* Secret Service agents accompanied First Lady Hillary Clinton and birthday-girl Chelsea as they enjoyed fresh powder on the slopes of Deer Valley (Left). President Clinton, who is a big golfer, is not a skier. "My girls can ski," he said, without elaboration. With the Monica Lewinsky scandal beginning to brew and dominating headlines, the president took advantage of the privacy in Park City—keeping as quiet as possible in front of the media—to spend time with family and relax.[250]

"[Utah is] a wonderful place."

DESERET NEWS

DESERET NEWS

DESERET NEWS

DESERET NEWS

DESERET NEWS

PRESIDENT CLINTON SOCIALIZES WITH CROWD ALONG PARK CITY'S MAIN STREET *President Clinton emerged from his solitude for a Saturday afternoon stroll down Park City's Main Street. Throngs of skiers and shoppers, who wanted to take his picture or shake his hand, greeted him. He was in a cheerful mood for the twenty-minute walk and said about Utah, "It's a wonderful place."[251] Before he left Utah, the president met with Democrat and Republican leaders for about twenty-five minutes at the Utah National Guard base adjacent to the Salt Lake International Airport. "He said he'll do everything he can to help us with the Olympics," Senator Bob Bennett (R-UT) said.[252]*

**CLINTONS RETURN TO UTAH FOR CHELSEA'S NINE-
TEENTH BIRTHDAY** (Above) *The Clintons gathered once
again at Jeffrey Katzenberg's mansion in Park City to celebrate
Chelsea's nineteenth birthday. Just a couple weeks prior, Bill Clinton had survived the vote in the Senate to convict him of perjury
and obstruction of justice in the Monica Lewinsky scandal, so he
understandably took a low profile on his vacation in Utah. After descending from Air Force One at the airport, Clinton greeted Governor Mike Leavitt; his wife, Jackie; and their children. The president
also shook hands with Lieutenant Governor (and future governor)
Olene Walker and her husband, Myron. He visited with State Senate Minority Leader Scott Howell as he walked from the plane to
his limousine. "He likes this place," Howell said. "He's very happy
to be here."[253]*

**AN EMBARASSING MO-
MENT IN DOLLY'S BOOK
STORE** *In Park City, the
Clinton girls skied while the
president mainly read inside
the mansion. On Monday, the
president ventured out onto
Park City's Main Street and
bought some books at Dolly's Book Store (Inset). He had chosen John
Grisham's* The Testament, *a couple books on India, and a Raymond
Chandler mystery. Unfortunately, when he went to pay, the store clerk,
Courtney Gannon, told Clinton that his American Express credit card
was declined. "It's not fun to tell someone their card has expired, especially when it's the president," Gannon said. A Secret Service agent
spotted the president the $62.66 cash he needed, and Clinton explained
that he had a new card to replace the one that had expired at the end of
February but forgot to bring it with him.[254]*

CLINTON SPEAKS AT TWO UTAH EVENTS AND CAMPAIGNS FOR HIS WIFE, HILLARY CLINTON *On Sunday, November 4, 2007, Clinton made his first visit to Utah since leaving the White House. He spoke at a fundraising event in Park City and at an event in the ballroom of the Olpin Union Building on the campus of the University of Utah. He campaigned for his wife's presidential run and spent time shaking hands and autographing his biography. He told reporters, "I love it here." When reminded that he came in third place in Utah in 1992, even after independent Ross Perot, he said, "I still like it." Then he continued, "Apparently, some of my decisions may be more popular now. To be consistent, I have to say it must be possible for me to like people who don't like me. That's one of the big things we've got to do in the world to bring things back together."*[255]

DESERET NEWS

DESERET NEWS

CLINTON RECEIVES A BOOK *(Below) At the University of Utah event, author Mike Winder presented Clinton with a copy of the book* Presidents and Prophets: The Story of America's Presidents and the LDS Church. *Winder explained the concept of the book and showed Clinton the chapter about him, to which the former president replied, "Hey, what a great idea for a book!" He then said, "I always liked the Mormons and tried to help them when I could. I remember helping them with some missionary visa issues in South America once." Salt Lake City native Ben McAdams was helping with Clinton's advance team and saw him backstage after the event showing people the book and acting genuinely pleased that he had received it.*

MIKE WINDER COLLECTION

President Clinton holds the record for the longest visit to Utah by a president—four days. His four-day visit in 1998 (February 26–March 1) was followed by a three-day visit in 1999 (February 27–March 1). Both visits were for pleasure, not business, but still broke the previous record, which was the three-day visit to Utah by William Howard Taft September 24–26, 1909. Gerald Ford also made a three-day visit to Utah December 4–6, 1978, although he was no longer president at the time.

DESERET NEWS

ationally, independent Ross Perot made waves in the 1992 presidential campaign by garnering 19 percent of the popular vote—the best showing by a third party since Theodore Roosevelt in 1912. In Utah, Perot was especially popular, and Democratic nominee Bill Clinton was just as unpopular. On Election night in Utah, George Bush won Utah's electoral votes with 320,858 votes (43 percent), but Perot was a

surprising second with 202,796 (27 percent), leaving Clinton in third with 182,590 votes (25 percent). Utah was the only state in the nation to relegate the incoming president to third place. Carbon County was the sole Utah county that cast a majority for Clinton. "I don't think he held a grudge against the Mormons about this, however," Senator Orrin Hatch said when asked about the third-place finish. "He was not the type to hold a grudge against a religious institution; and even if he did, he would get over it pretty quickly. He's the type of person that if it is to his advantage, he can like anyone."[256] Elder Ralph W. Hardy Jr., an Area Authority Seventy and chair of the Church's Washington DC Public Affairs Committee, agreed. "I met Bill Clinton as a representative of the Church on several occasions, and he was always very respectful to the Church, and never reflected a grudge for how Utah voted."[257]

CHURCH PRESIDENT PRAYS IN THE OVAL OFFICE   (Right) On November 13, 1995, President Gordon B. Hinckley and Elder Neal A. Maxwell (left) enjoyed a thirty-minute visit in the Oval Office with Vice President Al Gore and President Clinton. The Church leaders presented President Clinton with several volumes of his family history. President Hinckley said: "We advocate in the Church a program we call family home evening, reserving one night a week where father, mother and children sit down together and talk—talk about the family and about one another and study some together. You might get Hillary and Chelsea and sit down with those books and have a family home evening." President Clinton said that he would take the family history books with him to Camp David for Thanksgiving and have an evening with his family to "discuss our heritage." As they were concluding the visit, Elder Maxwell mentioned to President Clinton that the First Presidency and the Twelve had recently prayed for him and for the country in the Salt Lake Temple, following a longstanding custom regarding the occupants of the Oval Office. As the men rose to say their goodbyes, one of the senior White House aides suggested it might be appropriate to invite President Hinckley to offer a word of prayer. Clinton agreed, and the group gathered in a loose circle. "I had my arm around the back of the President and his arm was around my back, and I offered a prayer," President Hinckley recorded of the experience. "I thought it was a rather wonderful thing, to pray for the President of the United States in his office. When we left he expressed his gratitude for our coming. I thought he was sincere."[258]

OFFICIAL WHITE HOUSE PHOTO

When President Ezra Taft Benson passed away in 1994, President Clinton sent a warm statement of condolence. After outlining President Benson's service to his country and church, the President wrote, "We rejoice in his service, we remember his life and we extend our heartfelt sympathies to his family, his church and his admirers worldwide."[259]

When President Howard W. Hunter passed away the following year, President Clinton again sent condolences: "Hillary and I were saddened to learn of the death of Howard Hunter, and we extend our deepest sympathy to his family. President Hunter provided great moral and spiritual leadership to all Mormons as well as the entire country. His message of the need for greater kindness, gentleness, tolerance and forgiveness is an important one for all of us."[260]

On the occasion of the Mormon pioneer sesquicentennial, President Clinton sent greetings to those celebrating in Salt Lake City. "The story of the Mormon pioneers is in many ways the story of America," said the President. "Today, we marvel at what they accomplished. With faith, courage, and determination, they built a life for their families and made the desert bloom. . . . It is the story of a people who know that, with hard work and faith in God, they can accomplish anything."[261]

NATIONAL PORTRAIT GALLERY

GEORGE W. BUSH

G EORGE W. BUSH WAS PRESIDENT of the United States from 2001–2009 and served at the same time Mike Leavitt, Olene Walker, and Jon Huntsman Jr. were governors of Utah and Gordon B. Hinckley and Thomas S. Monson were presidents of the Church. He came to Utah seven times, including four times as president.

DESERET NEWS

DESERET NEWS

CAMPAIGNING FOR PRESIDENT *"Yes, I'm running for president, and I intend to win," was the message Texas Governor George W. Bush declared to cheering supporters on his first Utah visit, July 6–7, 1999. He arrived Tuesday evening and Wednesday morning had a private breakfast at the home of John and Marcia Price (Bush would later appoint Price as a U.S. ambassador) with six western governors to discuss water rights, public lands, nuclear waste storage, and rapid growth (Bottom left). Bush then held a rally at the Marriott Hotel, where he spoke for twenty minutes to several hundred attendees (Below and top opposite) before attending a $1,000-per-plate fundraising lunch. In between those two events, Bush spent an hour with the First Presidency of the Church. "These are great leaders. I can learn from them," he said. "We talked about the need for good strong values," Bush reported after his meeting, adding that he fully supported the values of the Church.[262]*

Governor **George W. Bush**

RESIDENTIAL EXPLORATORY COMMITTEE, INC.

Salt Lake City, Utah
July 7, 1999

RONALD FOX COLLECTION

DESERET NEWS

DESERET NEWS

LEAVITTS GIVE BUSH WARM WELCOME   (Right) Utah Governor Mike Leavitt and his wife, Jackie, (right) were especially welcoming of Governor Bush when he campaigned in 1999. As president, Bush appointed Leavitt to his cabinet, first to head the Environmental Protection Agency and later to be the secretary of Health and Human Services.

BUSH COMES TO UTAH AGAIN FOR RALLY IN PROVO   On March 9, 2000, George W. Bush spent ninety minutes in Utah at a rally at the Provo Municipal Airport where he spoke to 1,000 fans who had gathered there (Below). "I'm glad I came," he said in response to the enthusiasm. Bush told reporters he came to Provo because of the early support he had received from Provo Mayor Lewis Billings, who endorsed Bush when most Utahns were still backing favorite-son Orrin Hatch for president. The Texas governor said that his priorities would be "my faith, my family and the great land called America." He told the Utah crowd that their most important work "is not necessarily your day job, but to love your children with all your heart."263

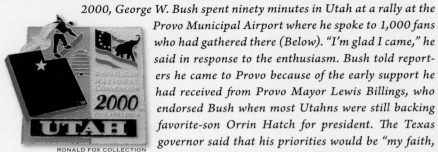

RONALD FOX COLLECTION

RONALD FOX COLLECTION

RONALD FOX COLLECTION

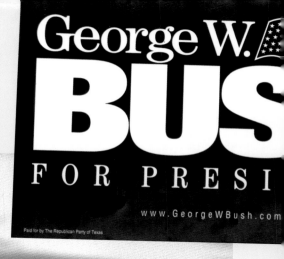

www.GeorgeWBush.com

Paid for by The Republican Party of Texas

DESERET NEWS

RONALD FOX COLLECTION

PRESIDENT BUSH ARRIVES IN UTAH TO PRESIDE OVER THE 2002 OLYMPIC WINTER GAMES OPENING CEREMONIES *(Right) On February 8, 2002, George W. Bush made his first visit as president to Utah to officially preside over the opening of the XIX Olympic Winter Games. Utah Senators Orrin Hatch and Bob Bennett arrived with the president and first lady on Air Force One. After landing at 12:35PM Governor Mike Leavitt and his wife, Jackie, as well as Salt Lake Organizing Committee President Mitt Romney and SLOC Chief Financial Officer Frazier Bullock, greeted them. From the airport, the Bushes traveled to meet with the First Presidency for a half hour before continuing on to events at the capitol.*[264]

DESERET NEWS

UTAH STATE HISTORICAL SOCIETY

UTAH STATE HISTORICAL SOCIETY

BUSH AND LEAVITT REVIEW NOTES IN THE CAPITOL'S GOLD ROOM *(Left and Above) At the capitol, the president and first lady met with Governor and Mrs. Leavitt, as well as their family, before speaking at an event in the rotunda. The two leaders spent some quiet time together in the capitol's Gold Room, reviewing their speeches and making last-minute notes and changes.*

State of Utah Reception

In honor of the

President of the United States

on the occasion of the opening of the

XIX Olympic Winter Games

Friday, February 8, 2002
Utah State Capitol

Governor & Mrs. Leavitt

Request the pleasure of your attendance at the

State of Utah Reception

For

The President of the United States

On the occasion of the opening of the

XIX Olympic Winter Games

On Friday, February Eighth

Two Thousand and Two

Doors open at Twelve-thirty o'clock p.m.

Guest must be seated by One-forty five o'clock p.m.

The State Capitol Building

R.S.V.P. 801-296-1276   Non-Transferable - Seating by ticket only

State of Utah Reception
For the
President of the United States
On the occasion of the opening of the
XIX Olympic Winter Games
Friday, February 8, 2002
Doors open at 12:30 p.m. · Be seated by 1:45 p.m.
Utah State Capitol Building

Nº 2150

Admit one
Photo identification required

RONALD FOX COLLECTION

RONALD FOX COLLECTION

PRESIDENTIAL OPENING RECEPTION FOR XIX OLYMPIC WINTER GAMES ❦ *The president and first lady wiped tears as they listened to the Mormon Tabernacle Choir's moving rendition of the "Battle Hymn of the Republic" in the capitol rotunda. In his fifteen-minute remark, President Bush said that Utah is the "perfect place" to host the Games because of its natural beauty, caring people, and rich history. With the recent attacks of September 11, the president said that "it's an important time for us to come together" as Utahns, Americans, and the world. He said it was the second time in history that a significant event in Utah brought the nation together. "In 1869 we were tied together by the railroad, and today the world is united in Utah through the Games," he said.*[265]

"In 1869 we were tied together [in Utah] by the railroad, and today the world is united in Utah through the Games."

PRESIDENT MEETS WITH U.S. OLYMPIC ATHLETES *An hour before the opening ceremonies, Bush visited the American Olympic athletes and coaches at the HPER gym on the University of Utah campus. They presented him with a U.S. Olympic Team jacket, and the president said, "I don't deserve to wear this." He talked about the flag that was unearthed from the World Trade Center rubble that would be used to christen the opening ceremonies of the Games and said, "This flag serves as a symbol of U.S. strength and our fight for freedom. These Games come at a perfect time; yes, one of sadness, but for the U.S., bringing out our best, and I can't wait for this flag to fly tonight." Then the president told the athletes, "You will represent us with class and dignity and courage. And you will come together in friendly competition to show that our spirit is bigger than evil and terror. You will become heroes overnight," he continued. "This is an awesome responsibility, but you are up to it, and you will do the best you possibly can." And then he concluded with the phrase used by one of the passengers who tried to overtake the hijackers on a plane on September 11: "Let's roll."*[266]

UTAH STATE HISTORICAL SOCIETY

WEATHER FORECAST: Partly cloudy today. Highs in low 30s; lows in mid teens. E8

INDEX
Business F1-6, B
Classified ads F8-38
Comics, TV E4
Comment A10, 11
Deaths F6, 7
Local B1-6
Movies E6, 7
Religion E1-3
Sports D1-8

INSIDE

No beer here Organizers of the Ethnic Village decide against selling beer in the area during the Games. **B1**

Uniting faiths Salt Lake's non-dominant religions unite for Interfaith Roundtable, designed to build bridges of friendship. **E1**

All-Star weekend Andrei Kirilenko, the only Jazz envoy at the All-Star media event, gets the spotlight in Karl Malone's absence. **D1**

MORNING EDITION
Deseret News
Utah's locally owned daily newspaper
SALT LAKE CITY, UTAH

151ST YEAR/No. 240

SATURDAY, FEBRUA

http://www.deseretnews.com

With the Mormon Tabernacle Choir behind him, President Bush declares Utah the perfect place to hold the 2002 Winter Games because of its natural beauty, its caring people and its rich history.

'The perfect place'
Bush hails S.L. Olympics

By Bob Bernick Jr.
Deseret News staff writer

In an emotional tribute to Utah as home to the Olympics, to Americans as heroes to the world and to the international visitors who wept along with us all in the wake of Sept. 11, President Bush arrived in Salt Lake City Friday and stood sentinel over the opening ceremonies of the Games.

At the Utah State Capitol Friday afternoon, Bush declared Utah the perfect place to hold the 2002 Winter Games because of its natural beauty, its caring people and its rich history.

Before presiding over the opening ceremonies in Rice-Eccles Olympic Stadium, the president met with members of the First Presidency of The Church of Jesus Christ of Latter-day Saints, then held a quick, private reception at the Capitol with local dignitaries, including Republican stalwarts and members of the Utah Legislature.

There, throughout his 15-minute address, the president touched on the disasters of Sept.

President Bush speaks to LDS Church President Gordon B. Hinckley after arriving in Salt Lake City.

Click on "Olympics"
Venues, maps, history, athletes

Olympics
▸ www.deseretnews.com

11 and how the Olympics are bringing together Utahns, Americans and the world. As he succinctly put it: "It's an important time for us to come together."

He went on to say that the next two weeks mark the second of two historically significant events that have unified Utah with the nation, and now the world. "In

1869 we were tied together by the railroad, and today the world is united in Utah through the Games.

While the Olympics always are significant each time they are held, no matter where, the events of Sept. 11 have made them especially important and heartfelt because of the sympathy and strong support that have come to the United States from around the globe.

Citing one of the first copies of the Declaration of Independence, which is now on view at the Capitol rotunda yards from where Bush spoke, the president asked: "Why are we so intent upon defending these values? We love liberty and freedom and we

Please see BUSH on A6

President Bush greets members of the U.S. Olympic team and poses with them for a picture after addressing all the American athletes in the Olympic Village in Salt Lake City on Friday.

OLYMPIC WINTER GAMES OPENING CEREMONY *(Left) During the opening ceremonies at Rice-Eccles Stadium, President Bush proudly marched in with International Olympic Committee President Jacques Rogge and Salt Lake Organizing Committee President Mitt Romney. Once his official duties were done, Bush sat amidst the Team USA athletes, posing for pictures and talking to their family members on cell phones. (Below) Downtown Salt Lake City transformed for hosting the XIX Olympic Winter Games. (Right) Thousands of pins were being traded during the festive weeks of the 2002 Winter Games, including pins depicting unique Utah icons, such as Jell-O, Brigham Young, and fry sauce. This unique pin was the official pin that commemorated the visit of President Bush to the Olympic Games.*

PRESIDENT BUSH SPEAKS AT VETERANS OF FOREIGN WARS CONVENTION

Bush's second visit as president to Utah came August 22, 2005, when he stopped in to address the 106th convention of the Veterans of Foreign Wars in Salt Lake City. Senator Orrin Hatch accompanied the president and first lady on Air Force One (Right and Below right), which had come from the president's ranch in Crawford, Texas. Utah Governor Jon Huntsman Jr. and his wife, Mary Kaye, greeted the president when he ascended the dais to speak at the convention. "A policy of retreat and isolation will not bring us safety," Bush said in his remarks (Below left), which centered on the wars in Afghanistan and Iraq. "The only way to defend our citizens where we live is to go after the terrorists where they live." Afterward, he spent more than a half hour shaking hands with the attendees before flying on to Idaho.[267]

The Committee for
The Presidential Inaugural
requests the honor of your presence
to attend and participate in the Inauguration of

George Walker Bush
as President of the United States of America
and

Richard Bruce Cheney
as Vice President of the United States of America
on Thursday, the twentieth of January
two thousand and five
in the City of Washington

UTAH DELEGATE

REPUBLICAN
NATIONAL CONVENTION

DESERET NEWS

BUSH LANDS FOR THIRD VISIT TO CHEERING CROWD OF 3,000 *The third visit Bush made to Utah as president came August 30–31, 2006, when he came to town for a fundraiser for Senator Hatch and to speak at the convention of the American Legion. Air Force One landed at 8:52PM with about 3,000 supporters cheering. The president thanked the crowd for "a fantastic Utah welcome," saying he wished his wife, Laura, were there to see it. He was very passionate and animated in his remarks as he discussed the need to support the troops and even as he acknowledged the need for help from the Almighty.*[268]

OFFICIAL WHITE HOUSE PHOTO

DESERET NEWS

BUSH RECEIVES STANDING OVATION FROM AMERICAN LEGION *(Above) Bush then spoke to the American Legion, rousing a standing ovation when he acknowledged the presence of the Utah family of Marine Cpl. Adam Galvez, who had just been buried the previous day after being killed by a roadside bomb in Iraq. President Bush also visited the parents of Galvez before speaking at a fundraiser for Senator Hatch at the Grand America Hotel. He then departed on Air Force One at 12:05PM, ending a fifteen-hour visit. Governor Huntsman rode with the president back to the airport and, along the way, discussed ecotourism and the great mountain biking in Utah. Huntsman said it was always good to have a presidential visit. "It focuses the national media's spotlight on Utah for at least a day," he said. "It's also a chance for the president to learn about some Utah issues." But not everyone welcomed Bush. Salt Lake City Mayor Rocky Anderson led a protest of 1,000 anti-war demonstrators.*[269]

MEETING WITH THE FIRST PRESIDENCY *(Above) On Thursday, August 31, President Bush met with President Gordon B. Hinckley, his counselors, and First Presidency Executive Secretary F. Michael Watson at Church headquarters in a half-hour meeting. It was the fifth time President Gordon B. Hinckley had met with President Bush. During the meeting, the First Presidency presented President Bush with the Hansen statue, which depicts a mother and father with their child running between them. The Church gave a similar gift to President Jimmy Carter during his 1978 visit to Utah. The statue represents the family as the essential building block of our society.*

BUSH ARRIVES FOR HIS FOURTH VISIT TO THE STATE *(Left) Bush's fourth and final visit to Utah as president came May 28–29, 2008. His Secretary of Health and Human Services and former Utah Governor Mike Leavitt and his wife, Jackie, once again greeted him at the airport. Governor Jon and Mary Kaye Huntsman also welcomed the president.*

PRESIDENTIAL MOTORCADE DRIVES TO THE AVENUES *(Left and Below left) The president's motorcade drove into the Avenues neighborhood of Salt Lake City, where a $500-minimum afternoon fundraising reception was held for about 300 at the home of Sam Stewart, founder of a finance firm. Children at the Madeleine School waved to the motorcade as it whisked by.*

MARINE ONE TAKES THE PRESIDENT TO PARK CITY *(Left) After the fundraiser in the Avenues, the president returned to the airport to board the helicopter Marine One for Park City. Accompanied by three identical helicopters, the president landed on the ball fields adjacent to Park City Middle School and waved to the gathered supporters and protesters before being whisked in a limousine to Mitt Romney's Deer Valley home for a fundraising dinner that cost $70,100 per couple to attend. Bush then spent the night in Deer Valley.[270]*

After President Bush landed in 2008, President Thomas S. Monson, second counselor Dieter F. Uchtdorf, and Relief Society General President Julie B. Beck toured Air Force One. Bush advanceman and co-author of this book Ron Fox (seen taking photograph) ar-

ranged for the tour, which is occasionally allowed for prominent VIPs during a president's visit. It was the three Church leaders' first time aboard the world's most famous 747 and was a special thrill for President Uchtdorf because of his career as a fighter pilot in the German Air Force and as an airline captain for Lufthansa.

BUSH SPENDS AN HOUR WITH PRESIDENT MONSON AND COUNSELORS *(Above) Thursday morning, President Bush flew in Marine One back to Salt Lake City and spent nearly an hour with President Thomas S. Monson and his counselors. They discussed the friendship President Monson shared with Bush's parents and also talked about foreign policy issues, Middle East peace, the economy, and energy. They also chatted about what the president planned to do after leaving office in January. The Church leaders told Bush that they prayed for him, they supported the presidency, and they were a very patriotic people.*[271]

BOOK SIGNING AT COST-CO *(Right and Opposite bottom) George W. Bush made his first post-presidency trip to Utah on November 19, 2010, as part of a national tour of book signings to promote his memoir, Decision Points, at the Sandy Costco. He signed 2,000 copies of his book as a parade of adoring fans came through the line, hugging, laughing, and shaking hands with him.*[272]

arack Obama cancelled a second campaign visit to Utah due to the passing of President Gordon B. Hinckley. Obama had planned to stop in Utah on Saturday, February 2, 2008, but out of deference to the funeral of Church President Gordon B. Hinckley, which was scheduled the day of the planned visit, the Democratic candidate changed plans. "Last night, I spoke with President Thomas Monson and I expressed my deepest sympathies to The Church of Jesus Christ of Latter-day Saints on the passing of President Gordon B. Hinckley," Obama said in a statement.[273] His wife, Michelle, did stop in Utah on Monday, February 4, and in the February 5 primary election, Obama won Utah by eighteen percentage points over Senator Hillary Clinton (D-NY) on his path to becoming the Democratic Party's nominee for president.

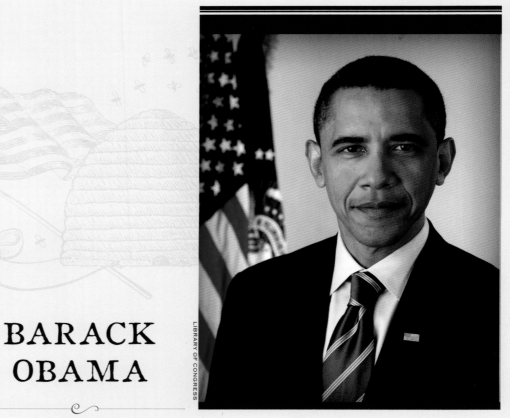

BARACK OBAMA

Barack Obama was president of the United States from 2009–present and served at the same time Jon Huntsman Jr. and Gary Herbert were governors of Utah and Thomas S. Monson was president of the Church. Besides at least two airport layovers, he came to Utah only once, and at press time for this book had not yet come as president.

OBAMA COMES TO PARK CITY FOR PRIVATE FUNDRAISER AND A "SORT OF SPONTANEOUS" CAMPAIGN RALLY *On Sunday, August 5, 2007, Senator Barack Obama (D-IL) stopped in Utah to attend a private fundraiser in Park City. Obama's popularity and credibility as a candidate grew tremendously that summer, and by the time the candidate arrived in Utah, there was an enormous demand for a campaign rally in addition to the fundraiser. A hastily organized event in the parking lot of the Park City Visitor's Center off State Route 224 near Kimball Junction drew more than 500 supporters. As he shook hands and signed autographs, Obama told a reporter that his reception in Utah was wonderful and that the turnout of the "sort of spontaneous" rally made it worth stopping. "This is part of what gives you energy in a campaign, seeing all these folks who are so eager for change," the senator said. "You know, it reminds you why you do what you do."[274]*

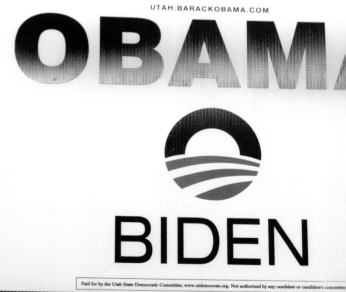

UTAH.BARACKOBAMA.COM

OBAMA
BIDEN

Paid for by the Utah State Democratic Committee, www.utdemocrats.org. Not authorized by any candidate or candidate's committee.

OBAMA CHARMS CROWD WITH QUICK WIT AND SENSE OF HUMOR *Obama spoke for nearly half an hour to the crowd at Kimball Junction, touching on healthcare, education, the environment, and the war in Iraq. He said that he had been to Utah before on layovers at the Salt Lake City International Airport, but this was his first time outdoors in Utah, and he praised the scenery as spectacular. "You guys have this all the time, don't you? It's unbelievable," he said. Americans must look out for one another, he said, an "idea that has to express itself not just through our religious bodies, not just through our families, it's got to express itself through our government." At one point in his remarks, a woman shouted that someone had fainted. Obama calmly responded, calling for assistance and asking if the person was all right. "Okay? Just give them a little room," he said then joked that it was "a sign that I might be speaking too long."*[275]

On May 16, 2009, President Obama announced the appointment of Utah Governor Jon Huntsman Jr. to the important diplomatic post of United States ambassador to China. Huntsman represented the United States in Beijing for nearly two years, earning praise from Chinese and American business and political leaders. He learned Mandarin Chinese as a missionary

OFFICIAL WHITE HOUSE PHOTO

in Taiwan and was formerly a deputy assistant secretary of commerce for Asia, deputy United States trade representative, and ambassador to Singapore. He and his wife, Mary Kaye, had also previously adopted a daughter from China, enabling him to connect with the Chinese people in an unprecedented way.

The Republican Utah governor was a national co-chair for Sen. John McCain's presidential campaign and said he never expected "to be called into action by the person who beat us," but added that "when the president of the United States asks you to step up and serve in a capacity like this, that to me is the end of the conversation and the beginning of the obligation to rise to the challenge."

"He has brought enormous skill, dedication, and talent to the job," the president said as Huntsman's service in Beijing came to a close. "And the fact that he comes from a different party I think is a strength, not a weakness, because it indicates the degree to which both he and I believe that partisanship ends at the water's edge, and that we work together to advocate on behalf of our country. So I couldn't be happier with the ambassador's service."

"You guys have this [spectacular scenery] all the time, don't you? It's unbelievable."

DESERET NEWS

CUMMING FUNDRAISER *At the Park City home of supporters Jon and Kristi Cumming, Obama attracted 450 people to a fundraiser with a minimum contribution of $500, though some paid as much as $2,300. The event raised around $250,000 for the candidate, who was a big hit with donors. "Usually this is a group that's not star-struck," Utah Democratic Party Chairman Wayne Holland said, but "it took a good half-hour just getting him 50 yards from the backyard podium to the living room to meet with public officials."[276] Holland and his wife, Katie, posed for a photograph with the future president (Above), as did State Senator Gene Davis (Top right), Salt Lake City Mayor Ralph Becker (Right) and others.*

OBAMA BIDEN

On July 20, 2009, President Barack Obama hosted a brief meeting in the Oval Office with Sen. Harry Reid (D-NV), left; Joshua DuBois, director of the White House Office for Faith-Based and Neighborhood Partnerships; President Thomas S. Monson; and Elder Dallin H. Oaks of the Quorum of the Twelve. The LDS guests presented the president with five large leather-bound volumes of family history and a table-long pedigree chart during the courtesy visit. "President Obama's heritage is rich with examples of leadership, sacrifice and service," President Monson said. "We were very pleased to research his family history and are honored to present it to him today."

PETE SOUZA WHITE HOUSE

"I enjoyed my meeting with President Monson and Elder Oaks," President Obama said. "I'm grateful for the genealogical records that they brought with them and am looking forward to reading through the materials with my daughters. It's something our family will treasure for years to come."

Elder Oaks was there in his capacity as chairman of the Church's Temple and Family History Executive Council and said, "The Church has great resources and experience in genealogy work, and we are proud to have researched such a unique and impressive family history."

Senate Majority Leader Harry Reid, a member of the Church, arranged for the meeting and said, "I thank President Monson and Elder Oaks for sharing our religion's tradition of genealogical research with the president and his family. I am also glad President Obama and Elder Oaks had an opportunity to discuss their shared passion of the law.

"Recognizing the president and first lady's deep regard for family," he continued, "I am honored that our church can have any part in documenting their family history."

The Presidential Inaugural Comm

requests the honor of your presence
to attend and participate
in the
Inauguration of

Barack H. Obam

as President of the United States of Ame

and

Joseph R. Biden,

as Vice President of the United States of A
on Tuesday, the twentieth of Januar
two thousand and nine
in the City of Washington

RONALD FOX COLLECTION

Deseret News

deseretnews.com Results for presidential, congressional, state and all local races. Also, stories, analyses and updates on the historic election, its aftermath and what lies ahead.

Obama wins

'Change has come to America'

President-elect Barack Obama waves to his supporters after giving his acceptance speech at Grant Park in Chicago Tuesday night. He promised to address the greatest challenges of a lifetime.

JERRY LAI/ASSOCIATED PRESS

■ Historic: President-elect vows to lead all Americans

By Nedra Pickler
Associated Press

CHICAGO — A triumphant Barack Obama vowed to be a president for all America, even those who voted against him, and asked for patience to address the nation's problems of war and finance that he called the greatest challenges of a lifetime.

The first black president-elect cast his election as a defining moment in the country's 232-year history and a rebuke to cynicism, fear and doubt.

"If there is anyone out there who

still doubts that America is a place where all things are possible; who still wonders if the dream of our founders is alive in our time; who still questions the power of our democracy, tonight is your answer," he said in his first public words after winning the election.

His victory speech was delivered before a multiracial crowd that city officials estimated at 240,000 people. Many cried and nodded their heads while he spoke, surrounded by clear bulletproof screens on his

Please see **OBAMA** *on A12*

More inside

● **HISTORIC:** A graphic history of black American milestones and a deeply personal vote for one Utahn in particular / **A4**
● **RESULTS:** A tally of major Utah election outcomes / **A8**
● **STATE RACES:** Most Republicans win re-election, but House speaker Greg Curtis loses to Democrat Jay Seegmiller / **A9**
● **ELECTION MATH:** A breakdown of the nation's Electoral College votes / **A12**
● **SALT LAKE COUNTY:** Voters OK bond proposals and give Mayor Peter Corroon another four years in office / **B1**

■ 'Pinch me': Blacks in Utah rejoice at the historic outcome

By Aaron Falk
Deseret News

In a corner of the University of Utah's student union, Wazir Jefferson counted aloud as the seconds ticked down and California's polls closed.

Dressed in a shirt that featured the words "I have a dream," the graduate student quietly raised his arms in the air.

"President Barack Obama. President Barack Obama," Jefferson repeated.

With the election of the United States' first black president, the

emotions that swelled inside blacks for years leading up to the historic election seemed to burst Tuesday.

"I never thought I would live to see this day," said Jeanetta Williams, president of the National Association for the Advancement of Colored People's branch in Salt Lake City.

Betty Sawyer, the adviser for the U.'s Black Student Union, believed otherwise.

"I'm an optimist," she said. "But when it finally does happen, it's

Please see **REACTION** *on A3*

JASON HADLEY, MASTERPIECE IMAGES

UTES PERFORM AT INAUGURATION *The University of Utah marching band represented Utah in President Barack Obama's Inauguration Parade on January 20, 2009.*

JASON HADLEY, MASTERPIECE IMAGES

ELECTION RESULTS

HOUSE 49		SENATE 10		HOUSE 51		GOVERNOR		1ST CONGRESSIONAL DISTRICT		2ND CONGRESSIONAL DISTRICT		3RD CONGRESSIONAL DISTRICT	
Greg Curtis (R)	Jay Seegmiller (D)	Chris Buttars (R)	John Rendell (D)	Greg Hughes (R)	Lisa Johnson (D)	Jon Huntsman (R)	Bob Springmeyer (D)	Rob Bishop (R)	Morgan Bowen (D)	Bill Dew (R)	Jim Matheson (D)	Jason Chaffetz (R)	B. Spencer (D)
5,447	6,827	18,089	16,596	7,730	7,325	657,337	168,352	186,031	87,139	108,997	201,525	155,074	67,968

NOTES

1   Jefferson to Lucy Jefferson Lewis, 19 April 1808, quoted on page 149 in Boynton Merrill's *Jefferson's Nephews* in Google Books: http://books.google.com/books?id=ts5km4_uzKcC&pg=PA148, obtained online 21 Nov. 2010.

2   Protea [Gentile governess of BY's children], "Brigham Young at home, the ways and words of the Prophet in his household: his conversations about himself, the government, Mormons," *The Weekly Sun* [daily newspaper of New York], 19 Sep. 1877.

3   Richard J. Ellis, *Presidential Travel: The Journey from George Washington to George W. Bush*, (Lawrence, Kansas: The University Press of Kansas, 2008): 6.

4   Schuyler Colfax to Ulysses S. Grant, 18 Aug. 1870, San Francisco, quoted in John Y. Simon, *The Papers of Ulysses S. Grant, 21* (Carbondale, IL: Southern Illinois University Press, 1988):105–6.

5   Young quoted in Stanley P. Hirshon, *The Lion of the Lord: A Biography of the Mormon Leader, Brigham Young*, (New York: Alfred K. Knopf, 1969): 278–79.

6   James A. Garfield, *The Diary of James A. Garfield*, ed. Harry James Brown & Frederick D. Williams, (East Lansing, MI: Michigan State University Press, 1967): 75–76.

7   Linda King Newell and Vivian Linford Talbot, *A History of Garfield County*, (Salt Lake City: Utah Historical Society and Garfield County Commission, 1998): 170.

8   *Deseret News*, 4 Jun. 1875, 5 Jun. 1875.

9   Davis Bitton, *George Q. Cannon: A Biography*, (Salt Lake City: Deseret Book, 1999): 247.

10   George Q. Cannon, *Journal of Discourses*, 22, (London: Latter-day Saints' Book Depot, 1854–86):137.

11   *Salt Lake Herald*, 3 Oct. 1875.

12   *Deseret News*, 6 Oct. 1875; also Salt Lake Herald, 5 Oct. 1875.

13   Bitton, *Cannon*, 195.

14   Ibid.

15   Preston Nibley, *Brigham Young: The Man and His Work*, (Salt Lake City: Deseret Book, 1970): 518.

16   Thomas G. Alexander, *Things in Heaven and Earth: The Life and Times of Wilford Woodruff*, (Salt Lake City: Signature Books, 1991): 228. Also, Susan Staker, ed., *Waiting for World's End: The Diaries of Wilford Woodruff*, (Salt Lake City: Signature Books, 1993): 309. Also, B.H. Roberts, *A Comprehensive History of The Church of Jesus Christ of Latter-day Saints, Century I*, vol. 5, (Salt Lake City: *Deseret News* Press, 1930): 503.

17   B.H. Roberts, *A Comprehensive History of The Church of Jesus Christ of Latter-day Saints, Century I*, vol. 5, (Salt Lake City: *Deseret News* Press, 1930): 504–05. Also, Nibley: 518.

18   *Deseret News*, 6 Oct. 1875; also *Salt Lake Tribune*, 5 Oct. 1875.

19   Susan Staker, ed., *Waiting for World's End: The Diaries of Wilford Woodruff*, (Salt Lake City: Signature Books, 1993): 310.

20   *Salt Lake Tribune* 5 Oct. 1875.

21   Thomas G. Alexander, "A Conflict of Perceptions: Ulysses S. Grant and the Mormons," *Ulysses S. Grant Association Newsletter* (Carbondale, Illinois), Vol. 8, No. 4, July 1971,39–40.

22   Staker: 310. First Lady quoted in Roberts, vol. 5: 505.

23   Brigham Young, *Letters of Brigham Young to His Sons*, edited and introduced by Dean C. Jessee, (Salt Lake City: Deseret Book, 1974): 224.

24   Governor Eli H. Murray to President Rutherford B. Hayes, 14 Aug. 1880; Correspondences of President Hayes, Hayes Presidential Center, Spiegel Grove, Ohio.

25   *Deseret News*, 4 Sep. 1880.

26   Roberts: 5: 611–12.

27   *Deseret News*, 7 Sep. 1880.

28   *Deseret News*, 6 Sep. 1880.

29   Ibid.

30   *Deseret News*, 7 Sep. 1880.

31   Arnold K. Garr, "Benjamin Harrison," in Arnold K. Garr, et. al., eds., *Encyclopedia of Latter-day Saint History*, (Salt Lake City: Deseret Book, 2000): 471.

32   Jean Bickmore White, ed., *Church, State, and Politics: The Diaries of John Henry Smith*, (Salt Lake City: Signature Books): 253.

33   Bitton, *Cannon*, 318.

34   *Deseret News*, 9 May 1891.

35   Alexander, *Things in Heaven*: 278.

36   Bitton, *Cannon*, 318. *Deseret News*, 9 May 1891.

37   Benjamin Harrison, *Speeches of Benjamin Harrison*, Charles Hedges, ed., (New York: United States Book Company, 1892): 431.

38   Harrison, *Speeches*: 433–34.

39   Bitton, *Cannon*, 318.

40   *Deseret News*, 16 May 1891.

41   Bitton, *Cannon*, 318.

42   Harrison, *Speeches*: 434–36

43   *The Ogden Standard*, 27 May 1901.

44   Ibid.

45   Ibid.

46   Ibid.

47   Francis M. Gibbons, *George Albert Smith: Kind and Caring Christian, Prophet of God*, (Salt Lake City: Deseret Book, 1981): 39.

48   *Salt Lake Herald*, 21 Sep. 1900 and 22 Sep. 1900.

49   Ibid.

50   *Salt Lake Tribune*, 30 May 1903.

51   Ibid.

52   Quoted in *Improvement Era*, Vol. XIII. September 1910. No. 11.

53   *Salt Lake Herald*, 30 May 1903.

54   *Box Elder Journal*, 19 Sep. 1912.

55   Ibid.

56   *Salt Lake Herald-Republican*, 25 Sep. 1909.

57   Harvard S. Heath, *In the World: The Diaries of Reed Smoot*, (Salt Lake City: Signature Books, 1997): 19.

58   Heath: 20, 22–23, 29–30.

59   Heath: 30–31. Also, Richard Neitzel Holzapfel, et. al., *On this Day in the Church: An Illustrated Almanac of the Latter-day Saints*, (Salt Lake City: Eagle Gate, 2000): 186.

60   *Francis M. Gibbons, George Albert Smith: Kind and Caring Christian, Prophet of God (Salt Lake City: Deseret Book, 1990), 66, 126.*

61   *Salt Lake Herald-Republican*, 26 Sep. 1909.

62   Heath: 31–32.

63   Heath: 32, 35 n127. Visit also noted in *Deseret News 2003 Church Almanac*, (Salt Lake City: *Deseret News*, 2002): 550.

64   Heath: 32–33.

65   Heath: 104.

66   *LDS Church News*, 26 June 1993, "Hotel Utah: Colorful History of Elegance."

67   Heath: 119.

68   Heath: 123.

69   Heath: 285–86. Also, *Improvement Era*, Vol. XVIII, "Passing Events," September 1915 no. 11.

70   *Improvement Era*, Vol. XXII. April 1919 no. 6, footnotes.

71   *Salt Lake Tribune*, 24 Sep 1919.

72   Milton R. Merrill, *Reed Smoot: Apostle in Politics*, (Logan, Utah: Utah State University Press, 1990): 228. Also, *Improvement Era*, Vol. XXV. "Passing Events." January 1922 no. 3.

73   Heber J. Grant, "Glimpses of Famous Contemporaries, Reed Smoot and William Howard Taft" in *Gospel Standards: The Ministry of Heber J. Grant*, comp. G. Homer Durham, (Salt Lake City: *Improvement Era*, 1941).

74   *Salt Lake Telegram*, 23 Sep. 1919.

75   *Ogden Standard Examiner,* September 24, 1919.

76   *Salt Lake Telegram*, 23 Sep. 1919.

77   *Salt Lake Telegram*, 24 Sep. 1919.

78   Daniel H. Ludlow, ed., *Encyclopedia of Mormonism*, 1–4 vols., (New York: Macmillan, 1992): 1560. Also, William Mulder, "A Glance At Heber J. Grant's Twenty Five Years As President of the Church," *Improvement Era*, Vol. XLVI. November 1943, no. 11.

79   *Salt Lake Telegram*, 24 Sep. 1919.

80   *Deseret News*, 24 Sep. 1919.

81   L. G. Otten and C. M. Caldwell, *Sacred Truths of the Doctrine and Covenants*, 2, (Salt Lake City: Deseret Book, 1993): 147.

82   *Salt Lake Telegram*, 24 Sep. 1919.

83   Nice summaries of this visit are found in Parry D. Sorensen, "Harding's last journey passed through Utah," *Deseret News*, 5 Aug. 1977, and W. Paul Reeve, "President Harding's 1923 Visit to Utah," *History Blazer* July 1995.

84   *Salt Lake Tribune*, 27 Jun. 1923: 1.

85   Heath: 540. Also, *Deseret News*, 25, 26, 27, and 28 Jun. 1923, 10 Aug. 1923; *Salt Lake Tribune,* 27 Jun. 1923; *Millennial Star*, 2 Aug. 1923.

86   Sheri L. Dew, *Go Forward With Faith: The Biography of Gordon B. Hinckley*, (Salt Lake City: Deseret Book, 1996): 41.

87   *Salt Lake Telegram*, 27 Sep. 1923: 3.

88   Hoover's Daily Calendar, Herbert Hoover Presidential Library and Museum.

89   Tim Gillie, "When Presidents Stopped By", *Tooele Transcript-Bulletin*, Feb. 22, 2011.

90   *Salt Lake Telegram*, 26 Aug. 1920.

91   *Salt Lake Tribune*, 30 Sep. 1935.

92   Ibid.

93   "The Church Moves On," *Improvement Era*, Vol. XLVIII. August 1945, no. 8.

94   "Rear Platform Remarks in Utah, 21 September 1948," Truman Presidential Library.

95   *Salt Lake Tribune*, 22 Sep. 1948: 10.

96   *Salt Lake Tribune,* "Visit First Lady," 3 May 1946: 8.

97   Harry S Truman, "Rear Platform and Other Informal Remarks in Colorado and Utah," September 21, 1948, Salt Lake City, Utah (Empire Room of Hotel Utah, 7:15 PM); in John Woolley and Gerhard Peters, University of California-Santa Barbara, *The American Presidency Project* available at http://www.presidency.ucsb.edu/site/docs/sou.php.

98   Michael K. Winder, *Presidents and Prophets*, (American Fork: Covenant, 2007), 187, 260–261.

99   Francis M. Gibbons , *George Albert Smith: Kind and Caring Christian, Prophet of God* (Salt Lake City Deseret Book, 1990).

100   David O. McKay Diaries, Special Collections, Marriott Library, University of Utah, 6 Oct. 1952.

101   Ibid.

102   "Address at Brigham Young University, Provo, Utah, October 6, 1952," Truman Presidential Museum and Library, online at http://www.trumanlibrary.org/publicpapers/index.php?pid=2287&st=Utah&st1=

103   *Salt Lake Tribune*, 7 Oct. 1952.

104   Francis M. Gibbons, *David O. McKay: Apostle to the World, Prophet of God*, (Salt Lake City: Deseret Book, 1986): 313.

105   "The Church Moves On," *Improvement Era*, Vol. XLIX. February 1946, no. 2.

106   George Albert Smith to Harry S Truman, 27 May 1946, Truman Presidential Museum.

107   George Albert Smith to Harry S Truman, 9 June 1947, Truman Presidential Museum and Library.

108   "The Church Moves On," *Improvement Era 49*. February 1946, no. 2.

109   "'This Is the Place Monument' Dedication, A Message From Harry S Truman President of the United States," *Improvement Era 50*, September 1947, no. 9.

110   Tim Gillie, "When Presidents Stopped By," *Tooele Transcript-Bulletin*, Feb. 22, 2011.

111   Ibid.

112   *Deseret News*, 10 Oct. 1952.

113   *Salt Lake Tribune*, 11 Oct. 1952.

114   Ibid.

115   *Deseret News*, 10 Oct. 1952. Priest's online biography is at wikipedia.org and historytogo.utah.gov.

116   *Salt Lake Tribune*, 11 Oct. 1952.

117   Ibid.

118   Ibid.

119   Ibid.

120   Francis M. Gibbons, *David O. McKay: Apostle to the World, Prophet of God* (Salt Lake City: Deseret Book, 1986): 351–52.

121   Ezra Taft Benson to Clare Middlemiss, May 28, 1966, *David O. McKay Scrapbook #169*.

122   Handwritten letter dated August 21, 1958 from Frederick W. Babel, former secretary to Ezra Taft Benson to President McKay regarding the impression President McKay made on President Eisenhower. *David O. McKay Scrapbook #169*.

123   *Provo Daily Herald*, 9/5/1954, p. 1 and Presidential Appointment Book found online on 18 Jan 2011 at: http://www.eisenhower.archives.gov/Research/Digital_Documents/Appt_Books_Pres/1954/September%201954.pdf.

124   Remarks at Natrona Airport, Casper, Wyoming, 9/4/1954 in John T. Woolley and Gerhard Peters, The *American Presidency Project* [online]. Santa Barbara, CA. Available from World Wide Web: http://www.presidency.ucsb.edu/ws/?pid=10049.

125   *Deseret News*, 10 Oct. 1952; also *Salt Lake Tribune*, 11 Oct. 1952.

126   Gibbons, *David O. McKay*: 374–75.

127   David O. McKay Diaries, 12 Nov. 1957. See also *Church News*, "President McKay Receives Sen. Kennedy at Church Office," 16 Nov. 1957: 4.

128   Ibid.

129   David O. McKay Diaries, 6 Mar. 1959.

130   David O. McKay Diaries, 30 Jan. 1960.

131   Ibid.

132   Oscar W. McConkie, Jr. interview with Gregory Prince, 24 Aug. 1998, copy in Michael Winder's possession.

133   Memo from Ted Cannon to Clare Middlemiss, 15 Sept. 1960, posted in David O. McKay Diaries.

134   *Deseret News*, 25 Sep. 1963.

135   John F. Kennedy, "Address in Salt Lake City at the Mormon Tabernacle," 26 September 1963, in John

Woolley and Gerhard Peters, University of California-Santa Barbara, *The American Presidency Project* available at http://www.presidency.ucsb.edu/site/docs/sou.php

136   Ibid.

137   David O. McKay Diaries, 27 Mar. 1968.

138   Ibid.

139   Ibid.

140   *Church News*, "Services Honoring President Kennedy Held In Tabernacle," 30 Nov. 1963: 4.

141   "Memorial services for President John F. Kennedy, George Albert Smith Fieldhouse, Brigham Young University, Monday, November 25, 1963": 8, 10. LDS Church Archives.

142   *Deseret News*, 20 Oct. 1954.

143   *Salt Lake Tribune*, 1 Nov. 1958.

144   *Provo Daily Herald*, 28 Oct. 1960.

145   *Deseret News*, 28 Oct. 1960.

146   Ibid.

147   *Deseret News*, 19 Oct. 1962.

148   *Deseret News*, 18 Sep. 1964.

149   Ibid.

150   Ibid.

151   http://www.gallup.com/poll/116677/presidential-approval-ratings-gallup-historical-statistics-trends.aspx retrieved on 22 Jan. 2011.

152   *Deseret News*, "Inauguration: Witnesses to history and a sense of hope," Scott Taylor, *Church News*, Thursday, Jan. 22, 2009.

153   *Deseret News*, 18 Sep. 1964.

154   Boyd K. Packer's report to the First Presidency on his White House meeting, in David O. McKay Dairies, 10 Mar. 1965.

155   *Salt Lake Tribune*, 30 Oct. 1964.

156   *Dave Leip's Atlas of U.S. Presidential Elections*, available online at http://www.uselectionatlas.org/.

157   Gibbons, *David O. McKay*: 311.

158   F. Burton Howard, *Marion G. Romney: His Life and Faith*, (Salt Lake City: Bookcraft, 1988): 200.

159   *Deseret News*, 18 Oct. 1952.

160   *Deseret News*, 10 Oct. 1960.

161   "President McKay Clarifies Nixon 'Endorsement,'" *California Intermountain News*, 13 Oct. 1960.

162   *Deseret News*, 16 Sep. 1966.

163   "Tooele High Band of '69 Recalls Playing at Nixon Inauguration," by Missy Thompson, *Tooele Transcript-Bulletin*, 20 Jan 2009 .

164   "The Choir Celebrates a History with U.S.Presidents" by Stephanie Price, *LDS Living*, 19 Jan 2011.

165   Francis M. Gibbons, *Joseph Fielding Smith: Gospel Scholar, Prophet of God*, (Salt Lake City: Deseret Book, 1993): 434.

166   Richard M. Nixon, "Remarks in Salt Lake City, Utah," 31 Oct. 1970 in Woolley and Peters.

167   Richard M. Nixon, "Pioneer Day Remarks."

168   *Church News*, "Pres. Nixon Praises Church," 7 Nov. 1970: 3, 5. Also, Richard M. Nixon, "Remarks in Salt Lake City, Utah," 31 Oct. 1970 in Woolley and Peters.

169   *Deseret News*, 2 Nov. 1970.

170   *Church News*, "Pres. Nixon Praises Church," 7 Nov. 1970: 3, 5. Also, Richard M. Nixon, "Remarks in Salt Lake City, Utah," 31 Oct. 1970 in Woolley and Peters.

171   *Deseret News*, 15 Oct. 1973.

172   *Deseret News*, 8 Jun. 1974.

173   Ibid.

174   *Deseret News*, 15 Jun. 1974.

175   Ibid.

176   *Deseret News*, 2 Nov. 1974.

177   Ibid.

178   *Deseret News*, 30 Nov. 1977.

179   *Deseret News*, 5 Dec. 1978.

180   *Deseret News*, 12 Feb. 1982.

181   Ibid.

182   *Deseret News*, 31 Jul. 1982.

183   *Deseret News*, 2 Jun. 1986.

184   http://golf.about.com/b/2006/12/27/gerald-ford-among-top-presidential-golfers.htm retrieved on 1 Feb. 2011.

185   *Deseret News*, 8 Oct. 1976.

186   Ibid.

187   *Dave Leip's Atlas of U.S. Presidential Elections*, available online at http://www.uselectionatlas.org/.

188   *Deseret News*, 27 Oct. 1978.

189   http://en.wikipedia.org/wiki/Presidential_limousine#A_symbol_of_the_presidency_.281969.E2.80.93present.29 retrieved on 29 Jan. 2011.

190   Mike Winder interview with James S. Jardine, 31 Jul. 2006.

191   *Deseret News*, 28 Nov. 1978.

192   Ibid.

193   *Church News*, "Pres. Carter lauds family," 2 Dec. 1978: 3, 4, 9.

194   *Deseret News*, 28 Nov. 1978.

195   Ibid.

196   *Church News*, "Pres. Carter lauds family," 2 Dec. 1978: 3, 4, 9.

197   *Deseret News*, 28 Nov. 1978.

198   *Church News*, "Jimmy Carter Drops by Temple Square," 28 Jul. 1990.

199   *Deseret News*, 21 Feb. 2003.

200   Ibid.

201   *Deseret News*, 5 Sep. 2004.

202   Ibid.

203   Ibid.

204   *Deseret News*, 29 Nov. 2005.

205   *Deseret News*, 29 Oct. 2010.

206   *Deseret News*, 13 Jul. 1968.

207   Ibid.

208   *Deseret News*, 14 Feb. 1974.

209   *Deseret News*, 17 Jul. 1976.

210   *Deseret News*, 28 Jun. 1980.

211   Ibid.

212   *Deseret News*, Jul. 15, 1988.

213   *Deseret News*, 18 Sep. 1982.

214   Ibid.

215   *Deseret News*, 11 Sep. 1982.

216   Ibid.

217   *Deseret News*, 30 Oct. 1982.

218   Ibid.

219   Ibid.

220   *Deseret News*, 4 Sep. 1984.

221   Ibid.

222   *Deseret News*, 9 Sep. 1984.

223   Ibid.

224   http://www.ldschurchnews.com/articles/21116/Reagan-visits-BYU-Church-leaders-.html, retrieved 3 Feb. 2011.

225   Ibid.

226   Ibid.

227   http://en.wikipedia.org/wiki/Ronald_Reagan#Announcement_and_reaction, retrieved 3 Feb. 2011.

228   *Church News*, "President Reagan respected Church," Jun. 12, 2004: 7.

229   *Church News*, "'It is our job to make a difference,'" Jun. 19, 2004: 4.

230   *Deseret News*, 15 May 1979.

231   *Deseret News*, 30 Jan. 1982.

232   Ibid.

233   *Church News*, "Vice President Calls on Church Leaders," 2 Mar. 1986: 7.

234   *Church News*, "Prophet Is 'At Home' in Capitol," 12 Mar. 1986: 3, 12.

235   *Deseret News*, 19 Sep. 1991.

236   Ibid.

237	National Archives and Records Administration, "Appendix A—Digest of Other White House Announce-ments," online at http://bushlibrary.tamu.edu/papers/1992/app_a.html. Also, *Church News*, "President Bush Lauds Church's Efforts to Bolster Family Values," 25 Jul. 1992.

238	*GBH Journal*, 17 Jul. 1992. Quoted in Dew, *Go Forward with Faith*: 487.

239	George Bush to GBH, 21 Jul. 1992. Quoted in Dew, *Go Forward with Faith:* 487.

240	*Deseret News*, 19 Jul. 1992.

241	*Deseret News*, 16 Sep. 1992.

242	*Church News*, "President Bush Lauds Church's Efforts To Bolster Family Values," 25 Jul. 1992.

243	*Deseret News*, 16 Sep. 1992.

244	*Deseret News*, 3 May 1997.

245	*Deseret News*, 22 Apr. 1998.

246	*Deseret News*, 16 Sep. 1992.

247	George M. McCune, *Gordon B. Hinckley: Shoulder for the Lord*, (Salt Lake City: Hawkes Publishing, 1996): 554.

248	*Church News*, "Clinton Meets with LDS Leaders," 19 Sep. 1992.

249	*Deseret News*, 27 Feb. 1998.

250	*Deseret News*, 1 Mar. 1998.

251	Ibid.

252	Ibid.

253	*Deseret News*, 2 Mar. 1999.

254	Ibid.

255	*Deseret News*, 5 Nov. 2007.

256	Hatch interview with Mike Winder. May 30, 2006.

257	Hardy interview with Mike Winder. July 2, 2006.

258	*Church News*, "White House Visit: Pres. Clinton Meets with Pres. Hinckley," November 18, 1995.

259	*Church News*. "Pres. Benson Dies at Age 94; Life Marked by Constancy," June 4, 1994.

260	*Church News*. "Civic, Religious Leaders Send Condolences," March 11, 1995.

261	Bill Clinton. July 26, 1997, letter to The Church of Jesus Christ of Latter-day Saints. Reprinted.

262	*Deseret News*, 7 Jul. 1999.

263	*Deseret News*, 9 Mar. 2000.

264	*Deseret News*, 9 Feb. 2002.

265	Ibid.

266	Ibid.

267	Ibid.

268	*Deseret News*, 31 Aug. 2006.

269	Ibid.

270	*Deseret News*, 28 May 2008 and 29 May 2008.

271	*Deseret News*, 30 May 2008.

272	*Deseret News*, 20 Nov. 2010.

273	*Deseret News*, 30 Jan. 2008.

274	*Deseret News*, 6 Aug. 2007.

275	Ibid.

276	Ibid.